to Richard
in the hope of
productive disagreements
and discussions

Bren van Fraassen

THE DYNAMICS OF LAW AND MORALITY

To Kees

The Dynamics of Law and Morality
A Pluralist Account of Legal Interactionism

WIBREN VAN DER BURG
Erasmus University Rotterdam, The Netherlands

ASHGATE

© Wibren van der Burg 2014

All rights reserved. No part of this publication may be reproduced, stored in a retrieval system or transmitted in any form or by any means, electronic, mechanical, photocopying, recording or otherwise without the prior permission of the publisher.

Wibren van der Burg has asserted his right under the Copyright, Designs and Patents Act, 1988, to be identified as the author of this work.

Published by
Ashgate Publishing Limited
Wey Court East
Union Road
Farnham
Surrey, GU9 7PT
England

Ashgate Publishing Company
110 Cherry Street
Suite 3-1
Burlington, VT 05401-3818
USA

www.ashgate.com

British Library Cataloguing in Publication Data
A catalogue record for this book is available from the British Library

The Library of Congress has cataloged the printed edition as follows:
Burg, Wibren van der,
  The dynamics of law and morality : a pluralist account of legal interactionism / by Wibren van der Burg.
     pages cm
  Includes bibliographical references and index.
  ISBN 978-1-4724-3040-3 (hardback) – ISBN 978-1-4724-3041-0 (ebook) – ISBN 978-1-4724-3042-7 (epub) 1. Law–Moral and ethical aspects. 2. Law and ethics. 3. Legal polycentricity. I. Title.

  K247.6.B87 2014
  340'.112–dc23

2013039372

ISBN 9781472430403 (hbk)
ISBN 9781472430410 (ebk – PDF)
ISBN 9781472430427 (ebk – ePUB)

Printed in the United Kingdom by Henry Ling Limited, at the Dorset Press, Dorchester, DT1 1HD

Contents

Preface   *vii*
Acknowledgements   *xi*

Introduction   1

PART I: UNDERSTANDING THEORETICAL PLURALISM

1. Two Basic Models of Law and Morality   19
2. Essentially Ambiguous Concepts   39
3. The Debate between Fuller, Hart and Dworkin   53
4. The Relations between Law and Morality   65
5. A Pluralist Framework   77

PART II: LEGAL INTERACTIONISM

6. What is Legal Interactionism?   95
7. Understanding the Dynamics of Law   119
8. Three Apparent Anomalies in Modern Law   135
9. The Necessary and Contingent Relationship between Law and Morality   151

References   *171*
Index   *181*

Preface

This book was born out of my disappointment with the theoretical discussions in the field of legal philosophy. Some 20 years ago, I was partaking in ethical and legal research on themes such as prenatal diagnosis, AIDS and genetics. In the emerging disciplines of bioethics and health law, I observed that law and ethics were strongly intertwined. In finding solutions to radically new moral and legal problems, both disciplines cooperated with and borrowed from each other. Many researchers in this field actually combined legal and moral analysis. As there was very little positive law at the time in those areas, legal views, court decisions and draft legislation all depended heavily on normative views about how the law ought to be: namely, perspectives in which legal and moral arguments were barely distinguishable from one another.

As I am both a jurist and a moral philosopher by training, my special interest was in the relation between law and morality. However, when I turned to the traditional philosophical theories of law and morality, none of them offered much guidance – they simply did not fit into the confusing reality of emerging bioethics and health law. Natural law was largely irrelevant, as the moral issues were so controversial that any hope regarding broadly convincing foundations seemed naïve. With only a fragmented and incomplete collection of authoritative legal sources, and a heavy dependence on normative argument, source-based versions of legal positivism were quite obviously useless. Even Dworkinian interpretivism failed – despite its strong emphasis on argumentation – as it presupposed the dominance of legal institutions and the perspective of legal officials such as judges, whereas the emergence of health law and bioethics took place largely outside of traditional legal institutions: namely, in health care practice and public debates. None of these traditions seemed to provide an adequate framework that could help us understand the dynamic intertwinement of law and morality in the practice of health care.

I experienced a similar disappointment when I moved on to study phenomena such as interactive legislation and international law. In many new and developing fields of law, there was a dialectical interplay between law and morality, which could not easily be forced to fit into the available theoretical frameworks. It seemed as if all those theoretical debates on a separation of law and morality, or on minimal moral qualities of the law, were disconnected from the real world.

The philosophical literature on the relation between law and morality is not disappointing only because it fails to provide adequate frames for many recent phenomena. It also comprises a curious and frustrating debate because it often remains unclear what the controversy is actually about. For example, the separation thesis, the claim that there is no necessary connection between law and morality, is usually considered to be one of the central ideas of legal positivism – currently the most influential legal theory. However, there are scores of different interpretations of this separation thesis.

Moreover, the debate is fraught with misunderstandings and caricatures of each of the opponents' respective positions. The main actors in the debate complain continuously that their critics misunderstand them. Even more curious, authors like Fuller, Hart and Dworkin have sometimes admitted their frustration: not only about being misunderstood but also about not being able to understand their opponents. In response to this, we may conclude that a fuzzy but pervasive form of theoretical pluralism exists in these debates.

Yet, most participants in the debate merely add another position of their own, rather than attempting to fully understand what divides the quarrelling parties. In the ensuing debates, some authors simply reduce their opponents to caricatures, while sometimes there are sincere attempts to bridge the differences. However, as long as we do not have an adequate understanding and explanation of this fuzzy and pervasive theoretical pluralism, such attempts at a synthesis will probably remain shallow. Moreover, most authors suggest that their theory is a general theory of law, whereas it often seems to the outsider that those theories are parochial and associated with a specific context. Most theories of law and morality offer more adequate descriptions in certain legal contexts than in others. Dworkin's interpretivism, for example, is much more adequate for the practice of constitutional adjudication in the United States than for Civil Law adjudication in countries where most of the law has been recently codified. Kelsen's theory, in turn, is much more adequate for the latter type of context than for the former. Consequently, most theories of law have blind spots, such as international law or emergent law. For example, few theories – if any – fit the recent emergence of health law and bioethics as closely intertwined practices in which there is a dialectical interplay between law and morality.

This disheartening and frustrating state of affairs in legal philosophy forms the background of this book, which has two aims. The first is to understand this pervasive pluralism of theories on law and morality. This is the task I set for myself in Part One of the book. My second goal, in light of this analysis of theoretical pluralism, is to construct a robust theory of law and morality that is adequate for Western liberal democracies at the beginning of the twenty-first century. This theory, which may be called legal interactionism, is the theme of Part Two.

The central thesis in Part One is that law is an essentially ambiguous concept, which means that there are at least two, partly incompatible, models of law: law as a practice and law as a doctrine. The partial incompatibility of these models may explain why various authors often simply cannot understand one another. Moreover, as this idea implies that a unifying and coherent theory is not possible, it explains why theoretical pluralism is pervasive, as each theory can only cover part of the complex phenomena of law and morality and their interaction. Consequently, a theory of law and morality can only be relatively adequate for particular contexts, but will never be fully adequate for every context. This pervasive theoretical pluralism is not something to be deplored but to be embraced, because it contributes to a fuller understanding of law and morality. The result of Part One is a weak analytical framework that may help us to understand various debates in legal philosophy, but it is relatively non-committal with regard to which theory is to be preferred in which contexts.

In Part Two, I develop a legal interactionist theory of law and morality. This theory is inspired by the work of Lon Fuller and Philip Selznick, but in various ways goes beyond their ideas. It takes interactional law seriously, however, without reducing all of law to interactional law. Thus, it is consistently pluralist in its approach. My claim is that legal interactionism provides the most adequate theory of law and morality at the beginning of the twenty-first century. Moreover, it offers a pluralist understanding of the relation between law and morality, which also does justice to the enormous variation in this relation.

Many studies on law and morality have a directly normative thrust. They present a normative theory about the moral norms and values that law should incorporate. My project in this book is a different one. It is primarily an exercise in descriptive analysis, in sociologically informed legal theory. It claims that, if we want to understand law, we have to pay attention to the variable and dynamic relations between law and morality. Law is not a normatively neutral phenomenon. However, a descriptive analysis of the variable relations with morality does not imply a normative agenda about, for example, how to evaluate these relations, or about how to improve the moral quality of law. Certainly, these latter questions are important ones. I can only hope that scholars and students interested in such questions may find my descriptive analysis helpful as a starting point that clears the ground for normative theory. Nevertheless, this book does not offer direct answers to those questions: my aim is simply to understand the dynamic relations between law and morality.

Acknowledgements

This book builds on 25 years of research and teaching on the theme of law and morality. During these years, I have incurred many intellectual and personal debts of gratitude. Regrettably, I can mention only a few of them. I began my career as a moral philosopher in the Philosophy Department of Utrecht University, with two very different doctoral supervisors. Whereas Robert Heeger was an analytical philosopher, highly critical of ambiguities or missing links in my arguments, the legal sociologist Anthonie Peters made me aware of the richness and variation in reality that always seems to evade neat categorization and sharp conceptual distinctions. The productive tension between those two approaches is still central to my academic identity. Although, inspired by legal sociology, I have gone beyond the analytical tradition and even advocate essential ambiguity and the inevitability of incoherence, I still try to do so analytically and as clearly as reality allows.

Various other colleagues and students in Utrecht helped to deepen my understanding of law and morality: in particular, Alex Huibers, Pieter Ippel, Frans W.A. Brom, Egbert Schroten, Marcel Verweij, Theo van Willigenburg and the members of the project group on Ethics and Law of the Centre for Bioethics and Health Law.

After nine years in the field of philosophy, I moved on to Tilburg Law School, where a substantial PIONIER grant from the Netherlands Organisation for Scientific Research (NWO) enabled me to set up my own research group, with some 20 researchers working on the theme of ideals in law, morality and politics. I learned a great deal from the stimulating cooperation and the conversations with my colleagues, postdocs and doctoral students. Special thanks are due to Paul van Seters, Willem Witteveen, Bert van den Brink, Frans W.A. Brom, Marc Hertogh, Ernst Hirsch Ballin, Roland Pierik, Lonneke Poort, Jellienke Stamhuis, Sanne Taekema, Bart van Klink, Anton Vedder and Bertjan Wolthuis. I should also mention the intensive discussions with contributors to the book *Rediscovering Fuller* (in particular, Ken Winston, David Luban and Francis J. Mootz III) both during the authors' conference in 1997 and in the many years since; these exchanges have been crucial to this book and to its Fullerian bent.

Since 2008, I have been working at the Erasmus School of Law. Again, Sanne Taekema has played a central role. She began 16 years ago as my doctoral student, and has since become my *collega proximus* and main intellectual sparring partner. Wouter de Been, Wietse Buijs, Jeanne Gaakeer, Marlies Galenkamp and Ellen Hey deserve a special mention among the colleagues who contribute to making Rotterdam such an inspiring research environment.

Three sabbaticals were essential for the writing of this book. In the spring term of 1993, I stayed at the Center for the Study of Law and Society in Berkeley, where I had the privilege of attending a class taught by Philip Selznick on his then recently published book *The Moral Commonwealth*. This class and a number of discussions with Philip influenced me deeply in many ways, especially in terms of my becoming oriented towards pragmatism and the specific Selznickian version of it. Selznick's continuous emphasis on the importance of having an eye for variation and for context has become a central subtext of this book.

In 2006–07, I spent my second sabbatical at Princeton at the Center for Human Values and the Program in Law and Public Affairs (LAPA). At Princeton, I wrote the first four chapters of this book. I profited greatly from discussions with colleagues at LAPA, especially Kim Lane Scheppele, Vanessa Barker, Paul Schiff Berman, Mary Ann Case, Laura Dickinson, Chibli Mallat, Jamie Mayerfeld, Margaret Jane Radin and Teemu Ruskola. Being the 'guy from Europe' in this interdisciplinary group with such a broad international orientation was an enriching experience, and it contributed greatly to my understanding of contextual variation in law and legal theory.

During my third sabbatical, at the University of Toronto during the spring term of 2011, I finished a rough draft of the remaining chapters. I am deeply indebted to the hospitality of the Centre for Ethics and to inspiring conversations with a number of colleagues, especially Jutta Brunnée, David Dyzenhaus, Anna Korteweg, Audrey Macklin, Dick Moon and Jacob Shelley.

Over the years, I have presented central ideas and parts of this book at universities in Amsterdam, Aarhus, Carlisle (Penn State Dickinson School of Law), College Park (University of Maryland), Copenhagen, Herzliya, Jerusalem, Linköping, Princeton, Rotterdam, Tilburg, Toronto, Uppsala, Utrecht, Washington (Georgetown) and Zurich, as well as at the Ersta Institute for Health Care Ethics in Stockholm and at meetings of the Societas Ethica, the IVR, the LSA, the Dutch Research School for Philosophy and the Netherlands Association for Legal Philosophy. I would like to thank the audiences and the organizers at these events for numerous helpful comments and critical discussions. Various other colleagues supported me and provided invaluable constructive criticism throughout the years. In addition to the above-mentioned individuals, I owe special thanks to Richard Bronaugh, Roger Cotterrell, Stefan Grotefeld, Alon Harel, Govert den Hartogh, Jos Kole, Martin Krygier, Henrik Palmer Olsen, Brian Tamanaha, Jeremy Waldron and Pauline Westerman.

Several colleagues commented on substantive parts of the final manuscript or even on the whole manuscript. For this, I owe a great debt of gratitude to Wouter de Been, Jutta Brunnée, David Dyzenhaus, Marlies Galenkamp, Vincent Geeraets, Ellen Hey, Harm Kloosterhuis, Lonneke Poort and Marc Van Hoecke.

A number of editors have corrected my English and tried to improve my style throughout the years, especially Hildegard Penn, Intisar A. Rabb and Donna Devine. The final manuscript was corrected by Beth Spratt, who did a wonderful job. Luigi Corrias, Lonneke Poort, Thomas Riesthuis, Astrid van der Wal and Danny Groenenberg were invaluable as student assistants.

The research for this book was financed partly by various grants from the Netherlands Organisation for Scientific Research (NWO).

This book is dedicated to Kees Notenboom, who for the last 30 years has been my great love and companion in life. He has always been highly supportive – even though this book project meant that for long periods I went abroad without him.

Chapters 1–4 incorporate two previously published articles (1 and 2 listed hereunder), but the texts have been completely reshuffled and substantively edited. In Chapters 5, 6 and 8, some smaller fragments of a number of previously published articles have been incorporated; these have also been substantively edited.

1. 'Two Models of Law and Morality', *Associations* 3 no. 1 (1999), pp. 61–82.
2. 'Essentially Ambiguous Concepts and the Fuller-Hart-Dworkin Debate', *Archiv für Rechts- und Sozialphilosophie*, 95 no. 3 (2009), pp. 305–26.
3. 'Bioethics and Law: A Developmental Perspective', *Bioethics* 11 no. 2 (1997), pp. 91–114.
4. 'The Role of Ideals in Legal Dynamics', in: Arend Soeteman (ed.), *Pluralism and Law. Proceedings of the 20th IVR World Congress, Archiv für Rechts- und Sozialphilosophie* Beiheft 91, Stuttgart: Franz Steiner 2004, pp. 28–33.
5. 'The Irony of a Symbolic Crusade. The Debate on Opening Up Civil Marriage to Same-Sex Couples', in: N. Zeegers, W. Witteveen and B. van Klink (eds), *Social and Symbolic Effects of Legislation Under the Rule of Law*, Lewiston: Edwin Mellen Press 2005, pp. 245–75.
6. 'The Work of Lon Fuller: A Promising Direction for Jurisprudence in the 21st Century', *University of Toronto Law Journal* (forthcoming).

I would like to thank the publishers Duncker & Humblot (1), Franz Steiner Verlag (2 and 4), John Wiley & Sons (3), Edwin Mellen Press (5) and the University of Toronto Press (6) for permission to reprint these materials.

Introduction

The relation between law and morality is one of the central themes in legal philosophy. It also plays an important role in many debates on topical issues such as biotechnology and health care, multicultural society, bank bonuses and other commercial practices, and the global economy. However, despite the fact that in recent years many new legal practices have emerged in response to these concrete issues, the current state of the theoretical debate is disappointing. Theorists from each of the three major traditions – natural law theory, legal positivism and interpretivism – rarely engage in truly open debate; instead, they are merely wrapped up in refining their respective positions.

The oldest tradition of the three, natural law theory, has been virtually dead outside of the contexts of religious orthodoxies and international human rights law. In most Western democracies, the basic tenets of classical natural law theories have been more or less incorporated into positive law. Consequently, natural law has become largely superfluous, and is no longer relevant for any practical purposes. Only on some highly controversial issues, such as same-sex marriage or issues relating to procreation, does it diverge from positive law or is it used to critique legislative proposals. Yet, precisely because of its controversial nature, natural law can hardly be the rational basis for law that its proponents claim it to be. Moreover, in international law, the only remaining field where natural law theory may seem to have some traction, the emerging practice of codification – in particular in the form of human rights treaties – makes appeals to natural law largely superfluous. As a result, few opponents deem it worthy of debate.

H.L.A. Hart formulated a highly sophisticated version of the second tradition, legal positivism, which is still highly influential. Though his theory was challenged seriously by Ronald Dworkin, legal positivists have endeavoured to rebut these criticisms. Most legal positivists who have responded to Dworkin appear to be satisfied that they have done so successfully, though it has been done through the diverging theoretical positions of inclusive and exclusive positivism. Since the initial rounds of discussion with Dworkin, positivism seems trapped in internal debates about subtle differences that are unlikely to capture the interest of outsiders.[1]

Finally, Ronald Dworkin not only criticized positivism, but in the process of so doing, also presented a highly interesting third approach, usually called

---

1 Wright, 'Does Positivism Matter?', p. 57 even argues that the debate has become irrelevant: 'the debate over legal positivism turns out not to be distinctively related, logically or in any other interesting way, to much of genuine philosophical or practical significance'.

interpretivism. This theory views law as an interpretive and argumentative practice. In response to his critique, Dworkin's positivist opponents have incorporated some of his criticisms into their theories, and, although from his point of view their doing so has still failed to respond to his core objections, these adaptations have made their positions far less vulnerable to attack. Since the initial, and still somewhat incoherent, presentation of his ideas in *Taking Rights Seriously*, Dworkin has tried to reformulate and refine his theory, and to rebut incorrect interpretations and unfair criticisms of it. Interestingly, at the same time he has often attacked his positivist opponents in terms that have hardly seemed fair to them. Consequently, the debate between positivists and interpretivists now appears to have reached an unproductive stalemate.

In addition to these three major philosophical traditions, a great number of other traditions have emerged in the past century, such as Legal Realism, Critical Legal Studies, Law and Economics, and systems theory. Interesting and original research is being done in each of these traditions but, again, there is little open discussion between their proponents.

Of course, a number of theorists have argued that we should move beyond the traditional approach, which involves an opposition between natural law and legal positivism, because it is an unproductive one.[2] Some theorists also make serious attempts at bridging the divisions between the traditions. However, these efforts usually originate with a strong basis in one tradition, and then, rather eclectically, include only one or two central ideas from a different tradition; hence, they are still a long way from constituting serious attempts at a full synthesis.

The field of legal philosophy, therefore, appears to be fragmented beyond redemption. Worse still, we are caught up in a deadlock. Proponents of each tradition seem hardly able to understand their opponents' positions, let alone learn from them. It is a telling illustration of this very problem that in the debates between Fuller, Hart and Dworkin there is an abundance of misunderstandings and complaints that their opponents caricaturize their views. In fact, these three authors even admit on occasion that they are at pains to understand their opponents.[3] The faithful within each school of thought are like orthodox theologians, who further entrench their respective positions in the debate by contesting minor differences of opinion that, to the outsider, seem hardly distinguishable from one another.

How is it possible that the various schools – each offering valuable insights – are not able to have a productive discussion? Why is each of them so blind to interesting new phenomena, such as the rise of international law during the past century and alternative modes of regulation and self-regulation? It cannot be because the theme of law and morality is no longer relevant: legal developments engendered by biotechnology and globalization have raised many new questions about how law and morality are connected. There must be something more that

---

2 For example MacCormick, 'Natural Law and Separation', at p. 130; Olsen and Toddington, *Law in its Own Right*, p. 14.

3 See Chapter 3 for these debates and for further references to those complaints.

might help us explain why current legal philosophy has become stuck in the trenches. Philosophical positions can develop into dogmas when they become immune to the corrective force of social reality. It seems to me that this is what has happened in the field of legal philosophy.[4] The various schools have all constructed largely coherent theories surrounded by giant fortresses for the purpose of warding off most external attacks.

How can we break this deadlock? It will certainly not be achieved simply by presenting another alternative theory to compete alongside the others. Indeed, that is how almost all legal philosophers thus far have responded: by critiquing their opponents' positions and then proposing what they consider to be a better theory. However, as all these attempts have failed to convince even a minority of their readers, it is unlikely that another similar attempt would succeed. It is my contention that before even thinking about how to develop new theories, we must analyse the fundamental differences that underlie the continuing disagreements in legal philosophy. In order to do this, we should search for a broader perspective that might explain why the various schools talk past each other and, in light of this analysis, construct a framework that enables us to include the various valuable insights provided by the respective schools. That is the primary aim of this book.

The first step in this process should be to examine why the schools cannot understand one another and why they become increasingly inadequate to the task of dealing with changing realities.[5] One reason for this is that a crude view of law is still implicitly presupposed in our discussions and legal practices, even though most lawyers and philosophers agree that it is incorrect. It is the idea of law as a largely coherent and relatively stable doctrine. I will argue that we should set aside this depiction of law in favour of a richer, more pluralist and dynamic concept. This richer concept of law may help us to understand both the biases inherent in each of the various philosophical theories and the failure within each school to understand the other's positions. This is the argument I will develop in Part One of this book.

The second step would seem to be the construction of an alternative general theory that combines the valuable, even if partial, insights offered by the various theories. However, I will argue that a universal theory of law is impossible in light of the pluralist and dynamic concept of law that I will develop in Part One. All we

---

4 For a similar suggestion, see Brian Leiter, *Naturalizing Jurisprudence*. However, for a number of reasons I do not follow his suggested solution to 'naturalize' jurisprudence, because it fails to take the more fundamental problem of pervasive legal pluralism seriously and merely provides yet another alternative and, in my view, a highly reductionist theory.

5 Shapiro, *Legality*, starts from a similar general question about the intractability of the debate. At p. 49 he suggests that it seems as if neither natural law nor legal positivism can be right. In this book he sets out to understand the biases of both traditions and to do justice to the valuable insights of both, including many insights derived from the work of Lon Fuller. In the end, however, his theory remains too strongly embedded in the positivist tradition.

can hope for is to construct theories that can claim to be more or less adequate in some contexts. Only such context-specific theories can be robust. In keeping with this general constraint, my aim in Part Two will be to develop a theory of law and morality for a specific context – that of Western liberal-democratic societies.

The Standard View of Law and Morality

There is a standard view of law that is implicit in most of our discussions on law. This standard view holds law to be a largely coherent and relatively stable doctrine. Of course, many legal theorists, like the Legal Realists and those belonging to Critical Legal Studies, have criticized this view on theoretical grounds. However, despite this, the perspective continues to have a powerful influence on how we talk about law in our everyday lives and within the context of everyday legal practice.[6] Judges and the police talk about 'the law' in this way. If a visitor to the US enquires what the traffic rules are, her depiction of 'the law' would likely follow along the same lines; and in most law schools students are taught that there is a coherent legal doctrine behind the collection of court cases, statutes and other legal sources.

This conception of law is deeply ingrained not only in legal practice but also in scholarly discussions of law. Such an image fits especially well with most positivist theories, as they focus on law as a system of rules or as an authoritative system of norms.[7] Of course, positivists acknowledge that this doctrine, based on statutes and case law, is not complete and that it is subject to a gradual evolution, made possible by secondary rules of change. They will admit that there are some gaps or areas in which discussion is possible: for example, in some newly emerging fields where the legislature and the courts cannot keep up with rapid changes. However, in their view, these are merely fringe phenomena – they do not seriously undermine the notion of a largely coherent and relatively stable legal doctrine as such.

Indeed, though many non-positivists have criticized the standard view of law, it is evident that they are still under its spell. In most discussions, these theorists simply accept the underlying framework that comes with it. For example, non-positivists frequently go along with the positivist notion that the general debate in jurisprudence is about what role moral standards play both in determining – or upholding – the core of law and in filling in the gaps of this doctrine. Consequently, they have to fight an uphill battle against the positivist

---

6 See Smith, *Law's Quandary* for a similar idea that we implicitly presuppose the idea of 'the law' as a (transcendentally) existing body of norms. Even though Holmes and many others have strongly derided this notion of a 'brooding omnipresence in the sky', in our everyday life and legal practice we still act largely as if such a body exists, or at least could be constructed.

7 Hart, *Concept of Law*; Raz, *Authority of Law*.

position that judges are not bound by moral (i.e. extra-legal) criteria. If non-positivists are then required to present their views within this frame, they face an almost impossible task. The classical natural lawyers among them are placed in a position in which they must then defend the stance that there are universal, moral and substantive standards that somehow have to be acknowledged as part of positive law. The interpretivists among them are then cornered into taking the position that judges are required to appeal to moral arguments in the cases of a gap or a controversy. Positivists can simply deny both of these claims regarding the importance of morality, or merely regard them as contingent and not important. By uncritically accepting the standard view of law as a largely coherent and relatively stable legal doctrine, both non-positivist schools are trapped in a frame in which they cannot win.[8]

This sketch is of course much too simplistic and, further, it fails to do justice to the elaborate refinements of each theory. It is sufficient for the present, however, as it succeeds, for our purposes, in highlighting the standard view of law. This view has two characteristics: relative stability and coherence. Moreover, it focuses on law as a doctrine consisting of norms with propositional content. The law says 'X is prohibited.' Positivists may believe that these features already characterize the law; others, like Dworkin, hold that in our interpretive practice we are required to construct the legal doctrine as if it were a coherent and relatively stable doctrine.[9] Despite their differences on whether we construct law or whether it exists, the positivists and Dworkin agree that it is useful to think of law in terms of a doctrine having these two characteristics.

A similar standard view can be discerned with regard to morality. Natural law theorists hold that there are certain universal moral standards. Positivists like Hart distinguish between critical morality (which may – but need not – consist of universal moral standards) and the social morality of a society; both are treated as if they consist of a coherent body of norms.[10] Dworkin argues that a judge should construct a coherent political morality as part of the justification of her decisions. Again, the ideal of morality as a largely coherent and stable body of norms and values seems to be presupposed implicitly by all three major traditions.

---

8 Of course, I should add that many non-positivists have proven successful in developing an alternative theory, precisely insofar as they have been able to develop an alternative frame; a good example is Dworkin's view of law as an interpretive and argumentative practice. I will elaborate on this in Chapter 3.

9 In the usual positivist interpretation of Dworkin's theory, he merely wanted to emphasize the importance of principles alongside rules in legal doctrine. As I will discuss in Chapter 3, his aim was a different one: we should regard law as an argumentative practice and lay aside the whole picture of 'existing law' (Dworkin, *Taking Rights Seriously*, p. 293). In this practice, however, a judge must still construct the law as if it were a coherent doctrine. In the argumentative practice, the focus is still on the legal doctrine, even though Dworkin emphasizes that it is a mere construction.

10 Hart, *Law, Liberty and Morality*.

From this standard perspective, the central analytical questions with regard to law and morality can be formulated as follows. Firstly, is there some form of essential connection between these largely coherent and stable bodies of law and morality? Secondly, if there is a connection, to which of the types of morality is law supposed to be connected? Thus, the central normative question can be phrased in terms that have become familiar since the Hart–Devlin debate: namely, should the law enforce moral standards? And, if so, which standards: those of social morality, those of critical morality, or perhaps even the precepts of natural law?[11]

The Inadequacy of the Standard View

This approach may have been largely adequate to structure the main jurisprudential debates in the nineteenth century and in the first half of the twentieth century. Positivism may have seemed plausible in relatively stable sovereign nation-states, where most of the law was formulated as a largely coherent and complete doctrine, and might have been found either in case law or in codifications and statutes.[12] The Hart–Devlin debate made sense in the context of a society with a largely shared and stable social morality, where reaching consensus on an ideal or on a critical morality seemed possible. However, modern societies no longer fit this archetype – if indeed our societies ever truly did. The notion that a relatively stable and coherent legal order exists – or that we can reasonably aspire to construct law as such – is at odds with reality.

Firstly, the premise that there is only one legal order can no longer be upheld. In recent decades, legal sociology has made us aware of the pervasiveness of legal pluralism in society, showing that internal norms of institutions or semi-autonomous social fields are legal orders in their own right.[13] Paul Schiff Berman and others have argued that legal pluralism is also a pervasive phenomenon in our globalizing world.[14] The coup de grace for the standard view comes from legal historians, who have argued that the notion of a Westphalian order, consisting of fully sovereign states and, thus, of completely independent legal orders, only became dominant in

---

  11 Hart, *Law, Liberty and Morality*; Devlin, *Enforcement of Morals*.

  12 See Cotterrell, *Politics of Jurisprudence*, p. 122: 'In times of stability positivist criteria of legal authority typically seem sufficient.'

  13 See Moore, 'Law and Social Change'; Griffiths, 'What is Legal Pluralism?'. Van Hoecke, *Law as Communication*, pp. 1–2 even concludes: 'Today a conception of legal pluralism is widely accepted, which does not limit the law to state legal orders but broadens it to differing forms of institutionalised social organisations, such as international law, sports associations, or numerous forms of unofficial law.' This may hold true for legal theorists but I am not so sure that among ordinary lawyers and members of the public legal pluralism has been as widely accepted as he claims.

  14 Berman, 'Global Legal Pluralism'; Twining, 'Post-Westphalian Conception of Law'.

the nineteenth century, and even then was never entirely realized.[15] Therefore, it is undeniable that legal pluralism is a pervasive phenomenon of modern societies.

Secondly, the idea that there is a stable core of law, and that room for uncertainty and change exists only at the penumbra, has also become highly questionable. In many respects, positive law is subject to rapid evolution, and often there is hardly any settled law in various newly emerging areas of law, such as that regulating biotechnology. Modern technology, changing moral views, globalization and informatization – to name just a few trends – have all led to a constant need for change and adaptation. The positivist idea that gaps are merely a temporary and marginal phenomenon no longer seems valid. Gaps and controversies are pervasive, and they often concern the core of the law.

Finally, partly because of the pervasiveness of pluralism, controversy and change, the idea that law is or should be coherent is also dubious. This is not solely because of the familiar criticism raised by Critical Legal Studies. Flagrant inconsistencies or contradictions are rare, at least within a single legal order. Coherence is, however, more than merely the absence of inconsistencies; it also reflects an ideal of mutual support between various parts of the law, of uniting ideals behind the plurality. Mutual support is weak and tensions may arise if there are too many gaps in the fabric and if the legal order is also partly open to other legal orders. Tensions may also arise if various parts of the law evolve at different speeds, or develop in different directions from one another.

Similar observations can be made with regard to the idea of morality as a coherent and relatively stable doctrine. As globalization and the modern communication era have brought together different groups that in the past would scarcely have been aware of one another's existence, pervasive moral pluralism is hard to deny. The partial secularization of Western countries combined with the rise of evangelical Christians in the US and the immigration of large groups of Muslims into most Western democracies have led to more religiously and culturally divided societies. In the face of this pluralism, the idea that there is one shared morality, or that we could evolve towards more unity, seems untenable. Natural law's aspiration of uncovering some universal moral truth, either through revelation or through the use of Reason, seems even more naïve. As the morality of the previous generation has changed in drastic ways during its lifetime – think only of sexual morality, traditionally one of the core subjects of natural law – it is highly likely that similar changes will occur during our lifetime. Thus, the idea of a stable morality seems even more outdated than it did when legal theorists simply proclaimed the morality of the dominant group to be 'our' shared morality.

The conclusion to be drawn from the above analysis can only be that the presuppositions implicit within the current debates on law and morality are at odds

---

15 Osiander, 'Westphalian Myth' argues that the Peace of Westphalia confirmed and perfected 'a system of mutual relations among autonomous political units that was precisely not based on the concept of sovereignty' (p. 270). See also Randall Lesaffer, 'Grotian Tradition Revisited', suggesting that sovereignty is best seen as a relative concept.

with reality. Dynamics, pluralism and incoherence are pervasive. Philosophical analysis can no longer ignore this fact, but must take it seriously. Therefore, legal theory is in need of a framework different from that which conceptualizes law and morality as largely coherent and relatively stable doctrines.

An Eye for Variation

There is an additional reason that we should attempt to move beyond the current debate. Most studies on law and morality are embedded in one specific legal tradition or culture – even if they claim to present analytical or universal truths.[16] Hans Kelsen's theory of law is a good example of this. His theory is quite obviously most relevant to lawyers from countries with a written constitution and elaborate codifications, where judges can play a subordinate role in the creation of new law. A sad illustration of how strongly Kelsen's theory was culture bound is that during his exile in the United States, this leading European legal philosopher was barely taken seriously by the American legal academy.

Ronald Dworkin presents another example of contextual bias. His theory fits into a Common Law tradition, with a Supreme Court as the ultimate authority in interpreting and recreating the law, and with elaborately argued majority and minority opinions. This is also an attractive model for lawyers who are trying to develop a philosophy behind the progressive interpretation of the European Court of Human Rights in Strasbourg. However, it certainly is less appealing to most lawyers from Civil Law traditions, who are used to a practice of law that involves judicial restraint and legislative supremacy.

A third example is classical natural law, which is most attractive in situations where legal order is virtually absent or highly chaotic. Therefore, it is understandable that it flourished during the Middle Ages (as legal sources were scarce in that period of extreme legal fragmentation) or during the early developments of international law (for example in the works of Grotius). In the relatively stable domestic legal orders of nineteenth-century Europe, however, classical natural law was largely irrelevant.

These three examples can be generalized. Legal philosophies – even if they claim universality – are usually more suitable for analysing certain legal orders and less so with regard to others. This is a matter of degree, however. Kelsen's theory may have at least some use in Common Law jurisdictions, as the fact that both Hart and Raz build on his work demonstrates.[17] Nevertheless, it certainly

---

16   For a similar critique, see Tamanaha, *General Jurisprudence*; Van Hoecke, *Law as Communication*, p. 5; and especially Cotterrell, *Politics of Jurisprudence*.

17   Richard Posner, however, argues with reference to the Kelsenian inspiration that Hart's theory has a typical Continental flavour, and doubts whether it really describes the English let alone the American Common Law tradition. See Posner, *Moral and Legal Theory*, pp. 97–8.

fits better within Civil Law traditions, which are characterized by legislative supremacy. Each legal philosophy has its blind spots. Most legal philosophies have blind spots with regard to international law, at least in its emerging stages[18] (natural law is the major exception), or with regard to customary law and emergent or incipient law (sociological jurisprudence is the exception here).

This bias may be inevitable. Indeed, the dream of a universal theory of law may be unrealistic. However, it is a limitation of the current theoretical debate that the participants rarely take the context relativity of their own positions seriously. Worse still, they almost never reflect explicitly on this, such as to recognize that competing theories might prove more adequate in different legal contexts.

In doing legal philosophy, therefore, we need an eye for variation in different respects.[19] We should be attentive to variation in the object of our theories, because of pervasive pluralism and dynamics, but also to variation at a higher level: that of the theories themselves. This means that we may have to accept the relative truth of different theories, relative to the type of legal order they describe. This requires us to recognize theoretical pluralism.

To keep our analysis open for this theoretical pluralism, we need a weak framework and strong theories.[20] At the most abstract level, we need a weak analytical framework that allows us to contend with statutory law, with customary and international law, and with Common Law and Civil Law as well as with Chinese law and Middle Eastern law.[21] At the level of the analytical framework, we should exclude as little as possible. Such a framework is bound to be highly abstract. In order to elaborate it into theories that are productive with regard to specific legal orders, we need to develop strong theories of law. Only by accepting that they have been constructed primarily in the context of specific legal orders does it become possible to develop strong theories that have considerable explanatory and normative force for these legal orders.

This distinction between weak frameworks and strong or robust theories comprises the structure of this book. In Part One, I develop a weak analytical framework that seeks to do justice not only to the plurality of legal orders but also to the plurality of legal theories. In Part Two, I construct a strong theory of legal development on moral issues, which takes the intertwinement of law and morality

---

18 Klabbers, 'Constitutionalism', p. 95.

19 The phrase 'an eye for variation' originated with Philip Selznick when, during my sabbatical in Berkeley in 1993, he succeeded in convincing me that I needed to pay more attention to context and variation in my research on ideals. I have, however, been unable to find the specific phrase in his publications. Even so, the idea is central to his work, in which Selznick consistently argues for being open to variation in social reality (see Krygier, 'Selznick's Subjects', p. 6).

20 This is inspired by Philip Selznick's plea for weak definitions and strong concepts to do justice to variation (Selznick, *Law, Society and Industrial Justice*, p. 4). I prefer the terms framework and theory rather than definition and concept for reasons that will become clear in Chapter 5.

21 See Mallat, *Middle Eastern Law*.

seriously and focuses on a broad process of interaction. In the final part of this Introduction, I will briefly present the basic ideas upon which I will expound in the rest of this book.

A Weak Pluralist Framework

If we want to make our analytical framework as open as possible, it should take as its starting point the pervasive pluralism in legal theory. Even on the seemingly simple issue of defining the most basic of concepts, that of law, agreement appears to be impossible. The central thesis of my book is that we can understand and explain this theoretical pluralism better once we accept that law is an *essentially ambiguous concept*. Law can be modelled in two different ways that are at least partially incompatible. The first model, which I will call 'law as a product', focuses on statutes and judicial rulings and on law systematized as a doctrinal body of rules and principles. The second model, which I will call 'law as a practice', focuses on the practices by which law is constructed, changed and applied. Competing legal theories and competing definitions of law focus on different models and combine elements from these models in different ways.

Acknowledging the conceptual ambiguity of law, and of other central concepts such as morality, may not only help us understand why pluralism is so pervasive but may also give us insight into the relative value of each of the competing theories. Indeed, each theory focuses on different aspects of this complex phenomenon named 'law' and, consequently, neglects some other aspects. This means that each theory may contain a relative truth. However, it is only a relative truth, as each theory can only provide us with a partial description of law. It is also relative to context, as legal orders differ as to how important various aspects are; hence they differ in terms of which theories are most adequate to describe their legal reality. Medieval European legal orders required a descriptive theory different from that of the French legal system of the nineteenth century, with its major codifications.

We must accept, therefore, the relative truth of each legal theory. It should be noted at the outset, however, that this is not relativity in the strong sense, often used in popular debates, which tends to imply that anything goes. Accepting that partiality and relativity to context are inevitable in legal theory need not imply that we should wholly embrace it and should become indifferent as to how much partiality and relativity is inherent in a theory. Partiality is a gradual concept. We can reflect on how partial our theory is. We can ask which biases are inherent in it, how do they influence the validity of our findings and how can we counteract these biases. A good strategy to correct our biases is to switch back and forth to a competing theory that is highly sensitive to precisely these aspects that our own theory neglects. Consequently, positivists may be required to correct their biases by switching to a natural law theory, and vice versa.

A similar idea holds true with regard to relativity as a gradual concept. If we accept that legal theories are relative to specific legal orders, the first step is to understand in which respects they are relative. A comparison with other legal orders and with the theories that seem most adequate to describe them may be a first step. The second step may be either to accept that our theory is bound to our own legal order or to try to generalize some of our findings in a way that spans a number of different legal orders as well.

By seeing law as an essentially ambiguous concept, we have to accept that a truly universal and inclusive theory of law is impossible. However, this does not preclude strong local theories that are self-reflectively aware of their biases and restrictions. But it does allow us to understand why some theories developed out of specific historical circumstances and why they were valuable contributions to the legal debates of their time, even if they seem untenable in light of our own legal orders.[22]

Such an open analytical framework requires and promotes a pluralist approach to legal theory and to law. For example, the neglect of natural law theories by most contemporary Western legal philosophers may be explained because contemporary legal orders consist of enormous bodies of positive rules and case law, which can be reasonably described with theories such as legal positivism or interpretivism. Natural law seems to have nothing to add to this. However, in emerging or chaotic legal orders, natural law theories may provide invaluable insights, for example, with regard to war crimes or human rights. Once we have learned to perceive that, in these contexts, a natural law approach has something to offer – such as a minimum content of natural law that every legal order must respect in order for it to be truly law – it may be possible to return our attention to our own legal orders. The experience that, in other contexts, a natural law approach offers invaluable insights may allow us to perceive some dimensions of those orders highlighted by natural law theories that, so far, have been imperceptible to us because of the predominant influence of positive law.

My suggestion that law is an essentially ambiguous concept and that, therefore, a truly universal and complete theory of law is impossible raises many issues of a methodological nature. If one coherent general theory is impossible, can we still uphold coherence as a methodological criterion? The answer is that as long as we understand that relativity does not mean that anything goes, and we remain self-critically aware of the biases in our own theory, coherence remains a valuable regulative ideal. Our strong theories should be both as coherent and as complete as possible. Accepting the inevitability of some incoherence does not mean a licence to state just anything. We must provide appropriate reasons as to why some parts of our theories are incoherent, just as we must provide reasoned arguments as to why our theories are incomplete and partial.

---

22 Cotterrell's contextualist description of jurisprudential theories offers a nice example of how such a presentation of different theories might work (Cotterrell, *Politics of Jurisprudence*).

A Strong Legal Interactionist Theory

To make a case for the abstract pluralist framework, I will show in the first part of this book how such a framework serves to enhance our understanding of debates between existing theories. The task I set out for myself in the second part of this book is to show how the framework also helps us to construct new theories. It enables us to build strong theories, even if – or precisely because – they are partial, contextual and not completely coherent.

The context of the theory of law that I develop in Part Two is one of Western liberal democracies governed by the rule of law at the beginning of the twenty-first century. The challenge for theories of law in this context is fourfold; or, put another way, they must be able to address at least four phenomena. Firstly, they must address global legal pluralism: the presence of a plurality of partly intertwining relatively autonomous legal orders, such as domestic law, international law, EU law and the law of the Council of Europe.[23] Secondly, they must attend to the production of enormous amounts of black-letter law in modern regulatory states. Thirdly, they must tackle the emergence of interactional law: legal norms emerging in more or less horizontal interactions between various parties, such as citizens, business, non-governmental organizations, state institutions and international organizations. Examples of these kinds of interactions may be found in normative development at the international level, in interactive legislation and in self-regulation. Fourthly, they must attend to the dynamics of law and society: namely, the highly dynamic character of Western societies and law, which makes very static images of law obsolete.

My claim is that legal interactionism provides the best response to these four challenges. Legal interactionism is inspired by the later work of Lon Fuller. In his book *Anatomy of the Law*, he endeavoured to do justice to the insights of both legal positivism and natural law theory.[24] Fuller's approach can be enriched with ideas from sociological jurisprudence, especially that of Philip Selznick, who also tried to combine insights from natural law theory and legal positivism.[25] Selznick

---

23   In a broader sense of global legal pluralism which I will defend in Part Two (see Berman, 'Global Legal Pluralism', p. 1172), we should also add legal orders emerging among non-state actors, such as customary law and *lex mercatoria*, and norms created by private regulatory bodies, religious groups and professional organizations. Many legal theorists do not regard these normative orders as law; however, they still have to address the challenge of global legal pluralism in a narrower sense, where at least domestic law, international law, EU law and the law of the Council of Europe are relatively autonomous, intermeshing and conflicting legal orders.

24   Fuller, *Anatomy of Law*.

25   Selznick, 'Sociology and Natural Law'. Both Fuller and Selznick characterized their views in terms referring to, but at the same time clearly distinct from, the natural law tradition: as 'procedural natural law' (Fuller, *Anatomy of Law*) and 'legal naturalism' (Selznick, 'Sociology and Natural Law'), respectively. In a review of *Anatomy of Law*, Selznick argues that Fuller's theory might also be best referred to as legal naturalism, even

argued that to understand a phenomenon such as law, we must recognize that it is oriented towards the distinctively legal ideal of legality. Jutta Brunnée and Stephen Toope's work on interactional international law (building on Fuller's earlier work *The Morality of Law*) provides a third source of inspiration. Brunnée and Toope argue that interactional law is the primary source of legal obligations. Legal interactionism builds on this insight by giving interactional law pride of place. It recognizes interactional law as a source for legal obligations, but also accepts that contracts and enacted law, such as legislation and case law, may constitute relatively autonomous legal orders in their own right. Even though, ultimately, the obligatory force of enacted law and contract is embedded in an interactional pattern, it does not reduce the obligatory force of contract or enacted law to that of interactional law. Consequently, legal interactionism, as I understand it, is more pluralist than the theories mentioned above, because it takes positive or enacted law more seriously.[26]

Legal interactionism implies a broad form of relative legal pluralism accepting that there is a great plurality of relatively autonomous legal orders – orders that are partly autonomous and partly intertwined. Rather than accepting one criterion as the 'distinctively legal', legal interactionism emphasizes that the concept of law is plural in character and can best be analysed in terms of a dynamic family resemblance. Because of this pluralist character, legal interactionism can do justice to both an enormous body of state-enacted law and the emergence of interactional law in various areas of law, including international law. Moreover, it can also do justice to the undeniable fact of global legal pluralism.

Legal interactionism can also meet the challenge of understanding dynamics. In a practice model, it casts a wider net than do most positivist theories in looking

---

though he admits that Fuller does not use the term himself (Selznick, 'Review of Anatomy of Law').

26 Legal interactionism is indebted primarily to the philosophical tradition of pragmatism and its sociological relative: symbolic interactionism. American pragmatism was an important source of inspiration for both Selznick and Fuller. On Selznick's pragmatism, see Krygier, *Philip Selznick*, p. 30 and *passim*; on Fuller's pragmatism, see Winston, 'Is/Ought Redux'. In this book, I will not elaborate on this wider theoretical setting, although my pragmatist leanings will be obvious. An interesting defence of pragmatism in legal theory is provided by Coleman, *Practice of Principle*, pp. 6ff. I agree with most of the five pragmatist commitments he formulates; however, I believe that such a pragmatist position does not support inclusive positivism. The holistic understanding of practices that Coleman rightly emphasizes makes it impossible to separate law and morality, as I will explain in Chapter 5. The meaning of legal concepts must, therefore, be understood in light of the meanings those concepts have in morality, and vice versa. To determine the meaning of moral concepts (and of legal concepts), we have to engage in a process of critical reconstruction that cannot rely merely on social morality, but that also requires reflection on critical morality. In other words, pragmatism leads to Dworkinian interpretivism as developed in Dworkin's early work, but without the more objectivist or metaphysical claims in his later work, especially in *Justice for Hedgehogs*.

not only at the tip of the iceberg – the products of legislative processes and court procedures – but also including the processes leading up to the decisions of courts and legislatures, as well as the processes after the decisions have been made. Moreover, with its acceptance of relative pluralism and interactional law, legal interactionism pays special attention to the emergent norms and normative discussions in society, and in particular social practices that may be the harbingers of legal change. In the product model, legal interactionism focuses on the importance of ideals as one of the doctrinal sources for critically reconstructing the legal doctrine in light of new circumstances and new problematic cases.

As pluralism and dynamics are pervasive in modern law, legal interactionism is a more adequate theory to describe modern law than are the traditional competitors of legal positivism and natural law. On a more concrete level, this ability to do justice to pluralism and dynamics is also reflected in the understanding of phenomena that, at first sight, may seem like legal anomalies or aberrations. For example, the dynamic interplay in many European countries between domestic law, European Union law and Council of Europe law can only be understood in the context of a perspective that does justice to both pluralism and dynamics. Three of these apparent anomalies are international law (especially in its early stages of development), the law based on the European Convention on Human Rights and interactive, horizontal legislation. Each of these phenomena, in various ways, does not fit into the standard view of law, and is often criticized for that very reason. As I will show in Chapter 8, legal interactionism provides a more positive approach. Not only can it see these phenomena as newly emerging variations of law – rather than as aberrations – it can also explain why these phenomena are an adequate response to the specific conditions of dynamic pluralism in the modern world. We may, therefore, regard these phenomena as part of a newly emerging paradigm of interactional law.[27]

Interaction is central in this paradigm of interactional law.[28] This means that legal norms emerge from the interaction of a great many actors on the basis of their shared understandings. This is in stark contrast to positivist theories that usually focus on law as the product of specific state authorities such as legislatures and courts. In this paradigm, 'law' refers both to the interaction of these actors, to the

---

[27] Various terms have been used for this type of law and for the related jurisprudential theory. The specific type of law has been named 'interactional' (Brunnée and Toope, *Legitimacy and Legality*; Fuller, *Anatomy of Law*, p. 221 and p. 237), 'interactionist' (Witteveen, 'Rediscovering Fuller: An Introduction') and, especially if referring to legislation, 'interactive' (Van der Burg and Brom, 'Legislation on Ethical Issues'; Poort, *Consensus and Controversies*). Interactional law seems the best general term.

[28] Such a reorientation towards interaction and communication has recently been advocated by various other authors: for example Jürgen Habermas, Niklas Luhmann and Gunther Teubner. See also Van Hoecke, *Law as Communication*, esp. pp. 8–11. However, in my view, these theorists still do not take seriously enough the notion of interactional law emerging from interaction between citizens. I consider that they focus too much on the institutionalized and systemic nature of legal orders.

various practices in which legal norms emerge, as well as to the norms themselves, and to the legal doctrine that emerges from these practices. Normative development is the result of an interplay between various societal stakeholders. Even if, in the end, the courts or the legislature may formulate the norms authoritatively, their role is much less important than it is commonly described to be in legal theory. For example, in the development of bioethics and bio-law, legal scholars and moral philosophers have played a leading role, in combination with various groups in biomedical practice and in society at large. This is typical of the interactional paradigm. Legislatures and courts certainly play a role, but it is frequently a more marginal one, and also different from the traditional roles accorded to them. They participate in a social dialogue and help to structure and guide it, often leaving open the direction that development should go. In a sense, to implement their general ideals, they rely more on practice than on theoretical doctrine.

Legal interactionism, as I understand it, differs from Fuller's theory in *The Morality of Law* and from Brunnée and Toope's theory in one important respect. In line with the later work of Fuller, I do not regard interactional law as the only source of law. Legal institutions often take on a life of their own. In some cases, law may even best be analysed in terms of general commands enforced with sanctions. Thus, I develop a more consistently pluralist account of legal interactionism, accepting that interactional law and enacted law can both be important sources of law and that there may be other sources as well, such as contract.

To summarize, we may describe legal interactionism in four theses. First, it is a theory of law accepting an irreducible plurality of sources or types of law, each with its own distinct characteristics. Each of these sources may create obligatory force. The most important sources are interactional law and enacted law. Second, there is not one (set of) characteristic(s) that constitute(s) the distinctively legal, but a dynamic family resemblance. Third, law is a gradual concept; therefore, there are different dimensions according to which a normative order can be more or less law or not law. Fourth, a multiplicity of stipulative definitions is legitimate, to be justified in light of context and purpose.

In legal interactionism, law and morality are not separate entities; nor is law the dominant partner deciding authoritatively which parts of morality to incorporate. Instead, there are various forms of interplay between the two in their common pursuit of new norms.

Legal interactionism, therefore, also provides a novel perspective on the relation between law and morality. Law is always partly intertwined with morality and partly relatively autonomous; the mix of intertwinement and relative autonomy varies. The stronger the reliance on interactional law, the emphasis on law as an argumentative and discursive practice and the orientation towards principles, ideals and open norms, the stronger the intertwinement between law and morality will be. The more that law is oriented towards distinctively legal ideals, recognizes distinct legal procedures, institutions and professions, relies on black-letter law and rigidly formulated rules and uses a technical language, the more it will be relatively autonomous. Legal interactionism is thoroughly contextualist. Law cannot be separated from morality, and, in this sense, there is a necessary intertwinement between law and morality. Nevertheless, the degree of intertwinement and the form it takes is variable and, thereby, contingent. Law is oriented towards certain ideals that are inherent in the legal practice and that promote the moral quality of law. We might say that there is a necessary potential, but the degree of realization is contingent. Legal interactionism, therefore, offers a perspective that does justice to the core of truth in legal positivism and in natural law.

PART I
UNDERSTANDING
THEORETICAL PLURALISM

Chapter 1
Two Basic Models of Law and Morality

Theoretical Pluralism

There is hardly any other discipline where the central concept is as controversial as that of law. The broad variety of definitions is just an illustration, as is the fact that many authors have resisted presenting a strict definition and prefer a more general approach of conceptual analysis. Some authors have described law as a practice or an activity: 'the enterprise of subjecting human conduct to the governance of rules' (Fuller); an argumentative practice and an interpretive enterprise (Dworkin); a practice oriented towards the ideal of legality (Selznick).[1] Others have described it as a hierarchical or institutionalized system of norms (Kelsen and Raz), or as the union of primary and secondary rules (Hart).[2] And it is not only legal theorists that have trouble defining the law. If we ask ordinary citizens, some refer to the collection of rules found in statutes, others to law-enforcement institutions like courts and the police. Some may also make reference to ideals of justice.

Even for legal theorists, it is difficult to fully understand this controversy. What precisely is at stake in dividing the different camps? Many suggestions have been made to structure the debate in terms of one central issue that divides the parties, but none of these suggestions have succeeded in obtaining full acceptance from all the battling parties. One reason may be that, on close inspection, there is not just one divide, but a plurality of them. They partly overlap in the sense that most positivists tend to be in one camp on all of the issues and the non-positivists in the other. I suggest that we discern at least four issues that keep the parties divided.

The first issue that divides the parties is whether or not law can and should be described in morally neutral terms (or whether it can be described as separate from morality). The interpretations regarding what this means vary greatly. Some natural lawyers argue that law has an essential or conceptual connection with morality, others that in order to qualify as law, it must meet certain substantive or procedural standards that have moral implications.[3] Interpretivists have a different

---

1 Fuller, *Morality of Law*, p. 145; Dworkin, *Law's Empire*, p. 13 and p. 91; Selznick, 'Sociology and Natural Law'.

2 Kelsen, *General Theory of Norms*; Raz, *Concept of a Legal System*; Hart, *Concept of Law*.

3 See Beyleveld and Brownsword, *Law as Moral Judgment*; Finnis, *Natural Law and Natural Rights*; Fuller, *Morality of Law*.

angle: they argue that it is impossible to separate legal and moral arguments in legal discourse.[4] Positivists similarly have offered scores of formulations regarding what the difference precisely consists of.[5] I will leave this discussion here, and will elaborate upon it more fully in Chapter 4.

The second issue of contention is whether some reference to legal ideals or purposes is to be included. For Gustav Radbruch, law is oriented toward justice as it is 'the reality the meaning of which is to serve the legal value, the idea of law [i.e. justice]'.[6] For Philip Selznick, it is the practice oriented towards the ideal of legality.[7] And Lon Fuller characterizes law as a purposive enterprise.[8] Most positivist authors, however, differ from Radbruch (who for that reason sits, even in his early positivist period, uneasy in the positivist camp) in emphatically excluding any reference to ideals.

A third dividing issue is whether law is always connected, directly or indirectly, to the authority of the state. Most positivists have held that it is and, thus, have found it difficult to recognize international law in its emerging stages as law. Moreover, the presumed connection of law with the state has blocked legal positivists from accepting legal pluralism. Many non-positivists have suggested, as do Lon Fuller and Philip Selznick, that we should leave behind the idea that all law must be connected to the state. Consequently, they find legal phenomena emerging in schools, factories and even among a group of friends, and argue that our society consists of a plurality of legal orders.

The fourth and most fundamental issue of contention concerns a difference in categories. Most legal authors, and especially legal positivists, focus on law as a doctrine, as a set of rules and principles, or as a collection of texts. Law is seen as an object, either in the physical sense of texts, or as a mental object, a thought construction. Most sociological authors as well as most non-positivists focus on law as a practice or institution, as an interaction, or even as a dimension of interaction. Again, this distinction overlaps largely with the usual distinction between positivists and non-positivists, but not completely. The most influential legal positivist, H.L.A. Hart, emphatically claims to defend a practice theory of law (I will show later that this is only true in part). And many classical natural lawyers discuss natural law as a doctrine of timeless precepts.

There are some additional controversies that complicate the scene, for example, regarding whether law is connected with sanctions or whether its focus is on external actions rather than on intentions. I will leave these issues aside here, however, as they are not relevant to the central argument of this book – even though they may be important in other contexts. The camps on the four issues overlap in part, though not completely. This is one of the reasons why it has been

---

4 Dworkin, *Law's Empire*.
5 See Lyons, *Moral Aspects of Legal Theory*.
6 Radbruch, *Rechtsphilosophie*, p. 119; in: Wilk, *Legal Philosophies*, p. 73.
7 Selznick, 'Sociology and Natural Law'.
8 Fuller, *Morality of Law*.

so difficult to understand the nature of the controversy and, for example, to classify an author like Radbruch (even in the period when he self-identified as a positivist) as he sometimes belongs to the positivist camp, and sometimes defends a position that nearly all other positivists eschew.

We may conclude that the concept of law is irreparably controversial. Of course, we could have the ambition to unravel the Gordian knot and come up with the conclusive distinction that everyone could accept. However, it is highly implausible that we would succeed where all others have failed. The only solution to the Gordian knot seems to be not to untie it, but to cut it through with some more or less arbitrary exercise of power. In fact, this is what almost all authors have done, even if most did not acknowledge it explicitly: they suggested or stipulated a definition of law that was incomplete or in other ways unsatisfactory, but that would work for their purposes.

It may be that in the end such an arbitrary exercise of power is the best we can come up with. However, I will choose a different strategy: to accept the fact of theoretical pluralism, and try to understand it. How can it be that the controversy (or better yet, the four controversies) seems intractable? There must be some more fundamental explanation. It is this explanation that I am after in this and the next chapter.

Two Basic Models of Law

The explanation for the existence of intractable controversies in legal philosophy is to be found in the fact that phenomena such as law can be modelled in at least two partly incompatible ways. Each model can offer good insights to some aspects of law, but cannot do justice to some other aspects. Thus, we need both models to fully understand law. However, as I shall argue in this chapter and the next one, the two cannot be combined into one coherent and complete model.

Before elaborating upon the two basic models of law, it may be helpful to illustrate the idea behind the models with an example from a completely different field, that of physics. In school most of us learned that an electron may be regarded as a tiny particle and as a wave. Yet, it cannot be regarded as both at the same time because a combined theory results in contradictions. Each of the models allows us to understand some aspects of the electron that the other model cannot explain. It is possible to translate ideas from the wave model into the particle model and vice versa, but there is usually some loss of meaning and elegance. Every attempt to try to do with only one model leads to partial and incomplete theories. Thus, to obtain a full theoretical understanding of electrons, we must alternate between the two models.

This is also the idea behind the two models of law. Each of them focuses on certain characteristics of law to which the other model is blind or has less-than-perfect vision. The first model focuses on statutes and judicial rulings, and on law systematized as a doctrinal body of rules and principles. The second model focuses on the practices by which law is constructed, changed and applied. Each model can partly incorporate the insights of the other model, but not all: they are not fully compatible; nor are their respective insights translatable into the other model without a loss of meaning and elegance. The practice model should not be seen as replacing the product model completely, but should instead be seen as a second, alternative model that will enable us to study dimensions of law that remain hidden in the product model. Therefore, we should alternate between the models to develop a full understanding of law.

Various authors have suggested similar distinctions between different types of knowledge. Gilbert Ryle has made a well-known distinction between knowing *that* and knowing *how*.[9] Knowing that involves theoretical knowledge of an activity, usually in the form of propositions formulating rules or criteria. Knowing how is practical knowledge of how a certain task must be executed. Ryle argues that it is a mistake to believe that theoretical knowledge is the basis for practical knowledge.[10] It is rather the other way round: 'Efficient practice precedes the theory of it'.[11] Knowing how to execute a certain task does not imply that someone can explain in theoretical terms how to do it or that she simply applies theoretical knowledge. Someone may perfectly know her way around a city but may be unable to draw a correct map or even to understand a map, let alone follow it.

A similar point has been made by James C. Scott. He stresses the importance of mētis: 'the knowledge that can come only from practical experience'.[12] He confronts this with formal epistemic knowledge, especially in the form of simplifications of social reality that involve written documentary, static, aggregate, and standardized facts.[13] State policies based on such 'maps' of social reality pretend to be more rational but usually fail because they cannot do justice to the actual complexity of natural and social processes.[14] Practical knowledge is often local and implicit rather than general and explicit. A good example is professional knowledge. An expression like 'the clinical eye' refers to this partly intuitive, experience-based type of knowledge. This professional wisdom is not easy to grasp in general theoretical insights, because it is so particularistic and contextual.[15]

Both Ryle and Scott present a rich analysis of the distinction between practical and theoretical knowledge, combining many themes. My suggestion is that the most fundamental difference between these types of knowledge may be understood as reflecting two partly incompatible models of dynamic phenomena, a practice model and a product model.

---

9   Ryle, *Concept of Mind*, pp. 28ff.
10 Ryle, *Concept of Mind*, p. 26: 'Intelligent practice is not a step-child of theory.'
11 Ryle, *Concept of Mind*, p. 30.
12 Scott, *Seeing Like a State*, p. 6.
13 Scott, *Seeing Like a State*, p. 80.
14 Scott, *Seeing Like a State*, p. 262.
15 Scott, *Seeing Like a State*, p. 316: 'Mētis resists simplification into deductive principles which can successfully be transmitted through book learning.'

Law as a Product

The model of law as a product is probably the most familiar among lawyers and the public alike. A question concerning the law of intellectual property will usually be answered with a reference to statutes and judgments by courts, or with the formulation of some rules and principles. In most law schools in the Civil Law tradition, this certainly is the predominant model: students have to learn law from studying the substance of statutes and precedent. Most textbooks on subfields of law present legal doctrine on a subject as a coherent body of rules and principles. And despite repeated criticism in the US literature since Oliver Wendell Holmes, repeated by legal realists and sociological jurisprudence, most of the work of legal scholars is doctrinal study.[16] Law is thus either a collection of texts or a coherent body of norms.[17] Traditionally, this model has been referred to by phrases like 'positive law' or 'law in the books'.[18]

This model may be called 'law as a product'.[19] Law as a collection of texts is the product of legislative and judicial activities. Law as a coherent body of norms can also be seen as a product. Legal doctrine is the product of constructive activity by scholars and legal officials, not in the 'real' world of texts but in the world of thought. Legal doctrine does not 'exist' as some kind of brooding omnipresence in the sky, of course. Nor does it exist in texts. It is merely a construction: a product of our minds.[20]

The latter remark is not entirely self-evident. There is a tendency to reify law as if it had an existence of its own and, as a result, an objective status. We use phrases such as 'The law states', which suggest an unequivocal, authoritative meaning.[21]

---

16 See Rhode, 'Legal Scholarship', p. 1338 for US law and jurisprudence. Differently, Glendon, *Nation Under Lawyers*, p. 205. In the Civil Law traditions the focus on doctrinal study is even stronger.

17 Accordingly, we may further subdivide this model into two subversions – law as a collection of textual materials and law as a thought-construction – but this would serve no purpose in this context. In other contexts, the distinction might be useful.

18 However, law as practice should not be identified with law in action. This phrase suggests there is an entity, law, which acts. I prefer to call it law-as-action.

19 I borrow this term from Peters, 'Law as Critical Discussion', who confronts a product orientation in law with a process orientation (which is part of what I call law as a practice).

20 Even so, we do not treat legal doctrine as merely a construction. In our everyday life we speak and act as if 'the law' is real in some sense. For an interesting analysis of how we talk about legal doctrine in ontological terms, even though it is no longer acceptable to the modern mind, see Smith, *Law's Quandary*, p. 50. However, his metaphysical claims are not the only way to explain this quandary. I suggest that the understanding of law as an essentially ambiguous concept provides an epistemological, rather than a metaphysical explanation.

21 Peters, 'Law as Critical Discussion', p. 250 argues that the focus on prevailing doctrines and official opinions 'congeal normative options as positive facts'.

We should always be sensitive to the fact that it rather reflects the subjective voices of its drafters and interpreters. Law as a doctrine is not something 'out there', but is the product of human interaction, and is inherently controversial in nature. Reification conceals this controversial nature and the ambiguity of legal concepts and, thus, gives legal doctrine an unwarranted objective status.[22]

In philosophy of law, this model can be found in the work of positivist authors, especially those in the continental legal tradition, in which the great codification projects tried to formulate legal doctrine in statutes and codes as completely, authoritatively and unambiguously as possible. (Hans Kelsen is a good example, whereas in the English tradition Jeremy Bentham, with his advocacy of codification, stands out.) However, it is even more prominent in the way many legal textbooks present their materials, as one glimpse in the law section of a bookshop would demonstrate.

Law as a Practice

The model of law as a practice starts with the basic role of law in society. When we buy bread or when we teach at a university, law makes sense of what we do and sometimes even creates the possibilities for us to do what we do. The interaction between the baker and myself when I buy bread can only be fully understood by someone who understands the legal meaning of this interaction; moreover, the transaction can only take place because such an interaction has a legal meaning. In modern societies, law permeates social reality, and almost every action has a legal dimension. In some activities, for example, trading, the legal aspect is rather obvious, if only because these activities are based on legal concepts such as property and sale. In other activities, for example, raising children, the legal aspect is largely implicit or hidden, but still there is a legal dimension – for example, because children have certain rights and obligations towards their parents.

The legal, in this sense, is not some distinct element that can be separated from social reality.[23] It is not a specific characteristic or quality of actions – not even a supervenient quality. Rather, it is a way of looking at reality which guides both our actions and our constructive interpretation of those actions; sometimes the legal framework is even constituted by our actions. The term 'aspect' is helpful here: the aspect cannot be isolated from the whole; it merely offers one way of seeing and

---

22 See Olsen and Toddington, *Law in its Own Right*, p. 49. They argue, using the distinction made here between law as product and as practice, that if we restrict ourselves to law as a product, 'the process of interpretation is arbitrarily excluded from the concept of law'.

23 See Dewey, 'My Philosophy of Law', pp. 76–7. Dewey views law as a social process (he also uses the word 'inter-activities') and, therefore, rejects the idea that law can be regarded as a separate entity.

understanding the whole.[24] We can reflect on the legal aspect of our activities and confront it with other aspects, as expressed in statements like: 'This is an illegal action, though it is morally (or aesthetically) good'. However, we cannot isolate 'the legal' as some distinct entity or sphere or characteristic of our actions; the law is not something that is 'there'.[25]

To make the legal aspect of our actions explicit, we must take a 'legal point of view' or a legal attitude.[26] This legal point of view is at the core of law as a practice. In this practice, we abstract from the legal as an inherent aspect of social reality so that legal norms can be explicitly formulated and recognized as legal, and can be critically discussed, changed or applied. If we focus on the activities of judges, legislators, lawyers, legal scholars and so on, law can be fruitfully modelled as a practice, as a cooperative human activity. These actors cooperate to create law; they change it, interpret and reconstruct it, and apply it to concrete problems. However, law as a practice is not limited to the work of legal experts. Applying and interpreting law is something every ordinary citizen has to do when interpreting human interaction and when taking law as an action guide.[27]

It will be clear that 'practice' is used here in a very broad sense. A practice can be defined as any coherent and complex form of socially established co-operative human activity.[28] In fact, we may distinguish a number of connected legal subpractices like legislation, court proceedings, legal advice and critical reflection, and creation of legal doctrine. These practices are partly institutionalized in distinct procedures; but each of these practices is also partly embedded in daily human interaction, such as when ordinary citizens interpret the law and apply it to guide their own actions, when they settle conflicts among themselves or with the help of friends acting as informal mediators, or when they critically discuss the merits of the law on a subject like euthanasia.

The essential idea of law as a practice is that we do not focus on the products of these activities, for example the statutes and judicial decisions, but regard these activities themselves as the law. This may seem strange at first sight, especially for lawyers with a Civil Law background, but it is not. If we look at science, we can focus on the activities of scientists (the practice) or at the theories they construe (the product) – both are called 'science'. Moreover, in the theoretical

---

24   The term 'aspect' is only partly helpful, because it suggests a passive observer in relation to the object. Social reality is not only observed but also influenced and constituted by the participating observers; law is also a way in which we make our reality.

25   See Shklar, *Legalism*, p. 33.

26   Compare the central role attributed to 'attitude' in the last paragraph of Dworkin, *Law's Empire*, p. 413: 'Law's empire is defined by attitude.'

27   See Peters, 'Law as Critical Discussion', p. 251.

28   This definition is based on the first part of the definition in MacIntyre, *After Virtue*, pp. 187ff. MacIntyre distinguishes between practices and institutions as oriented towards internal and external goods, respectively; by omitting the second part of MacIntyre's definition of practice, I have chosen a broader definition that includes what MacIntyre calls institutions.

literature, the model of law as a practice, as a coherent activity, is quite common. Lon L. Fuller regards law as a purposive enterprise;[29] Ronald Dworkin regards it as an interpretive enterprise and as an argumentative social practice.[30] Recently, Brunnée and Toope developed an elaborate theory of interactional international law, which describes law in terms of a practice of legality.[31]

Two Examples: Social Rules and Rules of Customary Law

The two models of law should be regarded as complementary. Each provides insights that the other cannot provide; each has its own blind spots. Yet, combining them into one supermodel is not possible. The main reason is that each regards law as fitting into two incompatible categories: as a product or thought construct with propositional content on the one hand; and as a practice or as an aspect of activities on the other hand. In the next chapter, I will more elaborately discuss the claim that the models are really incompatible; but I hope that at this stage it is at least plausible that it would be very difficult to combine them because of this difference in categories.

The idea of two complementary partial models is not only useful in analysing the concept of law; it is also helpful in dealing with other concepts in disciplines such as the social sciences and practical philosophy, and with more specific concepts in law itself. Concepts like these may be called essentially ambiguous concepts. This idea will be elaborated upon in the next chapter but, for now, I will simply define them as concepts which refer to a dynamic phenomenon which can be modelled only incompletely in two partly incompatible ways. I will illustrate this with two examples. The first one is the general concept of a social rule, and the second one is a more specifically legal concept, that of a rule of customary law.

Take the social rule of men taking off their hats before entering a church. It is a famous example analysed by both Hart and Dworkin, and the discussion between them illustrates their inability to really understand one another.[32] In Hart's analysis, this social rule may be determined easily with reference to observable facts. We simply observe what men do when they enter a church. If they all take off their hats, we can cite the social rule as the reason why, and criticize others who do not take off their hats. In this way, we may conclude that a social rule exists that requires men to take off their hats when they enter a church. The rule 'Take off your hat when entering a church' seems an unambiguous rule for men. As

---

29 Fuller, *Morality of Law*, p. 145.
30 Dworkin, *Law's Empire*, p. 90 and p. 14. For a different view of law as a practice, see also Patterson, *Law and Truth*.
31 Brunnée and Toope, *Legitimacy and Legality*.
32 Hart, *Concept of Law*, pp. 124–5 and in the 'Postscript' at p. 257; Dworkin, *Taking Rights Seriously*, pp. 50–58. In the 'Postscript', Hart complains that he finds Dworkin's words 'tantalizingly obscure'.

this example is used by Hart to illuminate the concept of a social rule in general, we may conclude that social rules in general are to be regarded as unambiguous concepts: they can be described in terms of observable behaviour or, in other words, in terms of a practice model.

Dworkin argues that this social rule is not merely a matter of fact; as a normative rule, it can only be fully understood in light of its underlying moral purposes.[33] For example, it may be unclear whether male babies wearing bonnets fall under the rule. In order to interpret the rule, we must look to its purpose, its justification. This is, in my view, not a very convincing example against Hart, because it can easily be discarded with an appeal to the 'open texture' of descriptive language, as almost everyone would agree that it is a penumbra case. The vagueness can be settled easily by providing a more precise formulation.

A more interesting case against Hart's analysis would be to question what the social rule would require of a Jewish man when entering a church. According to his own religion, he should cover his head when participating in a religious service. Now we have to determine the issue at the core of the rule. We must choose, for example, whether the social rule requires every man who enters this sacred building to take off his hat, or whether it merely requires every Christian to do so (in which case atheists need not bare their heads either), or whether every man should do so, unless his own religion obliges him to cover his head.[34] This is, unlike the baby's bonnet, not an example of vague language; it puts into question the central purpose behind the rule, which is controversial. Is it respect for a sacred building, for religious devotion to God, or for both? Now we must explore issues that go beyond observable behaviour and begin a project of interpretation of what the practice is supposed to imply, and of explicitly constructing a doctrine of the rule. Moreover, we need to understand the purpose of the rule, its justification; and for its justification, we cannot refer merely to the existence of the practice. When we dig beneath the superficial analysis, the seemingly unambiguous rule proves to be an ambiguous concept which requires us to switch between a practice perspective and a doctrine perspective in order to fully understand what seemed, on first analysis, only a simple rule.

How precisely should such an analysis go? We have two options. If we regard the churchgoers rule as merely a social rule, we have to address the purpose of the rule. We must provide reasons for the rule, and it is not sufficient to merely refer to

---

33 Although I agree with Dworkin's argument about the inherently normative character of social rules, I am not interested in the relationship between facts and norms here. My use of the example serves a different purpose: we cannot understand the rule merely in terms of actions and practices, but we also need to understand it in terms of a doctrine. Whether the construction and interpretation of such a doctrine is a morally neutral enterprise, as a positivist might hold, or an inherently normative enterprise, as Dworkin would hold, is irrelevant for my purposes in this chapter.

34 Other variations are also possible: perhaps he should bare his head only during the church service; perhaps priests or ministers are exempt and so on.

the existence of the rule. If we regard it as a religious obligation, we may also refer to the relevant biblical text or to authoritative statements by religious authorities.[35] In both cases we need to construct a theory, a doctrine about men taking off their hats in church, and enter into an argument about the normative reasons that can be used to justify why we should choose one interpretation, as applied to Jews and atheists, over the other.

Most likely, even after careful analysis and discussion, views will differ. Some will hold that Jews and atheists have to respect the 'rules of the house', whereas others will defend the position that each man has to serve God in his own way, so that the rule only applies to Christian men. A third position is that the rules of the house should be respected, unless one's own religious tradition obliges one to behave differently (and perhaps unless they are offensive or discriminatory); in that case the Jew should cover his head, but the atheist should uncover it. Different interpretive principles may conflict here: there is no clear criterion regarding which one should prevail; nor is there a suggestion that there is always the same hierarchy between them. For example, it seems to me that even those who would take the second position would be willing to take their shoes off when entering a mosque; in that context the rules of the house argument should obviously prevail. When a non-Muslim enters a mosque, it is only respectful if he takes off his shoes, even if his own religion does not require him to do so.

Clearly, the type of argument appropriate for use in the interpretation of social rules is a matter of controversy, and there is no easy or mechanistic interpretation. This means that we must enter an interpretive discussion in which we construct the best possible doctrine for the interpretation of the social rule. This example demonstrates that even for simple social rules we need both models for a more complete understanding: that of practice and that of doctrine. Especially in controversial cases we may have to switch between practice and doctrine in order to reach a more complete understanding.

My second example addresses a subcategory of social rules: rules of customary law. In the Civil Law tradition, as well as in international law, a customary rule must meet two requirements in order to be recognized as a legal rule: *usus* and *opinio juris sive necessitatis*. There must be a practice, i.e., at least some actions in conformity with the rule; and there must be a belief that there is a legal obligation to act in accordance with the rule. The first element can be understood in terms of the practice model and the second in terms of the doctrine model as a belief with a propositional content. The concept of rules of customary law, thus, requires both models for the purpose of a more complete explanation. I believe the ambiguity I have pinpointed here may also account for the problem customary law has comprised for many positivist theories.

---

35 It is remarkable that both authors treat it as a merely conventional rule, thus ignoring its biblical reference in 1 Corinthians 11: 7–10. If a social rule has a connection with a religious or legal authoritative text, it becomes even more problematic to analyse it merely in terms of a practice.

At first sight, it may look as if both *usus* and *opinio juris* can be reduced easily to observable social facts and that, in order to deal with the concept of customary law, we may rely on a simple model in which descriptions of observable actions and the statements of the beliefs behind those actions are combined into one legal doctrine. However, this will not do. Even if there are some statements as to why some subjects acted according to a perceived obligation, this may still leave us in doubt regarding the precise content and domain of application of the rule. Moreover, it may be unclear whether they are really acting on a rule or, in Dworkin's terms, on a principle that, in the cases presented so far, has not yet been overruled by a competing principle. For issues such as these, we cannot refer to the social facts alone. Neither the actions nor the dispersed statements regarding why the actions were made will enable us to acquire a complete picture of the rule of customary law. We must construct the *opinio juris* in terms of a doctrine. What is the purpose behind the practice, and what should we do if it conflicts with other valuable purposes? Thus, once again we need both models to fully comprehend the concept of a rule of customary law.

The resulting image is still too simplistic. In line with the usual scholarly explanations of customary law, I have treated *usus* and *opinio juris* as separate elements, even reified them as separate social facts. But, of course, they are not. They are two dimensions of the same phenomenon.[36] The *opinio juris* is what gives meaning to actions as instantiations of the customary rule. Each of the separate actions can only be fully described if the intention refers to the opinion that it was obligatory. If that intention was absent (for example because, in the circumstances, it was the most convenient action or merely a matter of courtesy) the action cannot be regarded as an instantiation of the rule of customary law. Conversely, the *opinio juris* is not some free-floating doctrine as a brooding omnipresence in the sky or a statement in the books. It only exists in the actions and in the mind of the actors, i.e., in their beliefs that they are obliged to act as they do. Scholarly books and texts such as preambles or court decisions do not constitute the *opinio juris*. Instead, they report that the *opinio juris* was present in the practice, and they may provide additional proof for the notion that the customary rule should be seen as part of the law.[37] Such texts may even contain a formulation of the rule that is widely regarded as authoritative. But in the end, the basis for the recognition of the customary rule is to be found in the repeated actions that embody the *opinio juris*.

Both the example of the churchgoers' rule and the example of customary law show that for most practical purposes we do not need a complete description using both models. One model suffices: in the first case, the practice model; in the

---

36 For a similar critique on treating *opinio juris* as a separate artifice, see Brunnée and Toope, *Legitimacy and Legality*, p. 47.

37 In international law, relevant actions may, however, also exist in statements made by state officials that they must uphold a rule. Especially where a practice involves omissions – not taking certain actions where it would be possible – it will often be difficult to identify a practice without heavy reliance on such statements.

second, the doctrine or product model. Observing behaviour in a mosque should be sufficient for me to understand that I must take my shoes off. We can usually stick to a simple practice conception in describing social rules. Only in some unusual situations will a practice conception prove inadequate, requiring us to switch between both models. It is only then that the ambiguity of the concept rises to the surface. Similarly, we can usually stick to a simple doctrinal model in order to describe the law. In the great majority of cases, judges may interpret the text of statutes almost mechanically. It is only in exceptional, hard cases that they must really engage in an explicit project of constructing the best possible interpretation of the law. It is only then that we realize that law truly is an interpretive practice as well as a doctrine.

Additional Models of Law

So far, I have only discussed two models of law. These are the basic models that usually suffice for an adequate description, but they are not the only models. There are others that may be useful for certain purposes. Although for most descriptions of natural phenomena models with four dimensions of space and time will suffice, for some purposes additional models adding a fifth or sixth dimension may be helpful. A similar point can be made with regard to law. Two additional models of law build on the distinctions between the actual and the potential and between the real and the ideal.

One model is that of the potential states. I am potentially an old man, but at this moment I am only middle-aged. Although I am not old now, the potential old man is also part of me. It would be wrong to act as if I were already old, but it would be equally wrong to act as if I will always remain the same middle-aged, healthy man that I am now.

In law, this potentiality model is of special importance. On many issues, in rapidly evolving fields, the law is not settled. Is an action for wrongful birth possible? Many jurisdictions have struggled with the issue (or are still struggling with it) and they have come up with different answers. In the Netherlands, until the Supreme Court held that such an action was possible, it was highly debated, and it was difficult to predict what the Court would do when confronted with such a case.[38] Two possible alternatives could find some support in case law, in legislation and in the writings of influential authors. They were both plausible and potentially true descriptions of positive law. Yet, neither of them could be seen as an adequate description of positive law prior to the Supreme Court's ruling.

In situations like these, it may be useful to abstract from positive law and extrapolate the various potential developments. Thus if we want to describe potential law we should describe positive law both as it would be if legal development were to take one course and as it would be if it were to take another

---

38 Hoge Raad 18 maart 2005, NJ 2006, 606 (*Baby Kelly*).

course. In fact, this would be the most adequate description of positive law prior to the rendering of a decision on the law. If someone were to ask a legal expert what the positive law on the issue was at that time, the correct answer would be: 'That is not clear, as there is no settled law. There are good reasons to argue that the best defensible view is X, and there are good reasons to argue that the best defensible view is Y. So I will present you with both stories, as they are both plausible and potentially true.' Perhaps the expert might add that there is also a third view, Z, which, in his eyes, is highly implausible. He might even add that he believes that X has stronger arguments than Y. But it would be an incorrect description to say that X forms part of the accepted legal doctrine.

Now, many legal authors – especially those of 'handbooks', this type of treatise being widely regarded as the hallmark of legal scholarship in the Civil Law tradition – fail to make this very distinction. They argue for X as if it were already positive law, and then add in a footnote that some authors disagree. Thus, they arbitrarily remove the uncertainty from their description of the law. They choose to present one of the potential models of law as if it were already positive law. I believe this is the wrong way to present such a controversy. It conflates the potential and the actual rather than distinguishing them. Consequently, it presents a false image of actual law. It would lead to more adequate descriptions and analyses of legal developments if authors of treatises would, rather, distinguish between the potential and the actual and clearly present the different routes legal development might take before presenting their own position about which development they think is most defensible.

Another model focuses on the ideals that are implicit in law. According to Radbruch and Selznick, we can only understand law if we see it as oriented towards certain ideals, such as legality.[39] These ideals are part of the law; they are implicit or latent in it. Yet they are not fully realized: reality falls short of the ideals. Therefore, they are immanent in reality and they go beyond reality as well. Describing law as if the ideals were fully embodied in existing law would not do justice to reality; but neither would a description that completely ignores the orientation of legal practice and doctrine to certain ideals.

Usually it will be possible to include the orientation on ideals in the description of reality, as partly realized ideals that may explain, for example, the coherence between elements of the doctrine. In only some situations, it may be helpful to abstract the ideals from legal reality and elaborate their partly implicit meaning in a more coherent theory. For example, in discussions on multicultural society, it may be helpful to reflect on what 'our' democratic ideals, as embodied in our legal institutions, imply for the possibility of doing justice for new religious minorities. In order to stimulate reflection, it may be helpful to reconstruct an ideal theory behind our practices and our traditions. This may make it possible to reinterpret our ideals in ways that enable more accommodation than previously thought possible.

---

39 On the role of ideals in the theories of Radbruch and Selznick, see Taekema, *Concept of Ideals*.

Both additional models are only useful for very specific purposes. They may produce insights that we cannot so easily perceive when we are stuck in either of the other two models. In this book, I will focus chiefly on the two basic models.

Models of Morality

In discussing morality, we can make a similar distinction between two basic models. As the basic idea of the two models will now be familiar, I will present only a brief description.

Morality as a Product

The most 'tangible' model of morality is that of morality as a product. We can construct morality as a set of rules and principles or as a complete moral doctrine.[40] This is the most common way of looking at morality: it is a set of guidelines for action that are supposed to form a coherent body of norms and values – a moral code. The Ten Commandments exemplify this type of morality.

This is also a dominant approach in ethical theory.[41] The influential book by Beauchamp and Childress is a good example of this: they 'believe that for biomedical ethics, which has concentrated on guidelines for action, principles and rules are both indispensable and central to the enterprise'.[42] Rawls's theory of justice and utilitarianism are examples in the field of political ethics; both present general principles for the basic structures of society, elaborate upon the practical implications of the theory, and construct a coherent normative theory.[43] Many articles by moral philosophers focus on morality as a product: they elaborate upon the implications of principles and rules and the meaning of central concepts; they test them against ingenuous (often fictitious) cases; and they suggest new distinctions, offer conceptual clarification, and so on.

---

40   See Frankena, *Ethics*, p. 8: '[M]orality starts as a set of culturally defined goals and of rules governing the achievement of the goals.'

41   See Williams, *Ethics and Limits of Philosophy*, p. 93: 'The natural understanding of an ethical theory takes it as a structure of propositions.'

42   Beauchamp and Childress, *Principles of Biomedical Ethics*, 1994 (fourth edition), p. 40 (this section was dropped from the sixth edition of 2008). It is interesting to note that, although they assert the centrality of principles and rules, at the same time they characterize biomedical ethics as an enterprise. This illustrates the fact that the two models are ideal-typical and that almost every interesting author, including those who clearly focus on morality as a product, tries to combine each model with some insights from the other. See Gert, *Morality*, p. 283), where he argues that the moral rules and moral ideals are the core of morality as a public system but must be supplemented with an attitude or a procedure.

43   Rawls, *Theory of Justice*; for utilitarianism see Singer, *Practical Ethics*.

Morality as a Practice

Morality is, often implicitly, embedded in social interaction and in our interpretations of this interaction. For example, medical practice is not merely a technical activity, but is also oriented towards the patient's good. Therefore, it makes sense to understand and evaluate the medical professional's actions not only technically but also morally. If we do so, we take a moral point of view or a moral attitude. Just like the legal point of view, the moral point of view offers a way of looking that guides both our actions and our constructive interpretation of those actions. From this moral point of view, we cannot isolate 'the moral' as some distinct entity or characteristic of our action.

In morality, there are no institutionalized equivalents of legislation or adjudication. (If there are, especially in religious institutions, this is usually a reason to doubt whether their norms really constitute a morality rather than law or some semi-legal institution.) But there is a systematic reflection on, and critical discussion of, the question whether suggested norms should be recognized as moral; how they should be interpreted, constructed and modified; and how they should be applied to old and new problems. A central part of this practice of reflection and discussion is the philosophical discipline of ethics, which is often defined as the systematic (or philosophical) reflection on morality. This is not limited to the scholarly discipline of ethics, however; neither is it institutionalized or monopolized by specialized experts. It may flourish in the academic sphere, but also in public debates. It can find a place in religious practices like sermons or pastoral counselling, but also in discussions among close friends. Ethical reflection can be found in many circumstances. It is not, as law usually is, an institutionally structured and, consequently, distinctly organized practice; it is, rather, a practice that pervades every other practice.[44]

Morality as a practice need not take the form of explicit theoretical and critical discussion of moral norms and the application of them. It can also be the practice of a living tradition in which traditional values are implicitly or explicitly endorsed, reinterpreted and passed on to the next generations through the acts of setting examples and telling stories. It can also be an internalized attitude in which one does not reflect (or no longer reflects) on what to do, but simply does 'what should be done'.

These two models of morality are ideal types as well. Most sophisticated ethical theories try to combine elements from both models; but every theory, in the end, neglects some elements because its primary focus is on one of the two. Many discussions in the ethical literature can – at least partly – be understood as

---

44 One may even wonder whether, if it is not distinctly organized, it is really a practice. Perhaps in the narrow sense of the term 'practice', it is not; but in the broad sense of the term, it is. Individual ethical reflection on separate actions is certainly possible (just like an individual can build a house without the help of others); but that does not mean that ethical reflection as such (or building as such) cannot be regarded as a practice.

debates between the different models, where one party (often correctly) claims that its opponents are blind to insights that are central to its own model. For instance, some critiques on Rawls imply that the Rawlsian primary focus on the product model of morality neglects the importance of morality as a lived practice. Rawls, especially in the third part of *A Theory of Justice*, but also in his notion of reflective equilibrium, certainly tries to accommodate many elements that are central to morality as a practice, such as virtues and intuitions. Nevertheless, the primary focus on selecting two basic principles for the political structure, and on constructing a normative theory for an ideal society, makes it impossible to do full justice to these elements. Alasdair MacIntyre correctly drew attention to the importance of the practice model neglected by this predominant focus on abstract ideal-theoretical systems of principles and rules.[45] However, as he was as one-sided as his opponents, he did not present an attractive alternative image to those who believed in the value of abstract theorizing and constructing general doctrines.

With regard to law, I distinguished two additional models. With regard to morality, the potentiality model is best known from Aristotle but, although some of his ideas are still highly relevant and widely discussed, his ideas about potentiality are much less so. The reason for this is that they build on a philosophy of nature that is no longer acceptable in light of modern science.

Ideal theory is more familiar and is still a widely used model. Ideal theory, the normative theory for an ideal society, is a well-known constructive device to get our moral intuitions and ideas clear to be able to test their coherence and justifiability. John Rawls's theory of justice is, of course, a well-known example of ideal theory. His claim is a double one: he wants to make explicit and test the implicit values of our liberal-democratic societies; however, he does this by a process of abstraction from the real society in which we live. In his view, this is the best method to analyse those ideas and submit them to a process of philosophical testing and refinement.[46]

The role of ideals in morality is not restricted to the philosophical elaboration of a complete ideal theory, however. Ideals are pervasive in our morality. Moreover, H.L.A. Hart makes the distinction between critical (or ideal) morality and positive or social morality.[47] This distinction can best be understood in terms of the two different models of morality: on the one hand, the model of social norms as, in fact, accepted by a society or by a group; and, on the other hand, the norms as they ideally would be accepted after a process of critical reflection – ideally, because such a process of critical reflection is never complete and will never enable us to see morality from a completely detached or ideal point of view. Even if it can never be reached, however, this critical ideal is an important one:

---

45 MacIntyre, *After Virtue*.
46 I will not go into the problems and advantages of such an ideal-theoretical move here. See Van der Burg 'Ideals and Ideal Theory'.
47 Hart, *Law, Liberty and Morality*.

we know that the norms we endorse may, in fact, be tainted by bias, prejudice and incorrect reasoning, and we believe that we should correct for these in order to get a more justifiable morality. The idea of a social morality then refers to the norms that are, in reality, accepted and endorsed, whereas the idea of an ideal or critical morality refers to an ideal typical thought construct of a morality that can withstand critical testing and that is completely justified (whatever the latter phrase would mean).

Restructuring Debates in Jurisprudence

The distinction between seeing law as a product and seeing law as a practice is the most fundamental distinction in the debates between positivists and non-positivists. Even if there is no strict logical connection between this position and positions on the other three issues, there is at least a natural tendency to combine positivist views on each of the four issues and a similar tendency to combine non-positivist views.

There is a tendency in legal positivism to focus on law as a product. If we regard law as a product, as a doctrine with propositional content, we must be able to determine what belongs to the doctrine and what does not. One of the advantages of positivism is that it promises to provide clear criteria to determine what the law is. This offers legal certainty, but also serves freedom. By inferring the contents of law from clear and objective sources such as statutes and judicial judgments, an objective basis is provided.

A legal doctrine is a thought construct. It is not to be found somewhere as a brooding omnipresence in the sky; it must be constructed. To provide for an objective basis for this construction – which in the end is a subjective process – positivism needs clear criteria or tests to determine which rules or principles are part of the law and which are not. The most objective criteria are tests of pedigree, which require that the sources of positive law must somehow be traceable to official authorities or authoritative practices. In modern societies, that means that they should be traceable to state authorities and law enforcement agencies. Therefore, there is a natural tendency to combine a doctrinal approach with a state-centred approach that rejects legal pluralism.

Positivism's focus on legal certainty also necessarily works to the exclusion of morality from legal doctrine. Moral norms are difficult to ascertain, are controversial and open-ended. Making references to morality, or even to moral arguments, somehow part of the legal doctrine would not merely make such doctrine uncertain at the penumbra, but would ultimately bring uncertainty to the heart of the law. Usually, moral issues are not merely marginal issues, such as whether an aeroplane is to be regarded as a vehicle or not. Many moral issues are essential to keeping society together: they are matters of life and death; they belong to the core of the law. Therefore, allowing references to controversial moral standards in the determination of the contents of law would endanger the great advantage of positivism – that of the promise of legal certainty.[48]

A similar point can be made with regard to open standards, such as principles and ideals. This is not merely an issue as to whether law is a collection of rules or a collection of rules, principles and ideals. Incorporating principles and, even more so, ideals into the law means introducing inherently open and controversial standards into the law. This brings controversy and argument in the determination of the contents of the law. Therefore, most positivists do not only wish to exclude morality from the objective sources of the law, but, equally, such open standards as ideals.

None of the above arguments offers a strict connection between the various positivist positions. It is possible to be a positivist and accept that moral principles play a role in the law; for example, soft or inclusive positivism provides a case in point.[49] It is also possible to accept that ideals play a role in the law, as Radbruch's positivist theory demonstrates. Further, it is possible to be a positivist and accept legal pluralism and accede that there may be legal orders not connected with the state – indeed, Hart's concept of law as a union of primary and secondary rules makes no mention of the state. Even so, it is clear that there is at least a tendency to combine the various positivist positions.

A similar story can be told with regard to those who focus on a practice view of law. If we focus on practices, we can stipulate, for example, that law is everywhere where some form of authoritative rule-making and enforcement exists. That can be on the shop floor, in a school context, as well as in a group of friends embarking on a camping expedition. Accepting legal pluralism and denying an essential connection between law and the state will follow almost naturally. Similarly, there is no need to make a strict distinction between law and morality. Even if we focus on law as an institutionalized practice, it is perfectly possible to regard it as open to moral arguments, and to accept that it is oriented towards ideals such as freedom or democracy, which are shared by morality and law. Thus, a practice view is at least more open to legal pluralism, to a strong connection with morality and to an orientation towards ideals.

Of course, this is only a rough sketch of two ideal typical models, and the possible implications of choosing one model for the positions on three other issues. This cannot possibly do justice to all the nuances and subtleties of the various positions in legal philosophy. I hope this sketch also demonstrates that the basic model chosen has implications for other issues that commonly are held to be the dividing issues between positivists and their opponents. Moreover, that there is a tendency, and not a strict connection between the various positivist positions, may explain why the camps on the various issues are not always divided along the same lines.

---

48   For a similar critique of soft positivism, see Dworkin, *Taking Rights Seriously*, p. 347.

49   See Waluchow, *Inclusive Legal Positivism*; Coleman, *Practice of Principle*.

I will elaborate upon this sketch in Chapters 3 and 4. However, at this stage it is necessary to point out that the story is further complicated by the fact that there are many intermediate positions. Most of the leading authors combine elements of both ideal typical models in their theories. Before delving into the various positions in jurisprudence, we should explore in more depth what the idea of the two models implies for our understanding of concepts such as law.

Chapter 2
Essentially Ambiguous Concepts

Peculiar Concepts

In the last chapter, I argued that phenomena such as law and morality may be described in at least two partly incompatible ways, and that each provides insights that the other way of describing cannot offer. Further, no coherent and complete theory that combines both models is possible. Nor is a coherent definition possible that combines both ways of describing these phenomena.

What does this thesis imply for the concept of law? It seems to be a peculiar concept. On the one hand, it refers to two different phenomena: law as a product and law as a practice. On the other hand, these are not two different phenomena, but are, instead, the same phenomenon described or modelled in two different ways. This type of conceptual ambiguity may seem peculiar but it is, in fact, quite common. Examples of this include concepts such as religion, science, language, and morality. Each may refer to both the practice and the activities on the one hand, and the product of that practice on the other. In ordinary language, we use 'science' to refer to both the practice of ongoing research and the results of that practice, i.e., the knowledge and the scientific theories. And we use 'religion' to refer both to the practices of religious believers and to the doctrines held by believers or formulated by religious institutions.

This is not merely a matter of words having more than one meaning, as in homonyms where a word has two unrelated meanings, or as in Wittgenstein's idea of family resemblance. The bank as a financial institution and the bank as a river side are unrelated, separate phenomena. By contrast, the electron as wave and the electron as particle are not *different* phenomena; rather, each model represents the *same* phenomenon perceived or modelled in two different ways. Similarly, law as an ongoing practice and law as a legal doctrine are not different phenomena; they are two models of the same, complex phenomenon.

Concepts such as law, religion or science may be characterized as essentially ambiguous concepts. They are all concepts which refer to a dynamic phenomenon which can be modelled only incompletely in two partly incompatible ways. One model is more adequate to describe movements or actions; the other is more suited to describe objects, whether tangible or merely thought constructions. We need both models; they require and complement each other, but it seems they cannot be combined coherently into a single model.

In this chapter, I will explore the implications of understanding that some of our concepts are essentially ambiguous. In disciplines such as law, practical philosophy and the social sciences, the essential ambiguity of central concepts has so far mostly been overlooked. I will suggest that the explanation for this oversight is that many of the phenomena to which these concepts refer are socially constructed. Moreover, because the idea of an essentially ambiguous concept and the familiar idea of an essentially contested concept have much in common, it is easy to overlook the fundamental difference between both. Exploring the commonalities and differences between both types of concepts may therefore provide a further clarification of this idea of essential ambiguity.

Definition

Let me simply introduce a definition, and then discuss its elements.

> An essentially ambiguous concept is a concept which refers to a dynamic phenomenon that can only be described and modelled in at least two different ways that are each essentially incomplete and that are partly incompatible with each other.

The dynamic nature of the phenomenon is the central issue. That all examples I have mentioned so far are of dynamic phenomena is not a coincidence. The explanation for the ambiguity is that some models are better equipped to understand the dynamics of a phenomenon, and others are better equipped to provide us with a detailed snapshot view. Not every phenomenon has such a complex nature. Objects like a table or a painting may be moved or changed and are the result of a creative activity, but are themselves not to be understood as a movement or an activity. Only dynamic phenomena may be connected with an essentially ambiguous concept.

There are at least two partly incompatible ways to model the phenomenon.[1] One model describes the phenomenon in terms of process, i.e., movement or action, the other in terms of an object, i.e., a thought construct or a product. With regard to social phenomena, the terms practice and product are usually adequate; but for natural phenomena other than actions and practices, terms like process and object may be more fitting. For instance, to return to the old models of the electron: we may regard an electron as a particle, an object, and as a wave, a process. Therefore, I would suggest the use of the more general terms process/practice model versus object/product model. A process/practice model describes a given phenomenon in terms of movements, processes, actions, or practices. An object/product model describes the phenomenon in terms of physical entities, texts, or thought constructions. The precise terminology is largely irrelevant. It may vary

---

1 I discuss essentially ambiguous concepts in this chapter in terms of only two models. However, as I have argued in the previous chapter, there can be more models, as there are other sources of ambiguity. Even so, the most important source of ambiguity is the dynamic character of phenomena, so I will ignore these other models here for reasons of simplicity.

as to which term is used, and in some cases, even other terms may be used. In law and religion it may be better to use the word doctrine.² What matters is that each of the phenomena referred to can be studied in terms of actions, movements, or processes on the one hand, and in terms of objects, doctrines, or products on the other.

In my definition of essentially ambiguous concepts, I have deliberately used the phrase 'described and modelled'. The ambiguity is to be found at both the levels of single-sentence descriptions and elaborate models or theories. If the law is described by Fuller as a purposive enterprise and by Hart as a combination of primary and secondary rules, these descriptions provide a shorthand for the more elaborate models or theories of the law for which they stand. The broader term 'conception', popularized by Ronald Dworkin, may be used to refer to both short descriptions and more elaborate models.³

A model, even a very detailed one, is, by definition, a simplification of reality. So, in a trivial sense, every model is incomplete, as it necessarily leaves out many details; usually, however, the model can be elaborated upon in various ways to include more details, if so desired. By 'essential incompleteness' I refer to a more substantive problem. A model is essentially incomplete if it leaves out important aspects or elements of a phenomenon which cannot easily be added to the model without distorting it, for example, by making it incoherent. A model of law is not incomplete, in this sense, if it does not strictly state the length, in days, of a prison sentence for a given crime.⁴ But it is essentially incomplete if (like Austin's theory of law as general commands) it cannot deal with customary law at all because it is framed in such a way that all law must necessarily be declared by national legal authorities such as legislatures and judges. The definition of essentially ambiguous concepts implies that each of the two models is essentially incomplete. The object model is unable to explain certain aspects of the practice or dynamics of the phenomenon, whereas the practice model is unable to explain some other aspects which are connected to the phenomenon as an object or as a doctrine.

Finally, the definition requires that the two models are at least partly incompatible. Of course, there will often be substantive overlap in the descriptions the models offer. Many aspects of the phenomenon may be equally well explained in terms of both models. However, the propositions of the two models can never be completely translated into one another; there is a loss of meaning. Combining

---

2 See Van der Burg, 'Interactionist View'.

3 For an explanation of the distinction between concept and conception, see Dworkin, *Taking Rights Seriously*, pp. 134–6.

4 For example, H.L.A. Hart regards the contents of the law as (fundamentally) incomplete because in hard cases the judge has discretion (Hart, *Concept of Law*, p. 252). Whatever the merits of his view, and Dworkin's critique on it, what is important to note here is that, when the judge makes such a discretionary decision, this does not lead to a distortion of the legal doctrine. We may only call a model essentially incomplete if inconsistency or other distortions result from making the model more complete.

both models into one supermodel or supertheory in which the models, as such, are included is not possible because it leads to incoherence. Why this must be so is fairly straightforward: the models refer to the phenomenon using different categories. If an electron is seen as a particle it can have mass, whereas a wave cannot have mass. If an electron is a wave, it has amplitude and frequency, whereas a particle cannot have these. Similarly, if religion is seen as a doctrine, it would be a category mistake to state that it has great musical variation and emotional appeal, which a liturgy like the Roman Catholic Mass may have. Perhaps the doctrine has an emotive appeal too, but that is not the same as the appeal of a musical liturgical experience. So we quickly run into incomprehensible statements and contradictions if we want to combine the two models in one model while still using the same language.

The distinction between the two models is a theoretical construction of two ideal types. We may distinguish theories with a strong focus on the product and theories with a strong focus on the practice. However, actual theories are seldom (if ever) framed exclusively in terms of one model, because otherwise certain important aspects would be absent from the theory. For example, almost all moral and legal theories that discuss practices, even if they primarily focus on action, provide a richer view than the ideal typical one presented here by including the intentions and beliefs connected with the actions. Thus, these theories include elements from the product model.

The idea of essential ambiguity has important implications for the scientific study of dynamic phenomena. It means that we have to choose between an incomplete description and an incoherent one. If we want to be complete, we have to accept incoherence. If we want to be coherent, we have to accept incompleteness. For an adequate description we should use both models, but we cannot use them in one complete and coherent supertheory; instead, we should regularly switch between the models to understand those aspects of the phenomena that can only be studied adequately in the other model. Completeness and coherence may be separate regulative ideals, but it seems that the attempt to completely realize both ideals leads to serious problems or antinomies.[5]

Social Phenomena

Some phenomena are social in nature. Science, religion, language, law, morality – they all would simply not exist without humans and human action. These phenomena vary with cultures and societies. Each country has, for example, its own legal order and its own legal culture. Religions vary greatly and develop over time. Critical reflection may play a role in the way such phenomena are perceived, criticized and then perhaps changed. Although natural phenomena may be the result of human construction in one sense – think of the electron in experimental

---

5   There is an interesting parallel here with Gustav Radbruch's idea that the tension between the three ideals constituting the *Rechtsidee* leads to antinomies.

situations – social phenomena are the result of human construction in a more radical sense.

Our conceptions of social phenomena influence the phenomena themselves. For example, if I believe that in religion orthopraxy is much more important than orthodoxy, I will structure my religion accordingly. If I can convince my fellow-believers to adopt my position in this regard, then our common religion will become one in which orthopraxy is central. Moreover, if such praxis-oriented religions become dominant in a given society, this may determine the broader view of what religion is in that society. The idea that religion is, primarily, a system of beliefs may, consequently, be hard to grasp in such a society.

Thus, a specific conception of an essentially ambiguous social concept may make itself true. If, to take another example, all lawyers, legislators and citizens in a certain jurisdiction are legal positivists, this will influence the phenomenon of law itself.[6] The legal actors will try to mould law into their positivist image. Lawyers and judges will present legal arguments in such a way that no explicit reference to morality is made, and after a while it will be difficult to find any precedent that is not consistent with a positivist viewpoint. Legislators will focus on broad codifications in order to ensure that we can always construe the law as based, directly or indirectly, on authoritative statements by legal officials. For example, a Dutch statutory provision of 1828 stated that customary law is only recognized as law if and only if it is explicitly recognized as law by statute.[7] Customary law does not fit easily in most positivist views of law; by this act the legislator simply validated a positivist view of customary law.

This general tendency that perceptions of social phenomena influence their own reality is especially significant for essentially ambiguous concepts. Usually, one of the two models will be dominant in a given society. In the positivist Civil Law traditions, law is primarily seen as a collection of statutory texts and as a doctrine based on their contents and their interpretation by the courts. In a Calvinist tradition, religion is primarily seen as orthodoxy, a belief in a certain doctrine based on God's Word, the Bible. If most actors hold such a perception of law or religion, that view will become self-reaffirming through their actions and statements.[8] In a sense, the model makes itself immune to criticism.

---

6 See Davies, 'Politics of Defining Law', p. 159: 'Positivism is a self-fulfilling prophecy or ideology which so influences behaviour that it has become true.'

7 See Taekema, 'Introducing Dutch Law', p. 25. Taekema reports that, of course, it had little effect. The provision was only repealed in 1992.

8 A curious example of such an influence on the broader society and even on the legal order is provided by a Dutch lower court case on the Hindu ritual of spreading the ashes of a deceased in a river, in violation of environmental regulations (Kantonrechter Zevenbergen, 3 februari 1982, *NJCM-Bulletin* 1982, 418). The court held that the spreading of a deceased's ashes could not be regarded as a religious obligation because there was no authoritative religious text in which the obligation was formulated. Thus the Christian conception of a text-based religion was uncritically applied in this case, despite the fact that, in Hinduism, texts do not have such a central and authoritative status.

As a result, we may easily overlook that a concept such as law or religion is essentially ambiguous. That customary law does not fit into a source-based positivism can be ignored because the positivist legislator has provided a seemingly clear criterion and customary law that does not fit this criterion may be easily discarded as not really law. That judges implicitly rely in their argumentative practice on moral values and principles (and thus do not fit into a source-based positivism either) may easily be overlooked if positivist judges make an effort to exclude explicit appeals to morality from their written opinions.[9]

This self-fulfilling process of actively choosing one dominant model is reinforced by the social construction of restrictive definitions. For example, a positivist author may argue that custom is not law unless it is explicitly recognized as such by statute. If she has sufficient authority, this view may lead to a generally held belief in her community in which law is, by definition, restricted to rules that find their basis in statutes. Any person who, nevertheless, calls such a custom customary law can be proven to be mistaken – he simply does not understand the concept of law.

Even so, some phenomena will remain that do not fit the dominant model. Even if customary law may not be central to our own legal order, we have to admit that it plays a role in some other legal orders. In some legal orders (for example, international law regarding war crimes or the case law of the European Court of Human Rights) explicit appeals to moral arguments are made. The final line of defence for the dominant model is to regard such examples as atypical, as problems of the penumbra, and, in a sense, as not 'really' law. It is the core that matters, and the critics simply have an obsession with a small minority of hard cases. In political debates on religion, this phenomenon is well known. Radical anti-Muslim authors in Europe argue that we must focus on the essential core of Islam, which is to be found in a literal interpretation of the Qur'an.[10] This core is supposed to be violent, anti-women, anti-democracy and so on. References to the large majority of more moderate or even secularized Muslims are discarded by suggesting that they are not 'real' or 'true' Muslims and that, in time, they will also become faithful to the real nature of Islam. A particular interpretation of the Qur'an is taken to be definitive of the character of Islam, and every possibility of reinterpretation in the light of modern society (which a more practice-oriented or historical-contextual view would accommodate) is denied. Moderates or modernists are just atypical cases – even if they constitute an overwhelming majority.

A dominant model can, consequently, be reinforced in three different ways: by acting upon it and, thus, making it a more adequate modelling of reality; by using restrictive definitions of concepts that conform to the model; and by discarding data inconsistent with the model as merely penumbra problems. These three

---

9   Similarly, if interpretivist judges emphasize the constructive and argumentative element in their judgments, interpretivism will make itself true, because it will become more difficult to conceive of law in terms of a source-based positivism.

10 For example: Hirsi Ali, 'Open brief'.

mechanisms used to reinforce one-sided conceptions may work effectively for some time in certain conditions. Nevertheless, they can only offer a temporary resolution.[11] The fact remains that the phenomenon, thus conceived, is modelled only incompletely, and there are still aspects of it which simply do not fit into the dominant model. In the end, it is likely that the debate about how, precisely, we should understand a given phenomenon will be forced to reopen.

So far I have only discussed descriptions and descriptive theory. In normative theory, it is even easier to stick to a single model. In that context we can simply conclude that those aspects of a phenomenon that our conception cannot deal with are historical relicts for which normative theory has no need. Customary law can be proclaimed a historical relict which, in a reliable, modern legal order, should not be accepted as law. Restrictive definition is even easier in normative theory.

My thesis is that some debates between normative theories can be better understood through the use of the framework of essentially ambiguous concepts. In these debates, both sides focus on one model of a phenomenon and legitimately argue that the other side is blind to certain important aspects of the phenomenon. Because all the defensive mechanisms mentioned above are available, it is almost impossible to convince the other side of the value of one's arguments. The debate between Rawls's abstract ideal theory and MacIntyre's practice theory, discussed in the previous chapter, is but one example of this.

In politics, we may understand the valuable core of conservatism as pointing towards the value of the immanent wisdom embodied in our practices and traditions, a wisdom based on experience. This conservatism provides a valuable counterbalance against those who focus on utopian systems and abstract liberal theorizing. But, when conservatives try to transform this immanent wisdom into an abstract theoretical system, it loses much of its initial attraction. Moreover, it becomes vulnerable to the same criticisms against theoretical overreaching that conservatives brought previously and successfully against liberal, utopian theories. The sad history of modern neoconservatives on issues such as the failure to construct an effective and democratic government in Iraq after the military intervention only illustrates this point.

Essentially Contested Concepts

The term 'essentially ambiguous concepts' reminds us, of course, of Gallie's essentially contested concepts (in this section I will refer to both concepts as EAC and ECC, respectively).[12] EACs and ECCs have much in common; however, they

---

11 For a similar analysis of how, to a certain extent, lawyers believe what they want to believe in light of the dominant theory, until the aspects which are underestimated by the dominant theory can no longer be ignored and a new theory becomes dominant, see Van Hoecke, *Law as Communication*, pp. 2–5.

12 Gallie, 'Essentially Contested Concepts'.

differ on one crucial point, as explained below.[13] It may be helpful to explore the commonalities and differences between EACs and ECCs to develop a clearer understanding of EACs.

Both EACs and ECCs allow for different interpretations of a concept, in which a given concept may give rise to conflicting conceptions. Their meaning is open to variation and change. The differences are not the result of intellectual confusion or even a lack of understanding; they are essential and unavoidable. Moreover, the debate between the proponents of the different conceptions is a productive one, because it may bring to light the defects of the different conceptions. Each conception highlights certain important aspects of the phenomenon, but neglects or completely ignores other aspects.

However, there is a fundamental difference between the explanations as to why the concept allows of conflicting conceptions. For an ECC, the explanation lies in the evaluative character of the concept, whereas for an EAC, it lies in the dynamic character of the phenomenon. The evaluative character of an ECC is the first characteristic mentioned by Gallie.[14] This, combined with the aspirational and complex character of an ECC, results in a legitimate plurality of interpretations. Different conceptions focus on different values inherent in the concept or they rank these values differently. For example, some theories of democracy regard equality as the essential or defining characteristic, whereas others focus on self-government. As the aspirational character makes it impossible to excel in all dimensions, these choices lead to different conceptions of democracy. The essential defect leading to the conflicting conceptions is the impossibility of making all valuable elements of the concept fundamental and of attaining full achievement of them all. In other words, different conceptions reflect different evaluative positions.

EACs are primarily descriptive concepts, although many have an evaluative dimension. The plurality of conceptions is explained by the dynamic character of the phenomenon described.[15] The essential defect leading to the conflicting conceptions is that we cannot model a phenomenon both as a dynamic process and as a static object or doctrine in a single theory. The conflicting conceptions reflect different descriptive positions.

The difference between ECCs and EACs is more than just a distinction between normative and descriptive concepts. Certainly, a purely descriptive concept cannot be an ECC. Thus, 'electron' may be an EAC but not an ECC.[16] But,

---

13   In an earlier publication ('Two Models of Law and Morality', parts of which have been revised and included in this book), I did not yet distinguish between these terms, and, incorrectly, referred to what I now call an EAC as an ECC.

14   Gallie uses the term 'appraisive'.

15   In those cases where a third or fourth model is at stake, the explanation is found in the impossibility to coherently combine in one descriptive theory models of the ideal and the real, or of the actual and the potential.

16   Conversely, there may also be ECCs that are not EACs, for example, evaluative terms such as beautiful.

of course, many primarily descriptive concepts, especially those referring to social phenomena, also have a normative dimension. They cannot be fully understood if we do not know the point of the phenomenon, its purpose. Therefore, there can be EACs that also are essentially contested. Democracy is one of Gallie's favourite examples of an ECC, but it is also an EAC. We may describe democracy in terms of the practices and actions that constitute a democratic polity, and also in terms of a set of rules, principles and characteristics; in other words, as a normative political doctrine.

In other cases, the relation may be even more complex. Many legal positivists like Hart claim that law is a normatively neutral concept.[17] Therefore, by definition, law cannot be an ECC. Legal positivists usually focus on law as a doctrine based on objective facts. Non-positivists, however, usually focus on law as a practice and argue that we cannot understand what is going on in that practice if we do not focus on the master ideal, the purpose, or the leading values of law.[18] Different conceptions of these ideals, purposes or values are legitimate. Consequently, law is an ECC.[19] In the view of non-positivists, positivists are merely blind to this unavoidable normative dimension of law, but their position would be understood and defended better if they would simply acknowledge it. An example of this is Ronald Dworkin's attempt to describe jurisprudential debates in terms of different conceptions of legality.[20] However, chances are slim that Dworkin will be able to convince his positivist opponents that this is the best way to reconstruct the debate. They will probably continue to deny the basic presupposition that law is essentially oriented towards a normative ideal or value. This brings us to an interesting second-order contestedness. Positivists like Hart regard law as a normatively neutral concept which, therefore, cannot be an ECC, whereas non-positivists regard it as an ECC. This means that it is contested, whether or not law, as a concept, is essentially contested. We may call this a second-order essentially contested concept.

Even leaving aside the controversy over the fact–value distinction, there is a further reason why we should not hold on to a simple dichotomy of ECC as evaluative and EAC as descriptive. The choice of one descriptive model over another may have important normative implications. For example, choosing the product model of law will more easily allow us to uphold a separation between law and morality, whereas regarding law as an argumentative practice will easily lead us to conclude that moral and legal arguments are intertwined and that law needs to meet some minimum moral standards in order to be effective.[21] Moreover, the

---

17   See Hart, *Concept of Law*, p. 240.
18   See Selznick, 'Sociology and Natural Law'; Fuller, *Morality of Law*; Dworkin, *Justice in Robes*.
19   See Dworkin, *Justice in Robes*, p. 221: 'Lawyers share the concept of law as what I call an interpretive (or essentially contested) concept.'
20   Dworkin, *Justice in Robes*, pp. 168–83.
21   See Chapter 4.

choice of a descriptive model may be influenced by normative considerations. For example, someone who values legal certainty or systematic coherence may have a preference for the product model; someone who cherishes diversity and change may have a preference for the practice model. That we can distinguish between a primarily evaluative ECC and a primarily descriptive EAC need not imply that the choices made for a descriptive model are normatively neutral.

Gallie's analysis of the ECC was an important contribution to understanding how concepts can give rise to different conceptions. But it only addressed one possible explanation regarding the pluralism of conceptions. Many concepts referring to complex social phenomena are both essentially contested and essentially ambiguous. The fact that social concepts are often essentially contested may be the reason why, so far, the other source of conceptual pluralism has not been understood, let alone explicitly addressed. As EACs are often also ECCs, the existing plurality of conceptions may easily be attributed to the concept's being essentially contested, and the essential ambiguity may be neglected or implicitly reduced to the essential contestedness. However, it is important to recognize both sources of conceptual pluralism, and analyse them in their own right. There are two distinct, even if not completely separate explanations for why one concept may have different legitimate conceptions, and we can only acquire a deeper understanding of the pluralism of conceptions if we recognize them both.

Two Possible Objections

One possible objection to my view is that it may only be due to our current defective state of knowledge that we perceive a concept as ambiguous. With regard to essentially contested concepts, Arnold Heidenheimer has argued that, on some concepts, debate may lead to a consensus. Such concepts he calls former essentially contested concepts.[22] Could it not be that for essentially ambiguous concepts, a similar development is possible – that concepts previously regarded as ambiguous can become unambiguous due to scientific progress? An example to support this objection would be the electron. I have used the models of the electron from the time of the debates between Einstein and Bohr. But, since then, quantum

---

22 Heidenheimer, 'Disjunctions Between Corruption and Democracy'. Although I agree that some concepts could become uncontested, or at least less strongly contested, the example he uses – democracy – is not a very convincing one. Even if we were to accept that it may no longer be strongly contested that democracy is valuable (in light of the rise of political Islam this is a highly questionable thesis), it is still strongly contested what, precisely, democracy means. The Dutch system of democracy differs in important respects from the US system (for example, constitutional monarchy, proportional representation, no federal system, no judicial review, a fully appointed judiciary and prosecution and no juries); yet both systems can claim to be democratic.

theory has moved on and it now seems that there is a unitary concept of an electron as a quantum mechanical particle.

I grant that there are no *a priori* knock-down arguments to deny that all essentially ambiguous concepts may, in due course, become disambiguated. My argument has been mostly based on a generalization of a few examples in which category mistakes would occur if we were to combine both models in one theory. Therefore, it may be that some of the concepts that now seem essentially ambiguous prove not to be so after all. However, I think that it is plausible to argue that it is highly unlikely that all the concepts to which I have referred so far can be proven to be unambiguous.

Let us start with the electron concept and assume that it is no longer ambiguous.[23] Even so, there has been a certain period in the evolution of quantum theory in which the electron could only be described as an essentially ambiguous concept. When talking about electrons during that time, the best available option when referring to an electron would be to regard it for the time being as an essentially ambiguous concept. We can apply this insight to essentially ambiguous concepts in general. I have argued that a coherent and complete theory is impossible, but probably many readers will not give up so easily on that ideal. For them, the regulative ideal of philosophical analysis or scholarly practice may be that we reach one complete and coherent conception of a concept. However, I would posit that as long as we have not realized that ideal, it may be inevitable to regard some concepts as essentially ambiguous. Perhaps a God's eye point of view or a Herculean perspective would be able to integrate the two models of morality or law in a higher-level theory. For the purposes of my analysis, however, it suffices to conclude that for ordinary human beings, with the current state of our theoretical knowledge, these conceptions must be seen as partly incompatible.

Thus, even with regard to quantum physics, the idea of an essentially ambiguous concept may still make sense, if only as a temporary stage in the evolution of the theory. However, let us leave physics aside and focus on social phenomena. The case for the inevitability of ambiguity is much stronger there. The strategy used for solving the ambiguity in the case of the electron has been that of extremely abstract theorizing of a phenomenon which, itself, was already a theoretical abstraction from visible natural phenomena. This strategy does not seem available for concepts such as law or morality. We could try to employ it,

---

23 It may be doubted, nevertheless, whether in the current highly abstract theory of an electron the ambiguity of the earlier two models is really completely solved or merely removed to a different level. We may either accurately determine the speed of a tiny particle or accurately determine its position. An increase in accuracy in one dimension leads to a decrease in precision in the other. This fits the idea that we may not be able to describe adequately both the static dimension and the dynamics of a phenomenon. So it seems the ambiguity is still there on a different level. However, it is not in quantum physics that I am interested here, so I will simply grant for argument's sake that the concept of the electron may no longer be ambiguous.

but it seems unlikely that the required abstract discussion would lead to really useful insights. What we might win in coherence, we would lose in descriptive and explanatory power. In the study of social phenomena, it seems likely that such highly abstract approaches would have to abstract from most of the practical insights and experiences that a useful theory should be able to address.

The reason why we need the two models to describe one phenomenon is that one can do greater justice to the dynamic aspects of the phenomenon and the other to the static aspects. Therefore, we must describe law or morality both as a practice and as a doctrine. Using both descriptions in one theory leads to category mistakes, as I have argued above. In ordinary language, it is impossible to transcend this difference in categories without becoming extremely vague. Therefore, it is unlikely that a theory is possible that does justice to both models without serious loss of meaning (and, thus, without being essentially incomplete).

Of course, many essentially ambiguous concepts have been described in terms that, at first sight, do not seem ambiguous; but, on closer analysis, it may turn out that they are ambiguous after all. Hart's analysis of law in terms of rules provides an example that will be discussed below. Another example is David Lewis's theory of language as a convention.[24] Lewis makes a similar distinction between a language as a semantic system and language as a human social activity, and argues that both belong to rival schools in the philosophy of language. He regards his theory of conventions as a synthesis between both. However, this 'synthesis' is merely the explanation of an essentially ambiguous concept in terms of a different concept which is, itself, essentially ambiguous. The concept of a convention can be analysed along similar lines as that of the concept of a social rule in the previous chapter and, therefore, it is essentially ambiguous as well.

Even so, I must admit that it seems unlikely that my argument will fully convince all readers. They may continue to believe that although, at this moment, we have not yet constructed the coherent and complete unified theory of law that does complete justice to product and practice, it will still prove possible to construct one in the future. For practical purposes, I have no quarrel with that. For the purposes of this book, it is enough if readers accept the insight that there are two seemingly incompatible models of law and that, therefore, until we have constructed a unified theory, for practical purposes we must treat law as an essentially ambiguous concept. We may call this a provisionally ambiguous concept. Nothing of any great importance in the remainder of the book hinges on the claim that the ambiguity is essential rather than provisional. As long as readers are willing to accept that it is very difficult, and with our current insights practically impossible, to combine both models in one coherent and complete unified theory, they may ignore my more radical claim that it is essentially impossible.

Another objection would be that, although the word law is ambiguous it does not refer to one concept of law, but rather to two different concepts: legal doctrine and legal practice. It seems, therefore, quite easy to solve the ambiguity

---

24 Lewis, 'Languages and Language', p. 188.

by henceforth consequently distinguishing between the two models of law. Or, to put it more generally: we can solve the superficial ambiguity of every essentially ambiguous concept by always distinguishing between the practice and the product. We stipulate two separate definitions for two separate, if closely related, phenomena, and the problem is solved. We no longer speak of law, but only of legal doctrine and legal practice.

As a research strategy, this will often be very productive. For research purposes, we need clear working definitions that can be applied to reality. For example, the sociologist Philip Selznick, who is certainly not a positivist, has used Hart's positivist analysis of law in terms of a union of primary and secondary rules to construct a weak definition that is useful for doing sociological research on law.[25] Similarly, we may define a legal doctrine in terms of a collection of statutes, judicial opinions and other texts.

However, there are two reasons why, as a strategy to solve the ambiguity, this will not work. First, in almost every meaningful, stipulative definition of law the same ambiguity returns in essential elements of that definition. If we define law as a practice (or an institution) in terms of rules, we again introduce an essentially ambiguous concept. If we define law as a doctrine – not as the collection of texts, themselves, but as the largely coherent body composed of the meaning of the texts – we will have to engage in a practice of interpretive construction about their meaning. The doctrine does not exist out there in the theoretical stratosphere of ideas, but has to be constructed. If we construct it, we have the choice between either making it incomplete (by leaving out all the controversial and undecided parts) or complete but arbitrary (by including only one interpretation on those controversial parts and leaving out the competing interpretations).[26] So a conception of a legal doctrine will, itself, be either incomplete or incoherent. Consequently, our attempt to solve the ambiguity would fail because the problem of ambiguity would not have been solved, but merely removed to a different level.

Secondly, this strategy does not do justice to the phenomenon itself. It would mean that many central concepts of our social discourse would have to be completely skipped and replaced by new pairs of concepts. Such artificial language might work in scholarly analysis, but outside academia it would not, and for good reasons. We are not dealing with separate phenomena, but with one complex phenomenon. Law can only be understood fully if we see it as the union of practice and doctrine. We would lose that understanding of law as a union of practice and doctrine if we were to artificially separate them. They are not two distinct phenomena, but two distinct aspects of the same phenomenon.

---

25 Selznick, *Law, Society and Industrial Justice*, pp. 5–7.

26 An interesting view of pluralism is offered by the Islamic legal tradition, where the four main schools of Sunni law are deemed equally valid and their conflicting interpretations are all viewed as law by the state. See Jackson, *Islamic Law and the State*, p. 147. This does not lead to incoherence in the doctrine of law, as there are four equally legitimate doctrines of law and conflict rules for cases of conflict between the schools.

Conclusion

In this chapter I have elaborated upon the idea of essentially ambiguous concepts. Law and morality are essentially ambiguous concepts, and so are many concepts that play a role in law and morality, such as rules and rights. This fact may form part of the explanation for many controversies in legal and moral philosophy. For socially constructed phenomena, the essential ambiguity can often be largely constructed away – though not completely. This makes it easier to defend biased conceptions of law or morality against criticisms. This may also explain – in part – the intractability of many debates in legal and moral philosophy.

In this chapter and the previous one, I have constructed a very general analytical framework which aims to explain theoretical pluralism. It is now time to see whether this weak framework has any bite at all. I will show that it has in the next two chapters. In Chapter 3, I will argue that this framework helps us to reconstruct the positions of three leading legal theorists – Fuller, Hart and Dworkin – and to better understand the debates and misunderstandings between them. In Chapter 4, I will show that the framework may assist us in better understanding the relation between law and morality.

Chapter 3
The Debate between Fuller, Hart and Dworkin

Towards a Better Understanding of Debates in Jurisprudence

The idea of an essentially ambiguous concept is highly illuminating for the discussions in legal philosophy on the concept of law. The two models, discussed above, are only ideal-typical models. They focus on two different sides of law: on how law can be construed as a coherent body of normative propositions; and on how the specific practices function that create, change and interpret those norms and apply them to concrete problems. The models are connected and presuppose one another. Law as a practice results in (and is oriented towards) law as a product in the form of statutes, judicial decisions and other legal texts, but also in the form of legal doctrines formulated by legal scholars. Law as a product is not self-contained as if its only goal were to build a coherent system, but finds its point of orientation and justification in how it works in practice.

Accordingly, most theories in jurisprudence combine elements from the different models. However, the models are not fully compatible. Another example from physics can illustrate this point. According to quantum theory, we can determine exactly either the place of an elementary particle or its speed, but not both at the same time. In other words: we can have a perfect static view on the particle or a perfect dynamic view, but we cannot have both. Law as a product presents a static model, and law as a practice a dynamic one. We cannot fully cover both the dynamic and the static dimensions of law at the same time. If we focus on law as a coherent body of rules, the ambiguity and controversy, and the processes of change and argument cannot be fully understood. If we focus on law as a practice, we can see how fraught with change and controversy law is. This makes it difficult for us to construct a coherent legal doctrine because many norms that we try to construct are not yet, or no longer, settled, and good arguments can be brought both for and against many possible formulations. Only by abstracting from this controversy and dynamics (and thus selectively representing law) can we offer a complete picture of law as a product.

The fact that the two models are not fully compatible implies that every theory of jurisprudence has its blind spots, however sophisticated it is in its attempt to combine elements from both models. Moreover, most theories focus primarily on one model, which leads to a relative neglect of insights from the other model. This neglect can lead to well-recognizable extremes. If law as a product loses contact with the reality of law as a practice, we risk legal formalism, or

Begriffsjurisprudenz.¹ If we overemphasize law as a practice we may fall prey to a ritualistic proceduralism (if we reduce the practice to the strict observance of certain specified procedures) or overlook the important fact that the law must not only be good, but also certain and predictable.²

It seems to me that many debates in jurisprudence, like those between natural law and positivism, have remained futile because each opponent focuses on different models. Each of the positions is defensible as a theory that can successfully elaborate the issues for which that specific model is most adequate, yet each of them is unable to deal adequately with those characteristics in which the other side in the debate has a special interest.

I will illustrate this thesis with the debate between the three most important authors in jurisprudence in the recent Anglo-American discussion on this issue: Lon L. Fuller, H.L.A. Hart and Ronald Dworkin. The struggle of these three authors with the concept of law illustrates the ambiguity of the concept and the problems that arise when we attempt to develop a theory that is both complete and coherent. I will discuss each of these three authors' positions in more detail and show how they all struggled with the concept of law.³ Moreover, through this discussion we will observe how each failed to comprehend the position of his opponents. The framework offered by the idea of essentially ambiguous concepts will also enable us to understand these authors from a new perspective and, hence, will sometimes lead to novel interpretations and criticisms.

Lon L. Fuller

Lon Fuller sees law in a way that many European law students find counterintuitive – as a purposive enterprise. In his book *The Morality of Law* (1964), he focuses on the legislative enterprise. Usually in legal theory the focus is on the product – legislation; but Fuller describes the failure to produce law in terms of the process of lawmaking. He illustrates these failures by the story of a fictitious King Rex who failed to produce law despite eight serious attempts. How can a legislator

---

1 Lyons, *Moral Aspects of Legal Theory*, pp. 52–3 argues that both formalism and instrumentalism start from the questionable assumption that law is fundamentally a linguistic entity, which is exhausted by the formulations of authoritative texts and their implications.

2 The tension parallels the basic antinomy between *Rechtssicherheit* on the one hand and *Gerechtigkeit* and *Zweckmäßigkeit* on the other, which is central to Gustav Radbruch's theory of law (which he sometimes regards as an antinomy between two elements and sometimes as an antinomy between three elements).

3 There is a great wealth of literature on Fuller, Hart and Dworkin, and on the debates between them. I will leave most of this literature aside as I am not interested here in a full description of their positions. I merely want to demonstrate that the distinction between the two models of law can shed a new light on the debates, as well as on some of the tensions within their theories.

effectively guide society? How can legal rules really govern human conduct? Fuller shows how the legislator can fail in at least eight ways. From these failures he derives eight principles or demands that legislation should meet in order to produce law at all. Laws should be general, promulgated, non-retroactive, clear and non-contradictory. They should not require the impossible; they should be constant through time and there should be congruence between official action and the declared rules. This internal morality of law Fuller calls procedural natural law. He contrasts this with substantive natural law, which focuses on substantive norms about the contents of the law, whereas his eight injunctions are primarily directed at the process of lawmaking.

These two forms of natural law, contrasted by Fuller, correspond with the two models I have distinguished. In the classical forms of natural law – usually with a reference to the Bible or to timeless precepts of Reason – a substantive moral doctrine was presented and it was argued that this was, in some way, part of the law, of the legal doctrine.[4] Fuller focuses on the enterprise – the practice – of law, and argues that there are certain procedural principles we must follow if we want to make any law at all that can serve as a guideline for human conduct. Much of the misunderstanding regarding Fuller's important insights and the relative neglect of his work are due to the fact that most of his positivist opponents misinterpreted his eight principles as a substantive doctrine of natural law.[5] Transformed into a substantive normative doctrine, his theory becomes vague and gradualist: it does not provide any strict formulas or criteria. Thus, it may have seemed – in the heyday of analytical philosophy – hardly worth taking seriously.[6]

Most of the problems that Fuller's King Rex encounters point to defects in the text or contents of the statutes, such as unclear formulations or contradictions. These are defects that, at first sight, can be adequately described in terms of a doctrine model. But Fuller elaborately demonstrates that, in order to establish that these defects are present in a given text, we must interpret the text in light of reality. This interpretive activity requires us to consider law as a practice. Moreover, some of the eight requirements can only be discussed in terms of actions or practices,

---

4 Winston, 'Introduction to Special Issue', p. 256 reports that 'Fuller regarded traditional natural law theories as varieties of legal positivism.' This is a highly controversial but, in my view, correct understanding of both traditions as most traditional law theories have in common with most versions of legal positivism that they construct law as a doctrine, based on authoritative sources. In the case of natural law, these sources may include Reason or sacred texts.

5 More fundamentally, as Rundle convincingly argues in her recent book on Fuller, the eight principles are not some kind of checklist. Fuller´s focus is on a relationship of reciprocity between lawgiver and the legal subject, 'one that is *reflected* in the observance of his eight principles but which is not *exhausted* by them' (*Forms Liberate*, p. 92, italics in original).

6 Another serious obstacle to the acceptance of his views by analytical philosophers was that 'Fuller could be undeniably sloppy in his choice of language' (Rundle, *Forms Liberate*, p. 6).

for example, the congruence between the rules and official action and the relative constancy through time. Therefore, though in some respects we could analyse the deficiencies of legislation in terms of the texts produced, such an analysis would be incomplete.

Looking at law as an enterprise inevitably leads us to take a gradualist and pluralist approach. If law is a purposive enterprise, the enterprise can be more or less successful. Law is, thus, a gradual phenomenon, which makes it all the more difficult to create a clear-cut criterion of when a legal order exists. Moreover, if law is simply a purposive enterprise, this enterprise can take place in various contexts. A school, even a group of friends on a camping tour, may develop some internal legal rules and, thus, create a legal order. A broad version of legal pluralism seems not only unavoidable, but is explicitly endorsed by Fuller.[7]

Both inevitable consequences of the law as practice model, however, seem to undermine central purposes of law. If the law should guide with rules, it is important that the rules be easily determined, and that conflicting interpretations are settled. In other words, it is necessary that we know what, precisely, the law requires of us. However, if we cannot be sure whether or not law exists and which legal order or interpretation of that order should prevail, this makes guidance by rules problematic. We would need a mechanism by which we could authoritatively determine those rules and settle conflicts. In other words, we need a way to model law as a set of easily applicable rules, as a public doctrine of non-retroactive and clear rules. Thus, the internal logic of Fuller's analysis forces us to return to the product model and, in fact, to precisely those aspects of law which are central to Hart's analysis.

Even if he has some room for law as a doctrine, Fuller's focus is on law as a practice – that is, as emerging from the interaction between citizens and between citizens and the lawgiver. He refers to his position as an interactional view of law.[8] But the content of law in a practice conception does not lend itself to very precise formulations because of its dynamic, gradualist and pluralistic character. In practice, there are often no neat distinctions; rather, phenomena merge and are intertwined.[9] Fuller repeatedly criticizes the shortcomings of a linguistic philosophy that attempts to create artificial distinctions that are not based on the reality of our ordinary language. However, his approach results in an analysis that remains often frustratingly vague.

In his later work, *Anatomy of the Law* (1968), Fuller tries to do justice to legal positivism.[10] The central distinction in that book is the one he makes between made law and implicit law. Made law is the law that is purposively created by legal authorities, such as legislators and, up to a point, judges and the parties

---

7   See Fuller, *Morality of Law*, p. 125, where he indirectly accepts, as an implication of his view, that there may be hundreds of thousands of legal orders in the US alone.
8   Fuller, *Morality of Law*, p. 221 and p. 237.
9   See Rundle, *Forms Liberate*, p. 29 and p. 124.
10 Fuller, *Anatomy of Law*.

to a contract. Implicit law is the law that is implicit in our daily activities, that sometimes emerges as a custom in our interaction. Most positivist authors treat custom as a historical relict and consider implicit law as merely non-legal norms. That he takes both equally seriously is one of Fuller's greatest accomplishments.[11]

Although implicit and made law may be distinguished, they are not two separate types of law. Fuller shows that each presupposes the other. Made law has implicit law dimensions and implicit law has made law dimensions. Each is intertwined with the other.[12] In the end, Fuller advances what is now called a modest version of natural law; but he does not deny the legitimacy of the positivist perspective, which focuses on made law.[13] According to Fuller, we must recognize both forms of law.

Fuller thus seems to suggest, in the framework developed in this book, that we need both a practice approach (a focus on implicit law) and a doctrinal approach (a focus on made law). It remains unclear, however, how precisely we could form one unified theory based on the two approaches, which are clearly at odds with one another. The result of his struggle to deal with the richness of the phenomenon of law is, consequently, a vague and incoherent theory. In comparison with *The Morality of Law*, he gains a broader perspective and does greater justice to the product model. The price for this attempt at achieving completeness is two theories uncomfortably sitting next to each other in one incoherent framework.[14]

H.L.A. Hart

H.L.A. Hart is, in many ways, the opposite of Fuller, and not only because they have been opponents in various debates on natural law and positivism. Whereas

---

11 Perhaps Fuller is better able to understand the importance of implicit law because, in his fields of expertise – labour and contract law – informal norms often play a major role. Classics such as the sociological studies of Sally Falk Moore on labour law and of Stewart Macaulay on contract law are illustrations of the importance of social norms that have emerged in such contexts, often even in contradiction to official state law or standard contracts. See Moore, 'Law and Social Change' and Macaulay, 'Non-Contractual Relations in Business'.

12 This idea is also clear in the 1969 'Reply to Critics' in *Morality of Law*, at p. 154. There is, of course, much more continuity between both books than this short sketch can demonstrate.

13 Fuller, *Anatomy of Law*, p. 119.

14 However, already in his early work, Fuller openly accepts that antinomies or tensions are unavoidable, if one wants to do justice to reality: 'I shall argue that it is better to accept frankly a state of unresolved conflict or tension in our reasoning than to purchase consistency at the cost of needed premises, for it is, after all, scarcely to the credit of legal philosophy that it achieves harmony within its domain if this is accomplished only by barring its frontiers to every vital and fruitful idea that might disturb the internal order' (Fuller, 'Reason and Fiat', p. 377).

Fuller has an informal essayistic style, Hart is an analytical philosopher with an extremely precise use of language. Although Hart calls his famous book, *The Concept of Law*, an exercise in descriptive sociology,[15] it is almost devoid of empirical insights, whereas Fuller's 'eunomics' project is strongly inspired by sociological studies.[16]

Hart repeatedly calls his theory a practice theory of law. He starts with a description of the practice of primary social rules. For him, the existence of social rules involves the 'combination of regular conduct with a distinctive attitude to that conduct as a standard'.[17] Such a system of primary rules is defective, he argues, because the rules are often uncertain, they are too static, and social control is inefficient as an enforcement mechanism. In order to remedy these defects, we need secondary rules of recognition, change and adjudication. The introduction of these remedies marks the transition from the pre-legal into the legal world.

The introduction of the secondary rules in the book marks a different transition as well, which is not explicitly noticed. This is the transition from the model of practice to the model of doctrine. After introducing secondary rules, Hart talks about primary rules no longer in terms of behaviour, but in terms of lists and texts.[18] The first stage in the transition from the pre-legal to the legal 'is the mere reduction to writing of hitherto unwritten rules'.[19] This is, however, not a mere reduction; it is a transformation from rules conceived as patterns of conduct to rules conceived as propositions that can be written down.[20] This transformation is a radical one that substantially changes the way in which Hart analyses the law. For example, the main criterion for the existence of a rule is no longer the pattern of behaviour, but a reference to authoritative writing or inscription. The discrete unconnected rules of action become a unified system, a coherent doctrine; and the concept of validity (which is difficult to understand exclusively in terms of practices) is introduced. It is this doctrinal conception of rules that is elaborated upon in the chapters following the introduction of the

---

15   Hart, *Concept of Law*, Preface p. vi.

16   Eunomics was the name Fuller gave to his research project on the variety of legal and other social processes, which he defined as 'the science, theory, or study of good order and workable social arrangements' (*Principles of Social Order*, p. 62). Fuller never finished this ambitious project; some 'exercises in eunomics' have been collected in *Principles of Social Order*.

17   Hart, *Concept of Law*, p. 85.

18   Shapiro, *Legality*, p. 103 makes a similar point when he argues that Hart makes a category mistake when he reduces social rules to social practices.

19   Hart, *Concept of Law*, p. 95.

20   Cane ('Morality, Law and Conflicting Reasons', p. 80) argues that Hart treats both morality and law as 'things in the world – they are, if you like, reified or personified'. Cane advocates a shift 'from reifying morality and law to thinking about them in terms of individuals' practical reasoning' or, in terms of the two models, a shift from a product model to a practice model.

notion of secondary rules. The famous open texture problem, for example, can only be discussed if we regard rules as linguistic propositions; it makes no sense to discuss the open texture of a practice.[21]

Thus, although Hart starts with rules in a practice model, he ends up with rules as constituting a legal doctrine in a product model.[22] This results in a highly attractive and largely consistent theory. Because Hart started to develop his theory from within a practice model, he can also claim it to be relatively complete. He has done justice to the practice dimension of law, transforming and reducing it to the doctrinal model. However, he does all of this without noticing the fundamental importance of the transformation from practice to doctrine.

Moreover, Hart's focus on the concept of law rather than on a strict definition of law (which could be shown as inadequate because it does not cover important examples) makes his theory more complete and more immune to criticism.[23] It enables Hart to provide a somewhat satisfactory analysis of international law, a phenomenon which his positivist predecessor, Austin, could not adequately analyse given the absence of an international sovereign. Thus, his theory of law is more complete than Austin's. Elements that do not fit his theory could be dismissed as matters of the penumbra or as an unhealthy focus on hard cases (against Dworkin) and purpose (against Fuller), which are not relevant to the core of the concept.

Hart's theory in *The Concept of Law* can be regarded as a choice for a highly consistent model, which can lay claim to being largely complete by ignoring the fundamental transformation in the analysis. The debate with Dworkin, thereafter, painfully demonstrates the limitations of this choice. Hart struggled until the end of his life to understand and reply to Dworkin's criticisms.[24]

The idea that law is an essentially ambiguous concept can provide at least part of the explanation for this struggle. It was difficult for Hart to understand Dworkin's criticisms and relate them to his own theory because most of the criticisms were formulated in terms of a practice model. Therefore, he could not perceive them otherwise than as missing the mark. In so far as he did understand Dworkin's criticisms, he could not address them adequately without giving up his choice of a positivist theory and a doctrinal model. Yet, he was painfully aware that Dworkin had made some very important points that could not be discarded

---

21   See Lyons, *Moral Aspects of Legal Theory*, p. 86, who argues that Hart 'conceives of the law essentially in linguistic terms – as a collection of rules with canonical formulations'.

22   With the exception of the ultimate rule of recognition, which is the only rule that should be analysed in terms of a practice. This illustrates the impossibility of restricting a theory of law to the product model – at some point reference to the practice is needed, even if this reference makes the architecture of the theory more problematic.

23   I believe this makes him invulnerable, as he claims in the 'Postscript', p. 246, to Dworkin's criticism in terms of the semantic sting, but this invulnerability comes at the cost of an increase in vagueness.

24   The posthumously published 'Postscript' shows clearly how difficult it was for him to come to terms with Dworkin's critique. The fascinating biography by Nicola Lacey (*Life of H.L.A. Hart*) describes how intense and painful this struggle was.

as lightly as had been done by other positivists. This example illustrates how a one-sided choice for one model may be defensible up to a certain point but that, in the end, it will be impossible to ward off all attacks.

Ronald Dworkin

The work of the third author, Ronald Dworkin, has given rise to much confusion and many misunderstandings of and by his opponents. His theories are notably difficult to interpret. There are various reasons for this, one being that he started with a number of only loosely connected critical essays, published in *Taking Rights Seriously*. Only sometime after publishing *Taking Rights Seriously* did he try to construct a coherent theory in *Law's Empire*. Moreover, many of his articles and books use the strategy of critiquing the work of others to further develop his own theory. This approach inevitably resulted in texts that were coloured by the conceptual frameworks of his opponents which, combined in one critique, did not always provide for a coherent presentation.

The main reason for the confusion, however, is that, in his early work, Dworkin continually switched between the model of doctrine and that of practice. In *Taking Rights Seriously*, he used a double tactic to attack Hart's position. On the one hand, he argued within Hart's model of doctrine and presented an internal critique. When lawyers argue a hard case, he maintained, they appeal not only to rules, but to rules as well as to more open standards such as principles. The appeal to these open standards forces the lawyer to move beyond the model of law as settled doctrine consisting of rules based on authoritative sources. The purposes and principles implicit in the law and in the public morality of his society cannot be found in a statutory text or in other sources, but must be continuously debated and reconstructed. Therefore, the lawyer must engage in an interpretive and discursive practice. In this argumentative practice, no sharp distinction is possible between legal and non-legal arguments, due to the open and controversial nature of principles. This is an attack from within on the model of doctrinal rules, and demonstrates that this model is seriously incomplete in a way that not only requires amending it to a model of rules and principles (the way many positivists, including Hart, thought the attack could be countered) but also, ultimately, requires us to abandon the model altogether. In presenting his internal critique, Dworkin necessarily uses the terminology of the model of doctrine, thus suggesting that he is committed to ideas of existing law and is merely arguing for some minor modifications. For example, his famous Right Answer Thesis is often misinterpreted by positivists as implying that somewhere in the doctrine of law the right answer is already there, merely waiting to be discovered by the judge. However, such an interpretation (consistently denied by Dworkin in his later work)[25] misses the point Dworkin wished to make. Instead, Dworkin's point

---

25 For example, in Dworkin, *Justice in Robes*, pp. 41–3.

is that, in order to construct – rather than find – the right answer, we cannot rely on the social sources of law as authoritative doctrine, but must engage in normative interpretation and argumentative discourse.

Dworkin's other line of attack is an external one. Indeed, at times he boldly states, in a very direct way, that law should not be regarded as a collection of rules (whether or not supplemented by principles), and that we should put aside the idea of an existing law altogether and replace it with law as an interpretive enterprise.[26] The critique is presented using the practice model, demonstrating that positivism cannot do justice to important characteristics of law as understood in that model. For example, positivism cannot explain (other than regarding it as an illusion) why both lawyers and judges, when arguing a hard case in court, act as if there is one answer that has more legal merits than another. This enables Dworkin to present his own views more clearly within the framework of a practice model. Within such a practice model, the Right Answer Thesis is not about an 'existing' answer, but about a regulative ideal that structures the argumentative practice of court disputes and the reflective practice of judicial decision-making.

So, in the same book, and sometimes even in the same article, Dworkin uses both the practice model and the product model. However, as law is an essentially ambiguous concept, the combination of both models in one theory leads to inconsistencies. The many critics who claim that Dworkin's early position was incoherent are, therefore, correct. The lack of coherence is the inevitable result of his attempt to use an internal critique to criticize Hart's doctrinal model of rules and, at the same time, present a different model of law as an interpretive practice.[27]

In his later work, Dworkin predominantly chooses a practice model, repeatedly arguing against doctrinal law as a brooding omnipresence in the sky. His collection of essays *Justice in Robes* makes this unambiguously clear.[28] I believe this emphasis on practice has led to a more coherent position. Whereas his initial ambition was to be complete and cover the full phenomenon of law, his later theory of the concept of law is more consistent but less complete.

However, to make the matter even more complex, in many publications Dworkin does not restrict himself to a theory about the concept of law as an observer. He also becomes a participant in the debate about how to interpret the (US) law in concrete controversies, for example, on abortion or affirmative action. And, as a participant in that practice, he must discuss law in terms of a coherent legal doctrine because that is the regulative ideal that structures argumentative legal practice. This demonstrates how, from an internal point of view, we are often

---

26 See his 'Reply to Critics' in *Taking Rights Seriously*, p. 293; *Law's Empire*, pp. 90–91.

27 For a related criticism of Dworkin of his own earlier work, see Dworkin, *Justice for Hedgehogs*, p. 402.

28 A similar position as in *Justice in Robes* may be found in *Justice for Hedgehogs*, Chapter 19, where he regards law as a part of political morality. Therefore, every theory of law is inevitably controversial, as it can only be the result of interpretive argument.

forced to construct law in terms of doctrine. In order to enable us to discuss critically competing interpretations of the law, we need to formulate them as precisely as possible into a coherent doctrine.[29] Each model is not merely incomplete; they also make reference to one another. This double role Dworkin takes on as philosophical observer and as participant in a specific legal discourse is an additional source of confusion. As an observer, he emphasizes law as a practice; as a participant in that practice, he necessarily focuses on constructing law as a doctrine. Often, it is difficult to distinguish which role he is taking on in his work. The accusation of incoherence will, therefore, linger on.

Conclusion

The work of these three authors vividly demonstrates the struggle to grapple with the ambiguity of the concept of law. Hart, as a highly skilled analytical philosopher, opted for consistency and clarity; in order to achieve this, he had to focus on the doctrinal model – even though he started with a practice theory. He had to admit, consequently, that he did not have any fully convincing answers to Dworkin's criticisms. What is more, he was at a loss to understand them.

Fuller, with his interest in the reality of law as interaction and as a purposive enterprise, initially opted for the model of practice, but this resulted in a certain level of vagueness and lack of precision in his theory. Moreover, just like Hart, he could not realize his overall ambition of constructing a complete and coherent theory. His explicit acknowledgement in his later work of the intertwinement of made law and implicit law was an important step forward, however. Whereas Hart, in the end, focused only on the product model, Fuller did justice to both models. In this respect, his theory was the most promising and the most complete of the three – even if it came at the price of incoherence and vagueness.

Dworkin's position has rightly been described as a third theory,[30] as initially he did not wish to opt for either of the two models, but oscillated between them. This inevitably resulted in justified accusations of inconsistency and incoherence. His choice in his later work to focus on a practice theory brought him gains in the realm of coherence, but losses in the realms of completeness and precision. Moreover, his criticisms of various positivists became even less effective as, once they were expressed mainly in terms of the practice model, his opponents could not comprehend them.

It is a telling characteristic of the debate between these authors and their affiliates that they frequently fail to understand one another. In his review of Fuller's *The Morality of Law*, Hart writes that they seem fated never to understand one another's work, and the Dworkin–Hart debate is replete with inadequate representations of

---

29 For how a dialectic interplay between the two models is required in order to make critical discussion possible, see Peters, 'Law as Critical Discussion'.

30 Mackie, 'Third Theory of Law'.

each of the opponent's views.³¹ Clearly, this mutual misunderstanding cannot be the result of a lack of intellectual skills, of personal animosity, or of intellectual dishonesty (as in deliberately misrepresenting the opponent's view). There must have been something highly fundamental that made it impossible for them to truly understand one another. With the help of the framework which I introduced in the previous chapters, based on the idea of law as an essentially ambiguous concept, we may understand why. Whereas both Fuller and Dworkin focus on law as being based on human interaction, Hart focuses on law as a set of rules with a determinate content.

It seems to me that Dworkin was, in his early work, on the right track, but took the wrong turn in *Law's Empire* and in his later work. In those works he tried to make his theory more consistent by putting more focus on the practice model. The analysis of law as an essentially ambiguous concept demonstrates that this choice will lead to a greater degree of incompleteness and some loss of precision. I believe a better solution would have been to accept that law is an essentially ambiguous concept and that, therefore, we cannot but alternate between the two models. Indeed, this is the alternative Fuller chose in his later work. Rather than trying to ignore incoherence, we might openly recognize it. That could well be the only way to contain it.

---

31 For some of these complaints about being unable to understand, and being misunderstood by the other, see: Lacey, *Life of H.L.A. Hart*, p. 198 (quoting a letter by Hart in which Fuller's reply to his famous Holmes lecture is called a 'piece of logomachy' of enormous length and obscurity); Hart, 'Review of Morality of Law'; Fuller, *Morality of Law*, p. 154 ('I must confess I am puzzled by it' – referring to Hart's criticism); Hart, *Concept of Law*, 'Postscript', passim (using terms with reference to Dworkin's interpretation and critique as 'perplexing' (p. 243), 'tantalizingly obscure' (p. 257); Dworkin, *Justice in Robes*, p. 166 (arguing that he can only stick to his own interpretation of Hart's theory, despite Hart's explicit denial that it is a correct interpretation). In fact, large parts of his latter book address how other authors, including Hart and Coleman, have completely misinterpreted his theory. In turn, in this book, as well as in various other publications, Dworkin often presents the views of his opponents in ways they could hardly recognize. See also Lacey, 'Out of "Witches' Cauldron"', p. 23, describing how Fuller felt that he was widely misinterpreted and misunderstood; this is also a recurrent theme in Rundle, *Forms Liberate*.

Chapter 4
The Relations between Law and Morality

Positivists versus Non-Positivists: What is the Issue?

The second theme on which I will illustrate the usefulness of the idea of essential ambiguity is the relation between law and morality. The debate on this theme has been going on in jurisprudence for such a long time that one may wonder whether anything new could possibly be added to it. Yet, paradoxically, it is unclear what, precisely, the issue in the debate is.[1] According to H.L.A. Hart, positivists hold (and their opponents dispute) that there is no necessary connection between law and morality; law and morality can be separated. At first glance, this seems to be a simple thesis. David Lyons has shown, however, that this thesis is vague and indeterminate.[2] In a minimal interpretation, it has no distinguishing force at all. Lyons demonstrates this by formulating a Minimal Separation Thesis: 'Law is subject to moral appraisal and does not automatically satisfy whatever standards may properly be used in its appraisal.'[3] In brief: law is morally fallible. Tenets like this can be found in Austin, Hart and many other positivist authors.[4] The problem with this thesis is that it is too broad: everyone could subscribe to it, including non-positivists such as Aquinas, Fuller and Dworkin. This interpretation of the separation thesis, therefore, cannot help us find a distinguishing criterion between positivism and its critics; we must construct a more substantive interpretation of the separation thesis. A similar remark can be made with respect to a second version of this thesis, also to be found in Hart, that states that law and morality are distinct. This, again, is too weak because almost everyone can agree with it.[5] We need a stronger claim than that of merely a distinction.

---

1 Kent Greenawalt even argues that the label legal positivism should be dropped altogether: 'We have failed to identify any thesis of legal positivism that both is plausible and that marks it off distinctly from various positions that are advanced as being alternatives to it' (Greenawalt, 'Too Thin and Too Rich', p. 19).

2 Lyons, *Moral Aspects of Legal Theory*, pp. 70ff. See also Taekema, *Concept of Ideals*, pp. 198–207; and Alexy, *Argument from Injustice*, p. 27 for similar attempts to reconstruct the debate in a number of different theses.

3 Lyons, *Moral Aspects of Legal Theory*, p. 68.

4 Consider Austin's famous phrase, 'The existence of law is one thing, its merit or demerit another', to which Hart refers as a central positivist tenet in *Concept of Law*, p. 207.

5 See Lyons, *Moral Aspects of Legal Theory*, p. 66.

Therefore, it may be useful to search for a new perspective on the debate between positivists and non-positivists. A starting point for such a reorientation originates with the idea that law and morality are essentially ambiguous concepts, and that different schools focus on different models. Positivists have focused on product models of law and morality and, as a result, have been blind to those elements of the relation between law and morality that are best seen when using practice models. Positivism regards both law and morality primarily as systems of norms, as bodies of rules and principles which can be formulated as propositions. The central question in the debate on law and morality from the perspective of positivism can be formulated nicely using positivist terms: Can we separate those two systems of norms? The answer I will provide in this chapter is that in a product model we can separate them, but only as a matter of construction. We can try to construct law in such a way that the separation becomes largely true.

The model of law or morality as a system of normative propositions is, as we have seen, not the only possible one. If we take our point of departure from the practice model, the relation between law and morality will be seen in a different light. In the practice model, the separation thesis cannot be upheld, not even as a matter of construction.

Reconstruction of the Separation Thesis

The separation thesis is unclear in various ways. It is unclear what, precisely, is meant by the idea of separation, but it is also unclear what is meant by the reference to 'morality'. Usually the meaning of this term is not made explicit, and authors seem to switch between different meanings. We may distinguish at least three different meanings of morality in the discussion on law and morality:

1. social or positive morality: the morality actually accepted and shared by a certain social group;[6]
2. ideal or critical morality (or normative ethical theory): the general moral standards used in the criticism of social morality which may be elaborated in a normative theory of morality as it ought to be;
3. ideal or critical law (or normative legal theory): the general standards used in the criticism of positive law which may be elaborated upon in a normative theory of law as it ought to be.[7]

---

6 The term 'positive morality' has infelicitous associations, for example, that morality is a social fact and that it is 'posited' in a similar way as law is supposed to be by positivists. To avoid these associations, I will use the term 'social morality' instead.

7 Some moral philosophers may find it strange to call the latter category 'morality'. However, legal theorists have often identified 'law as it ought to be' as a morality or as 'morals'. The phrase 'natural law' has a similar ambivalence; it has been used both to refer to what I call normative ethical theory and to normative legal theory.

The distinction I suggest here is clearly inspired by H.L.A. Hart's distinction between positive and critical morality, but it goes further in two respects.[8] First, it adds the idea of a normative theory to ideal or critical morality; thus it makes explicit that critical morality is not merely negative, but also offers a positive orientation. Second, and more important, it introduces a distinction between the critical standards used in evaluating morality and the critical standards used in evaluating law. This is a crucial distinction that in the literature is too often overlooked and gives rise to many misunderstandings.

The distinction between law and morality is an essential one, also when we study critical morality and ideal law. Law and morality can never fully overlap. Not every moral standard can (or should) be translated into law; nor can every legal standard be translated into morality. The realm of love and care carries many moral issues that should not be translated into legal norms, and many criticisms of the instrumental (ab)use of law have nothing to do with morality as such.[9] In many critiques of positive law this distinction is not taken into account as, for example, when it is argued that the law is deficient because it does not correspond with moral norms in the first two senses. However, there may be good reasons why there is not full correspondence.[10]

This distinction, of course, does not mean that the three senses of morality are separate. There are many connections, and in Western societies the three overlap substantially. There is, for example, a dialectical interplay between social morality and normative ethical theory.[11] On the one hand, most social moralities include mechanisms of self-criticism and self-improvement by reflection on normative ethical theory; on the other hand, the construction of a normative ethical theory usually starts from elements of social morality, like moral intuitions or deeply held moral principles and values. There is also a strong connection between normative ethical theory and normative legal theory. In most theories, the aspirations of positive law and social morality should be that the legal and moral demands on the citizen coincide or, at least, that moral and legal obligations do not conflict. This ideal of full legitimacy may be unrealizable but, even as an aspiration, it leads to a strong cohesion and interaction between normative legal theory and normative ethical theory.

---

8   Hart, *Law, Liberty and Morality*, p. 20. In *Concept of Law*, p. 169 he makes a different distinction between '*the* morality' of a given society (to which he also refers as the 'shared', 'accepted' and 'conventional' morality) and the personal morality of an individual.

9   Clearly it is an open question what we should regard as distinctive for critical legal and critical moral standards, respectively. This is not an empirical issue that can be determined with a neutral appeal to facts. I only wish to claim that the distinction – however it is to be made or justified – is a useful one in discussions on the relations between law and morality.

10   See below, Chapter 9.

11   Brom, Vorstenbosch and Schroten, 'Public Policy and Transgenic Animals'; Den Hartogh, 'Soziale und kritische Moral'; Selznick, *Moral Commonwealth*, pp. 392–4.

The failure to distinguish between these three senses of morality has caused much unnecessary confusion. An example is H.L.A. Hart's famous article 'Positivism and the Separation of Law and Morals'. Hart discusses the relation between law and normative legal theory ('law as it ought to be'), and between law and normative ethical theory or even social morality (all legal orders coincide with morality in respect of basic moral principles vetoing murder, violence and theft) without noticing that different senses of morality are at issue here.[12] As a result, his analysis of the relations between law and 'morals' remains unsystematic and unclear, because some remarks refer to social morality and others to normative ethical or normative legal theory, and it is often unclear to which he is referring.

We should be aware of the different senses of 'morality' but, in this context, we need not choose between them. Each of the three meanings is relevant in the debate about how we should conceive law and its relation to morality. When analysing whether any version of a separation thesis is valid, we should, therefore, discuss each of the three senses of morality.

The second vagueness in the separation thesis is regarding what the idea of separation entails. For clarification on this issue, we may turn to the work of David Lyons. Lyons suggests that at the core of positivism is the Explicit Moral Content Thesis: 'law has no moral content or conditions save what has been explicitly laid down by law'.[13] When courts use moral arguments but do not simply deduce these from moral ideas already recognized as legally authoritative by legislative or judicial decisions, courts must be understood as making new law.[14] Lyons argues that if there is a distinctive positivist doctrine on the separation of law and morality, it is this thesis.[15]

A problem with this version is that it only fits into a product model of law. Only if we regard law as a system of normative propositions can we enquire into its contents. This is no objection as such; nevertheless, we should also try to formulate a version of the separation thesis that fits into the practice model. An initial formulation might be: 'In the practice of interpreting law, moral arguments are not valid interpretations of the law save those arguments that have already been explicitly recognized under the law.'

This formulation is clearly too broad and, therefore, implausible. In the practice of legislating and in discussions between legal scholars, references to morality are made in various ways. In the daily practice of ordinary citizens who

---

12 Hart, 'Positivism and Separation', pp. 621–4. In *Concept of Law*, p. 193 he explicitly refers to conventional or accepted morality when discussing the minimum content of natural law.

13 Lyons, *Moral Aspects of Legal Theory*, p. 83; see also p. 101.

14 Lyons, *Moral Aspects of Legal Theory*, p. 80.

15 Similar formulations can be found in Hart's 'Postscript' to *Concept of Law*, p. 269, and in MacCormick, 'Natural Law and Separation', p. 107: 'Positivist theories of law [...] hold that law can be explained, analysed and accounted for in terms independent of any thesis about moral principles or values.'

try to apply law to concrete situations, there are also implicit or explicit references to moral argument. If we want to give this version at least some initial credibility, we should make it more specific and restrict it to the practice of the courts. A better formulation, then, is: 'In the practice of the judicial process, and especially in the practice of judging, moral arguments are not valid interpretations of the law save when they can be deduced from interpretations that have explicitly been recognized by law.' If courts nevertheless, as they sometimes do, recognize new moral arguments as valid, they must be understood as making new law, rather than as interpreting the law. I suggest that we call this the Explicit Moral Argument Thesis because it holds that, in the practice of legal argumentation, only those moral arguments that have explicitly been recognized are valid.

The Relations between Law and Morality in the Practice Model

Before we can discuss a possible separation between law and morality, we should determine whether law and morality are, in fact, distinct practices. It is worth noting that the answer to this question depends on the historical development of a society or of a societal sector. Primitive societies may make no distinction between law and morality – in fact, one of the characteristics of developed societies is that there is a differentiation between law and morality and that, therefore, they can be distinguished.[16] This means that even the mere distinction between law and morality has only a contingent historical character.

An important factor in the differentiation process is the emergence of what H.L.A. Hart calls 'secondary rules'.[17] As long as the normative dimension of social reality is merely a matter of primary rules, it is impossible to distinguish between law and morality. A distinct legal order only emerges when there are secondary rules that can identify the legal aspects in social reality. Even if there are such secondary legal rules, however, it is still difficult to distinguish the legal from the moral aspects of reality, let alone separate them.[18] There is much overlap; many moral obligations are legal obligations as well, and vice versa. How should we determine, in such cases of overlap, what is law and what is morality?

Of course, in one sense, we do know how to distinguish the legal and the moral aspects of a given issue. We can say: 'You ought not to drive faster than 50 kilometres per hour now' or 'You ought to give money to that beggar.' It is usually plausible that, in the first statement, reference is being made to the

---

16 Hart, *Concept of Law*, p. 169.
17 Hart, *Concept of Law*, p. 94; see also Selznick, *Law, Society and Industrial Justice*, p. 5.
18 Cane, *Responsibility in Law and Morality*, p. 6 note 16 suggests that we should 'picture our normative life in terms of a tapestry in which law, morality and so on, are intricately interwoven'.

legal aspect and, in the second, to the moral aspect of reality. We can only be certain, however, if we know more about the content of the legislation, the moral opinions of the speaker and so on. From the utterance alone we cannot tell. It could well be that the first statement was meant as a moral or prudential one (for instance, if the speaker thought it morally obligatory to obey the law or if he knew that there would be speed control in a kilometre). We can only know for sure what the legal and moral aspects of these statements are if we take account of the full context and take an internal point of view. This means we can only say that something is to be considered legal or moral (or perhaps both legal and moral) if we take a legal or moral point of view. To take a legal point of view, we have to take the secondary rules as our starting point. As long as we remain merely at the level of primary rules, morality and law cannot be separated – in many cases they cannot even be distinguished.

If there is a basis for separating law and morality in the practice model, it should thus be found in the secondary rules, and especially in the practice of adjudication. This corresponds with the emphasis in the Explicit Moral Argument Thesis which we formulated as: 'In the practice of the judicial process, and especially in the practice of judging, moral arguments are not valid interpretations of the law save when they can be deduced from interpretations that have explicitly been recognized by law.' Yet, is this a valid thesis?

The answer to that question depends on the way the practice is structured. There can be highly formalized, almost ritualized court proceedings, in which there is no room for normative argument at all. Such practices would maintain a strict separation between law and morality. In modern Western societies such ritualized proceedings are, however, uncommon. Actual judicial processes include normative argument, discussion, construction of coherent doctrine in light of the available data, and so on. As Ronald Dworkin has convincingly argued, in such argumentation processes, moral and legal arguments fuse.[19] There is no clear demarcation criterion to determine when a principle is strictly legal or when it is strictly moral. Every argument – even if it is openly derived from ethics textbooks – could be recognized as legally relevant. We cannot determine *ex ante* whether an argument or the formulation of a principle is a legal one or 'merely' a moral one that is not legally relevant. Only after the decision has been made can we conclude that, in this concrete case, the argument was or was not considered legally relevant by the judge – but that does not imply that in the next case it will have the same status.

The conclusion here is that, at least for judicial practice in modern Western societies, the Explicit Moral Argument Thesis is invalid. A separation between legal argument and moral argument is impossible, regardless of which of the three senses of morality is involved. In a given case, arguments from ethics textbooks on normative ethical theory may be invoked, as well as arguments referring to public opinion or, in other words, to social morality. Only following the verdict can we

---

19   For example Dworkin, *Taking Rights Seriously*, p. 185.

try to determine whether these arguments were accepted by the court, but even then it is often difficult to tell. Not every judicial opinion is as elaborately argued as those of the US Supreme Court.

With respect to the distinction between law and normative legal theory, we can go even further. The purpose of legal reasoning is to determine how the law ought to be (constructively) interpreted. Consequently, the dichotomy between law as it is and law as it ought to be disappears. Instead, they merge into one view on how the law ought to be interpreted. A lawyer will never argue: 'This is the law, but it ought to be different. I urge the court to accept that view, which implies that my client should be acquitted.' Her argument will rather be: 'Even if some courts have mistakenly interpreted it differently, the law should really be interpreted as meaning what I tell you, and therefore my client should be acquitted.' If a court accepts the lawyer's argument, it will seldom acknowledge that it changes the law; it will, rather, say that it is now presenting a better view of how the law ought to be interpreted.

The conclusion here is that, in a practice model, a strict separation between law and morality is not possible. The need for interpretation in legal argument opens it up to references to social morality as well as to normative ethical and normative legal theory. However, there can be variation in how intense the connections between law and morality are. In highly formalistic and legalistic practices, the reference to morality may be minimal and largely shielded from perception. Deliberate attempts, motivated by a positivist ideology, to make law conform to the desired image of a complete separation from morality may make this image more true. As I discussed above, if all legislators, judges, lawyers and citizens believe in a positivist theory of law, they will act upon it and consequently they will construct their legal order in terms that largely correspond with that positivist image.[20] But, then, it is a matter of our construction, not of a conceptual truth. The idea of a separation between law and morality becomes truer because reality is shaped by the image. However, even then it is hard to imagine a legal practice in which, in the long run, all references to morality could be effectively banned.

Therefore, rather than seeing the separation of law and morality as an analytical or conceptual truth, we should regard the idea of a partial separation and partial intertwinement as a starting point for empirical or legal studies. There will always be variation between legal orders with regard to which way they structure the relation between law and morality. Sometimes, law will be constructed as largely autonomous with respect to morality; sometimes, it will be more open. So, in studying concrete legal orders we may ask in what ways the legal order is open to (various versions of) morality. How strong or weak are the intertwinements between law and morality? We need to be sensitive to variation here rather than use an *a priori* conceptual scheme that tries to fit reality into a Procrustean bed.

---

20   See Chapter 2.

The Relations between Law and Morality in the Product Model

In the product model, the positivist case for a separation of law and morality is stronger. Usually, the main body of law as a product is easily identifiable by what Ronald Dworkin has called a test of pedigree: the fact that a text has been produced or a rule has been announced by a legal institution such as the legislature or a judge.[21] There are some periphery problems, like the open texture problem described by Hart or the standard cases of customary law and 'soft' international law. These periphery problems, however, can be considered mere demarcation problems; the large core of law is easily identifiable, or so it seems.

With respect to morality, a similar story seems possible. Of course, usually there is no test of pedigree with respect to morality (except in some religious moralities). Social morality can, in principle, be described using sociological methods. With regard to normative ethical theory and normative legal theory, the story is more complex. These theories cannot be 'found' by empirical methods; they are always the provisional product of continuing argument. The best we can do is to choose a specific normative theory as 'the' normative theory. We can speak of the normative ethical theory as constructed in Rawls's *A Theory of Justice*, of the normative ethical theory of rule-utilitarianism or Kantianism, and so on. Similarly, we can speak of a Dworkinian or Posnerian normative legal theory with respect to issues such as abortion or constitutional rights. Even so, such a choice for one specific normative theory will always be open to contestation.

However, the separation thesis is about the character of law, so we can leave aside the problems regarding identifying morality for the moment. It may seem that, in the product model, it is not only possible to distinguish law as a separate code, but also to describe it without reference to morality (however identified). Under this model, there is no essential connection between law and morality. This still leaves open the possibility that there are contingent connections. The crucial point is that it is possible to describe what the law 'is' without making reference to morality. This has many theoretical and practical advantages. It promises to offer clear and objective criteria for determining what the law is; for the description of its content we need not refer to morality, save to those moral standards that have been explicitly recognized by the law. It also enables us, in a neutral way, to pose evaluative questions about the law such as: 'How should we evaluate the moral quality of positive law?' or 'Do we have a moral obligation to obey immoral laws?'[22]

So far, the positivist claim of a separation between law and morality seems strong in connection with law as a product. There is a crucial caveat here, however. As I have argued earlier, the uncertainty of law is not merely an issue of the

---

21 Dworkin, *Taking Rights Seriously*, p. 17.
22 See the discussion in Hart, *Concept of Law*, pp. 208ff. of the post-World War II discussions on Nazi crimes and resistance against the Nazis.

penumbra. If we admit that law is more than a system of rules and that principles and ideals are also part of the law, we introduce a crucial element of controversy to the core of the law. Principles and vague normative terms like 'equity' are not just vague concepts with an open texture. The latter may be true of descriptive concepts like Hart's example of 'vehicle', but normative concepts and legal principles are usually essentially contested concepts.[23] This means that controversy is at the heart of the law, and not merely in the penumbra. It is, therefore, not so easy to determine what the law 'is' (and a similar argument might be made in connection with morality). The test of pedigree may suffice to identify at least some elements of the law, but to obtain a complete image of the legal doctrine as a whole we need to deal with the uncertainty and plurality of legitimate interpretations resulting from the incorporation of principles and ideals. The legal doctrine is, after all, the result of our construction, not of finding it.

If we cannot determine what the law 'is', *a fortiori*, it is no longer possible to determine that law and morality are separately identifiable. Determining the content of law is not 'finding' it but constructing it, deciding in which way to remove the multi-interpretability, to make vague concepts more concrete, and to solve conflicts between principles. It, therefore, depends on us, and how we construct law and morality, whether there will be a separation between law and morality. The separation is only in the eye of the constructor, because it is the result of his constructive work.

The implication for the separation thesis is that the truth of the thesis is merely the result of our own constructive action, and not a reflection of something in the world 'out there'. The Explicit Moral Content Thesis holds that law has no moral content or condition – save what has been explicitly set out by law – once we have constructively interpreted the law as a coherent system of rules and principles. This is true, but only in a trivial sense – because we have made it

---

23   This is the reason why I criticized earlier, in Chapter 1, Dworkin's example about whether a male baby should wear a bonnet in church. This is an unfortunate counter-example against Hart's analysis of the social rule requiring men to wear a hat in church because it focuses on descriptive concepts such as 'man' or 'hat'. These concepts are not normative and, therefore, cannot be essentially contested. Hart's theory with regard to the open texture of language may be illuminating with regard to predominantly descriptive concepts such as vehicle or man, but it fails with regard to predominantly normative concepts such as many central concepts in law. In his recent work *Justice for Hedgehogs*, Dworkin distinguishes between criterial, natural-kind and interpretive concepts. Using this distinction, we might say that 'man' and 'hat' are normally criterial concepts, just like 'vehicle'. They may, however, temporarily become an interpretive concept when embedded in a legal or social rule (*Justice for Hedgehogs*, p. 165 and p. 166). The fact that in those cases the interpretive problem can be settled, after which these concepts become criterial again, can be understood in terms of Hart's notion of open texture. Normative concepts are usually interpretive and, therefore, essentially contested; as a consequence, they give rise to more fundamental interpretive problems that more radically challenge a positivist analysis of social rules.

true. The Explicit Moral Content Thesis must, therefore, be rejected as a general thesis about law as it is.

Thus, my conclusion is that, in the end, even regarding law as a product, the positivist separation thesis is invalid. Yet, it may play a useful, if limited role. For some analytical purposes, it may be helpful to stipulate that law and morality are to be regarded as if they were separately identifiable systems of norms. This stipulation is acceptable because there is at least a core of truth in it. Though it is not the full truth, it is a partial truth. As long as we remain aware that it is merely a stipulation, we can use the separation thesis as a tool for analysis. What we should not do, however, is go beyond the restrictions and make it a basic thesis rather than a stipulation for modelling purposes.

In the context of the analytical project of Part One, I leave aside here the issue of whether it is desirable or not to construct a legal doctrine as if law had no essential relation to morality. There may be many good reasons for constructing a doctrine in this way, for example, that it allows us to offer greater legal certainty about the contents of the law. A simple test of pedigree offers more certainty than an inherently controversial normative argument referring to moral standards which will always be open to contestation. On the other hand, however, there may also be good reasons to construct law as more open to moral argument, as such a construction may assist in enhancing legal dynamics or responsiveness. These matters will be taken up in Part Two. For analytical purposes, it is sufficient to conclude that the separation thesis can be made more or less true as the result of our constructive efforts as participants in the legal practice.

The fact that law and morality as products cannot be separated does not preclude their differentiation from one another. The role of principles and open standards can be stronger or weaker and, consequently, the connection with morality can be stronger or weaker. Some fields of law have strong connections with morality – for instance, in modern Dutch tort law, where terms like reasonableness and fairness (*redelijkheid en billijkheid*) play crucial roles. In other fields, like traffic law, the connection with morality is weaker or less obvious. No generalizations are possible for law as such: we need detailed analyses of specific subfields at specific stages in their historical development. A century ago, Dutch tort law was much less intertwined with morality than it is nowadays. The core of truth in the positivist separation thesis may be smaller or larger. But the important thing is to realize that it is only a partial truth.

As in the practice model, this means that, for research purposes, it may be useful to use the ideas of a partial separation and a partial intertwinement of law and morality as a starting point for further legal or empirical analysis. For example, we may inquire as to which extent open standards that invite reference to morality play a central or a marginal role in legal doctrine. Rather than a thesis, the idea of separation becomes a heuristic for research. How far, and in which ways, is a specific legal order characterized by a strong or a weak openness towards morality? And to which of the three types of morality, distinguished earlier, does law refer?

Conclusion

The result of this analysis will be clear. For each of the two models, a strict separation of law and morality is hard to defend as a general analytical thesis. If we focus on law as a product, the separation thesis has a strong core of truth. However, in the end it should be rejected. If we focus on law as a practice, it is obvious that we cannot uphold the separation thesis in any meaningful way.[24] Therefore, we must conclude that the positivist separation thesis is invalid.[25]

For both models, however, it makes sense to analyse to what degree law and morality are interconnected and to what degree their connections are weak. In modern societies, they are never fully separate or fully identical, but there is a continuum between the two extremes that is worth investigating. This provides us with a framework for further research. How strong is the connection between law and morality in a given legal order? What are the variables and factors that may be relevant in determining this? Here, we need an eye for variation. We need it not only in sociological research (there it may be more common), but also in legal research. Before we can do research, however, we need to explore what the implications of this framework are for the concept and definition of law and for the methodology of legal research. These topics will be tackled in the next chapter.

---

24 This conclusion resembles Selznick's suggestion that it is indispensable to distinguish statements about facts and values (statements are part of a product model, in my terminology), but that fact and value as aspects of our existence (the practice model, in my terminology) do not belong to separate realms (Selznick, *Moral Commonwealth*, p. 21). Tamanaha, *Realistic Socio-Legal Theory*, p. 51 similarly argues, with reference to Dewey, that facts and values should be distinguished 'as functionally distinct aspects of our experience'. Tamanaha rightly criticizes those who claim there is no distinction between fact and value, but fails to distinguish between the idea of a distinction and that of a separation between both. The use of the word 'aspects', however, suggests that both cannot be separated.

25 See Olsen and Toddington, *Law in its Own Right*, p. 158: 'The crucial interdependence of law and morality, both conceptually and practically, is not seriously open to question.'

Chapter 5
A Pluralist Framework

Weak but Not Uncontroversial

In the previous chapters, I have argued that law and morality are essentially ambiguous concepts. This idea provides an analytical framework that leads to a better understanding of debates in jurisprudence between natural law, legal positivism and interpretivism. Moreover, it provides a new understanding of the relations between law and morality.

This analytical framework is undoubtedly weak in the sense that it is very broad and inclusive. It allows for many different and conflicting conceptions of law rather than preferring a specific one. These conceptions complement one another: each may offer insights that the others cannot provide. Moreover, the framework offers an explanation as to why these different conceptions co-exist and why proponents of competing conceptions can, at times, hardly understand one another. It includes each of these conceptions as a legitimate, yet necessarily partial theory.

The framework is, thus, relatively non-committal and it has, as I demonstrated in the previous chapters, great explanatory power. However, that does not mean that it will be uncontroversial. On the contrary, it is likely that many legal theorists will strongly oppose it. The main reason why we may expect it to be controversial is that it claims that each of the various competing theories in legal philosophy can be no more than a partial perspective on law, whereas the self-understanding of most philosophers is that their theories are correct and that the others are simply mistaken. This claim to supremacy is not completely denied by the framework; it may be that one of the existing theories is currently the best defensible and least partial theory. However, its essentially pluralist claim is certainly at odds with the idea of most theorists: that further elaboration of their own theory should ultimately lead to the most adequate understanding of law. The pluralist framework implies that to arrive at the most adequate understanding of law we need to switch between the various positions.

Whether the argument for the pluralist framework is convincing, I can only leave to the reader to judge. There are no *a priori* knock-down arguments for it. However, I have attempted to make it plausible in two ways. First, I have shown that the best way to understand concepts such as law is that they refer to at least two partly incompatible models, and that this may give rise to a variety of legitimate conceptions that combine elements from these models in different ways. Second, I have shown that the pluralist framework leads to a better understanding of some debates in legal philosophy and offers a promising perspective on the relation between law and morality. In other words, it works.

In a sense, I would not be disappointed if I could not convince every reader that all we can come up with in legal theory is a collection of legitimately partial theories between which we must switch to attain a full understanding. It seems likely that there would be more progress in developing each of the competing theories if some – if not most – researchers believed in them and tried to construct them in so far as possible in light of the criticism from competing theories. Otherwise, researchers could easily answer every criticism with 'That is a legitimate complementary insight which does not fit into my theory but, of course, we have to accept that every theory is partial, so I will simply ignore your criticisms.' Such an attitude would be unlikely to lead us to the strongest elaboration of each of the theories. For maximum progress on each of the theories, we need true believers. Of course, I hope that I have convinced at least some readers that every legal theory is, by necessity, only incomplete and, in addition, sometimes incoherent. However, it might be detrimental to progress if I were to convince all readers.

There is, therefore, a tension between the way the pluralist framework looks at competing theoretical positions and the self-understanding that many of the faithful to those positions have. This tension is a productive one and need not worry us too much. There are, however, two issues that I want to discuss in this final chapter of Part One. The first is that of definition and demarcation of the law. It may be that the analytical framework is weak, but what does that mean for the attempt to clearly define and demarcate the law? The second issue is that of methodology. It may seem that the thesis that full completeness and full coherence cannot be combined leads to a postmodernist 'everything goes' approach. Can there still be methodological guidance or is, in fact, every method (or every lack of method) equally defensible? These are the issues I will take up in the next sections.

The Holy Grail of the Distinctively Legal

Many authors have sought to identify the specific characteristics of law, the properties that distinguish law from other normative orders. They have been looking for the distinctively legal. Some authors even argue that this is the central task of legal philosophy. Indeed, according to Julie Dickson, the core business of analytical jurisprudence is 'to isolate and explain those features which make law into what it is'.[1] She further argues that legal philosophy must analyse the nature of law, that is, 'those essential properties which a given set of phenomena must exhibit in order to be law'.[2]

---

1   Dickson, *Evaluation and Legal Theory*, p. 17.
2   Dickson, *Evaluation and Legal Theory*, p. 17. See also Shapiro, *Legality*, Chapter 1.

I believe that this is a fundamentally mistaken idea of what jurisprudence is all about.³ It may not be entirely useless; the search for the distinctively legal has resulted in many valuable theories about phenomena that may be associated with specific legal orders such as secondary rules, the claim to authority, and practices of legality. However, these are mere spin-offs of a research process aiming at the wrong goal, just like chemistry has gained important insights from the medieval attempts to turn lead into gold. Rather than looking for the essential properties of laws, we should study the richness of legal phenomena with an open mind to variation, the specific context, and the dynamics in those phenomena.⁴ In other words, rather than trying to frame all legal phenomena on a Procrustean bed of essential properties, we should focus on the pluralism of legal phenomena.

There are various reasons for the impossibility of constructing a set of essential properties as defining the 'distinctively legal', but, to avoid misunderstanding, I might add that the reason is not that law is an essentially ambiguous concept. From the latter thesis, we may derive a plurality of definitions, as I will show hereunder; but the idea of essential ambiguity does not exclude the possibility that law as a product and law as a practice have at least some characteristics in common that determine the distinctively legal.

The first reason why it is impossible to define the distinctively legal is that it is a second order essentially contested concept.⁵ It is essentially contested whether or not it is essential for law to be oriented towards certain values, such as legality, or whether law embodies a certain substantive content of natural law. Among those who hold that law is oriented towards certain values, it is essentially contested which values they are and how they should be interpreted. Is the master ideal of law legality, as Selznick and Fuller hold, or are there other ideals such as justice, legal security and purposiveness, as Radbruch holds?⁶ What, precisely, is the substantive natural law? Is it merely a minimum content as held by Hart, or a more substantive set as defended by Finnis?⁷ Moreover, not only is there debate among theorists on the value-oriented character of law (an essential property for most theorists in the natural law tradition), but there is also broad disagreement on other suggested characteristics of law.

Of course, the fact that theorists disagree does not, in itself, imply that there is no one right answer in the quest for the distinctively legal. This disagreement may be a reason to doubt that one answer is possible, but no more. After all, most of the theorists could have been mistaken so far. We could say that all the other theorists simply do not fully understand the concept of law – a strategy which, in fact,

---

3   For similar criticisms, see Schauer, 'Nature of Nature of Law'; Leiter, 'Demarcation Problem'.

4   For a similar view, see Cotterrell, *Politics of Jurisprudence*, pp. 15–16.

5   See Chapter 2.

6   Selznick, 'Sociology and Natural Law'; Fuller, *Morality of Law*; Radbruch, *Rechtsphilosophie*; Taekema, *Concept of Ideals*.

7   Hart, *Concept of Law*; Finnis, *Natural Law and Natural Rights*.

most participants in the debate use. Nevertheless, the fact that there is continuing controversy might, at least, place the burden of proof on those who claim that there is something like the distinctively legal that holds true for all legal orders. This burden of proof requires theorists to provide not only a convincing theory of the distinctively legal, but also an explanation at a higher level – a meta-analysis – as to why so many brilliant minds have been mistaken and are still mistaken. Otherwise, their assertion will be just one more claim in the chorus of conflicting theorists. Again, in itself, this does not provide a knock-down argument against the attempt to formulate the distinctively legal as the primary task of jurisprudence. In a debate between conflicting theories, mere theoretical arguments can only rarely demonstrate fatal flaws in certain positions – that is, flaws that are fatal in the eyes of the defenders.

Therefore, we must turn to reality in search of more convincing arguments. At this stage, we should proceed in two steps. The first step is to accept that we should consciously reject the implicit paradigm that law is identical to state law.[8] In most of the older legal positivist theories of law, some connection with the state is presupposed. Of course, the connection with the state is one of the characteristics that, even though not essential, are often important for understanding legal orders. However, most contemporary theorists accept that this connection with the state apparatus is not essential for law, if only because the rise of international law makes it difficult to ignore this phenomenon as a major exception. Even so, the connection between law and state still has a strong hold on the minds of both legal theorists and the general public, as the state legal order is the most important order in our lives. We must be aware of this bias and deliberately try to correct it.

Once we have accepted that the law is not only associated with the state, we can find a host of phenomena that might be called law, and that are called law by at least some theorists. Customary and international law co-exist with bureaucratic regulations within the state legal apparatus. Arbitrary rules set by authoritarian dictators are called law, but so are the emergent norms in semi-autonomous social fields. Here again, the obvious solution would be to argue that some of these phenomena are not law because they do not have the properties deemed essential for law. In fact, most theorists have chosen this strategy but, alas, they all come up with a different list of essential properties and, thus, each one ends up excluding phenomena that other theorists include. Therefore, this strategy is circular and question-begging. However, so is my own critique, as I implicitly presume that all these phenomena might be called law and that those theorists who disagree should come up with convincing arguments which disprove this presumption. It seems we are stuck here.

We might learn, however, from the analysis of some candidates for the distinctively legal. Just to illustrate this point, I will discuss two influential

---

8 For a critical analysis of this focus on state law, see also Tamanaha, *Realistic Socio-Legal Theory*, p. 99: 'State law is the currently dominant paradigm for law.'

candidates: Hart's idea of the union of primary and secondary rules and Fuller's ideal of legality. Of course, there are other candidates and variations on each of these theories. However, an analysis of these two may suffice to show a pattern for each theory of the distinctively legal, whether it belongs to the tradition of legal positivism or to that of natural law.⁹ Each of them is usually either overinclusive or underinclusive, and frequently both. They include phenomena which are, according to many scholars, not law, and exclude phenomena which are legal.

Let me start with Hart's idea that law exists when a system of primary rules is complemented with secondary rules. Of course, this is an important insight about a dimension that is often characteristic of legal orders. However, it is obvious that for both customary law and classical international law in its early stages of development, this would imply that many phenomena that are considered to be legal are excluded. Hart's own solution in *The Concept of Law* is to avoid the issue by stating simply that he provides a concept, rather than a strict definition.¹⁰ Nevertheless, even this weaker claim still implies that both customary law and international law are fringe phenomena. He argues that international law is merely sufficiently analogous in function and content to municipal law to call it law, implying it is still lesser law.¹¹ Moreover, he banishes customary legal orders as they have existed throughout most of the history of civilization to the jurisprudential fringe. At the same time, he is overinclusive, as there are also non-legal normative orders which would fit this description and which Hart himself would not want to call law. For example, Tamanaha refers to many legal sociologists who have discerned law in a host of institutions that 'exert social control through administering a system of secondary and primary rules', such as community associations and corporations.¹² Undoubtedly, Hart would have rejected the claim that all of these forms are law, yet they satisfy his criteria.

The main alternative from the non-positivist camp is, in my view, the appeal to the value of legality by Fuller. Here Martin Krygier, an author who is very sympathetic to Fuller's position, provides a strong counterexample, referring to a study by Edward Rubin.¹³ In modern regulatory states, legislation is sometimes not directed at ordinary citizens but, rather, at large government-implementation mechanisms, such as administrative agencies. This type of bureaucratic law relies largely on top-down regulations and directives, and shares hardly any characteristics with Fuller's eight principles of legality. Fuller might, therefore, prefer to call it managerial control. However, this seems an arbitrary exclusion as almost everyone regards those administrative directives as law – and for good

---

9   For example, see Tamanaha, *General Jurisprudence*, pp. 139–40 for a similar critical analysis about the deficiencies of Joseph Raz's idea that law is distinct because it is the most important institutionalized order in a society.
10 Hart, *Concept of Law*, p. 81.
11 Hart, *Concept of Law*, p. 237.
12 Tamanaha, *General Jurisprudence*, p. 138.
13 Krygier, 'Hart–Fuller Debate', p. 133, referring to Rubin, 'Law and Legislation'.

reasons, in light of their form, function and contents.[14] We may conclude that Fuller is underinclusive; but he is also overinclusive – at least in the minds of a large majority of legal scholars. He is famous for including the internal rules of a camping group as a distinct legal order, something which very few legal scholars would agree with.

Of course, each of these authors (and especially their followers) might believe that both the underinclusive and the overinclusive character of their theories is simply a consequence of fully understanding the concept of law as they see it.[15] Anyone else is mistaken to believe that other phenomena are legal as well, or that some of the phenomena that they include in law are not law. However, for an impartial outsider, each of these theories seems to make partly plausible but, in the end, arbitrary choices about the concept of law that includes within its ambit both too much and too little. Yet, each of these attempts to understand the distinctively legal provides important insights into the phenomenon of law as, in most cases (even if not in all), both secondary rules and a practice of legality are associated with a legal order.

The problem with my thesis that there is no general property or characteristic of law is that it is usually impossible to provide definitive proof for a negative thesis. In theory, it is still possible that someone comes up with a theory which no one ever thought of and which almost everyone should reasonably assent to – although it is extremely unlikely. It is plausible that none of the existing proposals can generate wide assent, and it is plausible that there is a wide variety of phenomena called law that are difficult to fit into one set of properties or criteria. However, the latter observation on the two theories may point in a different direction. Even if some authors think such an essentialist concept of the distinctively legal is possible, would this be a good focus for legal philosophy to take?

What we can learn from these two theories is that each of them grasps something important and provides us with insights into characteristics that are important in many legal orders. The same holds true for traditional criteria such as the existence of sanctions, or the association with the state. Neither of these criteria is universal, yet for those legal orders where they do exist, they are an important aspect of the law that we need to study in order to understand law more fully. My main difficulty with the search for essential properties of law is, therefore, not so much that it searches for the impossible but that, in doing so, it neglects all the other important characteristics that we need to understand in order to better comprehend a specific legal order. The search for the universal may blind us not only to the particular,

---

14   A similar criticism with regard to Selznick's claim that the specific ideal of legality is always bound to develop when there is law is brought forward by Rokumoto, 'Philip Selznick's Conception', p. 177. Rokumoto refers to the Japanese Tokugawa rulers realizing the values of order and control by means of law.

15   As I have argued in the previous chapters, such an imperialist claim would have been uncongenial to both Hart and Fuller, as they were very ecumenical in their approach. However, we may find a similar implication in the secondary literature.

but also to those general characteristics that are often present, even if they are not universal.[16] While searching in vain for a black tulip, we simply neglect the beauty of all the tulips that do exist, and that come in many wonderful variations.

Perhaps a legal philosopher in the isolation of her study room may believe that we had come by a major insight if we were to, finally, construct the distinctively legal. I think that even if this were possible (or if we would simply do it by arbitrary stipulation), they would likely be such minimal and abstract characteristics that they would not tell us much about the real phenomena that we call law.[17] We need to be attentive to variation and we need to be attentive to degrees in which legal orders may exhibit certain characteristics. The essence of a concrete, legal phenomenon is as much in the particular details as in the general, or even universal, characteristics it exhibits.

We should, therefore, aim for a pluralistic and variable understanding of the characteristics of law. Sociological, historical, comparative and philosophical analysis may provide us with insights into both characteristics of law that are fairly general and characteristics that only some specific legal orders possess. Wittgenstein's idea of a family resemblance is illuminating here.[18] Blond hair may be present in almost all current members of a family, but a big nose in only two of them. None of the characteristics is present in all. The family metaphor is, both by Wittgenstein and in the secondary literature, usually only discussed in terms of an existing set of family members. However, we can obtain a richer understanding if we realize that families are dynamic phenomena. Families expand and decrease in size. New members are born into the family; other members die. Some members are adopted into the family and they may (although biologically unrelated) come to exhibit behaviour that seems typical to that family. In-laws become part of the family, too. For example, when we speak about dynasties such as the House of Orange or the Kennedys, the in-laws like Queen Máxima or Jacqueline Kennedy are as much a part of the family as those who are a biological part of the family – though in a different way.

This dynamic understanding of the family resemblance metaphor is illuminating when applied to the phenomenon of law. Older types of law, such as customary law, may become less important, while newer types, such as state bureaucratic law and international law, may emerge. Those types of law that continue to exist, such as constitutional law, may change in important ways, for example, by becoming explicitly formulated in a written constitution or by becoming intertwined with international human rights treaties and European Union treaties and, thus, forcing us to rethink the concept of the constitution of a sovereign state. Perhaps in the future, completely new types of law will emerge that we can hardly imagine today. The emerging law of virtual networks is a phenomenon in which law may lose some of its older characteristics (like the association with a territorially bound

---

16   See Schauer, 'Nature of Nature of Law'; Twining, *General Jurisprudence*, p. 103.
17   A similar point is made by Tamanaha, *General Jurisprudence*, p. xvii.
18   Wittgenstein, *Philosophical Investigations* I, nr. 67.

state) and acquire new ones that we cannot yet fully grasp. It is important to have a concept of law that is open to such variation and dynamics. A concept that focuses on essential properties is simply not adequate to the task at hand. A pluralist concept based on the dynamic metaphor of family resemblance is much more productive.

A Variety of Definitions

From the thesis that law is both an essentially ambiguous concept and a second order essentially contested concept, it follows that there can be more than one definition of law. As a variety of conceptions of law is possible, different stipulative definitions may highlight different aspects of the complex phenomenon of law.[19] Law is such a variable and dynamic phenomenon that one general definition is simply impossible. Judith Shklar makes a similar point when she argues that both law and morality vary too much to find one general distinctive criterion.[20] She discusses various differential characteristics that have been suggested by legal theorists as distinguishing law from morality. Examples are the idea that law focuses on the external dimension of behaviour, whereas morality focuses on the internal dimension, and the association of law with sanctions and state enforcement. Shklar demonstrates that none of these characteristics is universally valid. Again, this does not mean that these characteristics are irrelevant. On the contrary, they are often highly relevant for understanding the specific legal orders in which they are present, and it is important to study them and their variation when one studies legal orders. The point is merely that they are not universal characteristics that are essential for law, or that can distinguish law from morality.

Brian Tamanaha presents a similar critique of attempts to formulate the distinctively legal in terms of a single standard or central case, or in terms of an essentialist and functionalist analysis.[21] He argues that most definitions of law suffer from the defect that they implicitly presuppose state law as their central case. However, he offers an interesting alternative which, at first sight, may seem to falsify my thesis that there is no general definition. He suggests that '*Law is*

---

19   This is the reason why, in the Introduction, I replaced Selznick's idea of a weak definition with a weak framework. I also replaced strong concept with strong theory, but this is more in line with Selznick, as he argues that strong concepts shade into theory. Selznick, *Law, Society and Industrial Justice*, pp. 4–5. I replaced the word concept here as I use the same word in a different context when discussing the idea of essentially ambiguous concepts.

20   Shklar, *Legalism*, pp. 29ff. For an extensive discussion of possible characteristics of law, see also Van Hoecke, *Law as Communication*, Chapter 3. Some of these characteristics may be important to characterize a concrete legal order and they may be useful to construct stipulative definitions for specific purposes, but they do not have a universal character.

21   Tamanaha, *General Jurisprudence*, p. 151 and p. 155.

whatever people identify and treat through their social practices as "law" (or droit, recht, etc.).'[22] If they call something law, a legal scholar must simply accept their label. If they do not call something law, even if it looks like law to a researcher, she still has to accept their label. This sounds very sympathetic, as it avoids the theorist as an outsider imposing a definition on certain groups.

Sympathetic as it may appear, this approach has three major problems.[23] The first is that it may depend on which ideologies are dominant in a certain society whether something is labelled as law. For example, in a country dominated by major codifications and a tradition of legal positivism, hardly anyone will refer to customary law as law, whereas in a less positivistic country, citizens are more likely to label it as law. Therefore, it may not be the theorists' explicit ideological bias that colours what is regarded as law, but the implicit ideological bias of the citizens in a given context. The latter seems even worse because, under this proposition, the ideology is hidden in the data and, thus, can less easily be criticized and corrected.

The second problem is that the qualification of certain phenomena varies in time and this qualification is often controversial and, therefore, indeterminate. Not only can the same phenomenon (let us say customary law) be called law by one society and not by another (or by one group in a society and not by others), it may also change with the passage of time within one and the same society. Take the controversy in the debate between Hart and Fuller: were immoral Nazi statutes law? According to Tamanaha's suggestion, this question is not for the legal theorists to decide, but for the members of society. However, we must ask which members (do they include the Jews, the silenced opposition, and the Germans living in exile) and when (in 1940, in 1944, or in 1946)? If we accept, as seems inevitable, that it may be controversial whether some phenomenon is law because the participants in the relevant practice disagree, we have only made the demarcation problem worse. In most cases, there will be controversy over phenomena such as customary and international law, and their status will be indeterminate. And then, if we take Tamanaha's idea seriously, it cannot even be solved by an arbitrary stipulation by legal scholars or by authoritative legal institutions.

The third problem is that Tamanaha's suggestion is not, by any means, theoretically uncontroversial or neutral. Instead, it is arbitrary because it excludes phenomena that are, in function or form, very similar to phenomena that are called law, simply because the participants do not use the word law for them. Thus, Tamanaha excludes all functionalist or formalist conceptions of law. For example, in his catalogue of types of law, he does not mention the internal law of organizations or the implicit law of semi-autonomous social fields.[24] They are probably supposed to be not law because most participants in those practices,

---

22 Tamanaha, *General Jurisprudence*, p. 166 (italics in original). For a similar position, see Berman, 'Global Legal Pluralism'.

23 See also Twining's criticisms: Twining, 'Post-Westphalian Conception'; Twining, *General Jurisprudence*, pp. 97–103.

24 Tamanaha, *General Jurisprudence*, pp. 224ff.

indoctrinated by the dominant view that law is identical to state law, do not identify them as law. But why should we refer to their ideological biases even though from an external point of view these normative orders are, in many respects, so much like law that we could as well identify them as law, or at least as emergent or implicit law? Law can exist in degrees. It is usually not the insider who first perceives that something is slowly acquiring a legal character, just like the frog in the water does not notice that the temperature is slowly rising to a boil.

How, then, should we define law? I posit that we should make a fresh start. We should accept the legitimate pluralism in possible conceptions and definitions of law. Rather than define 'law' in general, we should determine which definition is most useful for our research purposes and for the phenomena that we want to study. For some sociological purposes, a simple stipulation that law is a normative order enforced by the state or a system of primary and secondary rules may be most adequate. For the context of international law, such a definition is clearly inadequate. For the latter, a definition as suggested by Brunnée and Toope in terms of a practice of legality may be much more productive.[25] If law is, indeed, a concept characterized not by one single trait but by a very complex and dynamic family resemblance, such a contextual and functional approach to defining law is the best we can do.

This may all be well from the perspective of legal scholars. They can simply stipulate their definition. As long as they attempt to justify their choice with good arguments and are aware of the biases and blind spots involved in their definitions, these choices may be understood by their academic forum and may perhaps be criticized. The result will be a plurality of definitions. In fact, this is the situation we also have in the current academic debate, except that many scholars currently profess to have the only correct definition.

However, law is a major social institution and the act of defining law may, therefore, have important consequences. It does matter whether I have a legal duty not to insult my neighbour or to pay my gambling debts. An objective identification of a legal order, and especially of its content, is a highly consequential and practical issue.[26] I believe that some sort of practical issue is also behind the continuing quest

---

25 See Brunnée and Toope, *Legitimacy and Legality*, p. 6: 'What distinguishes law from other types of social ordering is not form, but adherence to specific criteria of legality: generality, promulgation, non-retroactivity, clarity, non-contradiction, not asking the impossible, constancy, and congruence between rules and official action. When norm creation meets these criteria and is matched with norm application that also satisfies the legality requirements – when there exists what we call a "practice of legality" – actors will be able to pursue their purposes and organize their interactions through law.'

26 We should not exaggerate this practical problem: 'Whatever view is taken about the value of positivism as a theory of law, no-one has any difficulty identifying the law of the state in which they live as a set of social practices because the 'domain of law' is thick with formal institutions of three broad types: law-making institutions, law-applying institutions, and law-enforcement institutions' (Cane, *Responsibility in Law and Morality*, p. 5). The problem merely arises in the context of certain types of non-state law.

to identify the distinctively legal or to provide objective universal definitions. This is also the reason why Brunnée and Toope diverge from Fuller in providing a definition of law.[27] They argue that in order to uphold an admittedly weak rule-of-law tradition in international law, a distinction between legal obligations and broader social norms is crucial.

These are practically important questions, but it is a mistake to think that the answers rely on legal philosophy providing a general definition of law. These questions are always asked from a specific perspective. It is that of the insider who participates in a certain normative practice and wants to know what the consequences are if someone violates or follows a certain norm. For this question, the character of the practice as legal or non-legal will hardly ever matter. Whether it is mere custom or customary law, in both cases it will be clear (or unclear) whether there are sanctions to be expected, which type of sanctions, and who will decide upon them. Whether we qualify this as 'law' or not does not matter very much.

Let us now elaborate upon Lon Fuller's example: the norms that emerge within a group of friends embarking on a camping trip.[28] Most positivists would not call this law, as Fuller does. A group of friends goes on a four-week camping expedition in the Amazon area, one of the purposes of which is to do some gold-digging. We may wonder whether the internal rules that emerge within this group constitute a legal order or not. Let us assume that one of the members ate a double ration of food. The group, or perhaps one or two informal leaders, may then decide on how to sanction him, perhaps by withholding half of his ration for the next two days (if they merely want to compensate) or three days (if they also want to punish him). Whether or not we qualify this process as legal is simply irrelevant; in these circumstances he will simply have no choice but to accept the sanctions as, on his own, he would probably get lost.

Let us further complicate the story. Around the campfire, the group has agreed that if they find gold, the profits will be divided evenly among all members. One member finds gold worth a million dollars and decides to keep it for himself. If the group is still out in the bush, social sanctions may still be possible, but what if he only announces his decision the moment he has sold the gold and deposited the money in his bank account? Social sanctions such as ostracizing will not help much. Therefore, the group will probably turn to the state law apparatus to enforce their agreement. It is at this stage that the bindingness of the legal character of their internal norms comes into question.

It is important to note that our practical question has now shifted in a major way. The question is no longer whether the group's normative order may be recognized as a legal order, but whether the state legal order will recognize the

---

27 Brunnée and Toope, *Legitimacy and Legality*, p. 26 and p. 46. This need for a strict definition may also explain why they speak of 'criteria' of legality, whereas Fuller uses aspirational terms like 'principles', 'demands' and 'desiderata'.

28 Fuller, *Anatomy of Law*, p. 48.

norms as legally binding. In very specific cases, state legal orders may recognize internal rules as an independent legal order, but these are exceptional in Western legal orders (although they were common in the era of colonialism). These exceptions are restricted to phenomena such as church regulations (for example, canon law) and, perhaps, the rules of professional associations. Therefore, it is safe to say that most advanced legal orders will not recognize the camping group's norms as a legal order in its own right. However, whether the legal order does so or not is largely irrelevant to the legal outcome, for, even if the state legal order were to accept the group's norms as an independent legal order, the state legal order would still not be bound automatically to apply all norms. It is like in international private law: Western democracies recognize the legal orders of countries with Islamic family law, but some states withhold full recognition from specific elements of it, such as polygamous marriage. On the other hand, if the state's courts do not recognize the camping group norms as an independent legal order, they may still accept the campfire agreement as an agreement that, pursuant to the state law order, counts as a binding contract. Again, however, not every contractual agreement will be uncritically accepted, regardless of its contents.

The details of how such a court case would go in this case will vary from legal order to legal order. Some formalistic orders may require written proof of the existence of the contract and, therefore, may withhold recognition of the informal agreement. Most legal orders will not recognize oral wills for that reason, even if in the circumstances there was no effective possibility for drafting a written will. What is crucial, however, is that a philosophical analysis of whether the agreement constitutes a legal order in its own right is completely irrelevant to the legal question. Each legal order has its own norms, both about what to recognize as a valid independent legal order and about which informal agreements can be recognized as binding contracts.

Therefore, for the practical questions, we cannot rely on universal theories about what counts as law. It depends on the internal criteria of the legal order. In a highly formalist legal order, only explicit statutory formulations may count as enforceable law. In most, if not all, Western societies, there are more open criteria. There are variations in how open they are and whether moral and customary standards may be included as sources of the law. In some domestic orders, Dworkinian theory may provide the correct theory of interpretation, whereas, in other orders, exclusive positivism may provide the best description.[29] The question as to which theory is right is not a question that jurisprudence can answer in the abstract. It requires a hermeneutic theory related to the specific legal order.

---

29 Exclusive positivism holds that all law is source-based: 'its existence and content can be identified by reference to social facts alone, without resort to any evaluative argument' (Raz, *Ethics in Public Domain*, p. 195). In the nineteenth century, in countries with a Napoleonic codification and strongly positivist legal cultures such as the Netherlands around 1850, Raz's theory may have been the best description.

This holds true also for international law. Whether the international legal order is recognized as law is not something legal theorists can decide.[30] It is an internal question to be decided by the participants in that order. Therefore, the specific criteria, as suggested by Brunnée and Toope, are good starting points as they start from the internal point of view, not from the external. But again, we must be careful here not to overstate the point. Although, as descriptive scholars, they may hold this is an adequate conception of law, in the end it is up to all participants in the legal practice of international law (including scholars, but certainly not limited to them) to agree or not on a given definition of law. As Paul Schiff Berman rightly notes, 'the question of what constitutes law is itself revealed as a terrain of contestation among multiple actors'.[31]

The conclusion, then, is that definitional pluralism is legitimate, but certainly not unrestricted. We must provide good reasons for preferring one definition over another; there is no free licence here, as I will further explain in the next chapter. The fear that anything goes is, thus, unfounded, at least while we focus on the definitions of law. Idiosyncratic definitions may be suggested, but if there are no good reasons to accept them, they will simply be ignored by the community of scholars and/or the community of practice.

Methodological Pluralism

Does this pluralist framework necessarily lead to a postmodernist relativism with regard to methodology? It may seem so at first sight. Some amount of incoherence seems unavoidable, so I have argued, and that may seem to undermine traditional standards of rationality, such as the principle of consistency. If incoherence is no longer a conclusive argument to refute a theory, what other arguments can there be?

Indeed, the framework invites a strong form of methodological pluralism. An obvious consequence of the idea that we need more than one model to describe the law is that we also need more than one method. For some aspects of law as a practice, a qualitative sociological method may provide interesting insights; for other aspects, abstract economic models are helpful. In understanding legal doctrine, traditional doctrinal analysis based on some form of hermeneutics may be the preferred method; but, for example, historical and philosophical methods may also provide useful knowledge.[32]

---

30 For a similar argument, see Berman, 'Global Legal Pluralism', p. 1177, arguing that 'pluralism frees scholars from needing an essentialist definition of law'.

31 Berman, 'Global Legal Pluralism', pp. 1178–9.

32 For similar arguments in favour of a plurality of methods to study law, see various contributions to Van Klink and Taekema, *Law and Method*, esp. Taekema and Van Klink, 'On the Border', and Taekema, 'Relative Autonomy'. See also Van Hoecke, *What Is Legal Theory?*, Chapter 2, and Cotterrell, 'Legal Ideas'.

However, the method is relative to the model and, thus, the methodological pluralism is bound to the pluralism of models. There is no complete freedom to choose; the method or methods must be adequate to the model used. If we switch between different models we may also need to switch between different methods. Each method will give us some insight, some partial truth, while, at the same time, withholding other insights and blocking other partial truths from our perspective.

This methodological pluralism does not imply that the search for truth is in vain and that there is no longer a distinction between true and false, as a relativist might hold. On the contrary, the justification for pluralism is that it allows us to reach a fuller understanding of complex phenomena. We need a plurality of methods in order to do justice to the full richness of experience. The methodological pluralism I advocate for is not based on relativism, but on the idea that complementary perspectives, and the use of complementary methods, may lead to a fuller and truer account of law.

This moderate type of methodological pluralism is, in fact, very common in research. In social sciences, qualitative methods co-exist alongside quantitative methods. That co-existence is not always easy because adherents of most methods claim that their own method is much better than alternative methods. In fact, they often claim that theirs is the only method that meets scientific standards. The resulting methodological battles can be intense. However, viewing those battles from some distance, most observers will usually accept that each of the methods has produced some valuable insights. So the idea of methodological pluralism need not trouble us. Similarly, in the study of law, different methods may co-exist depending on which model or mix of models of law is involved. This need not imply that every researcher must be a strong methodological pluralist in her own work. On the contrary, for most researchers it will be best to focus on only one or a few methodologies that they know well. As I noted in the first section above, research is probably best served if many researchers devote all their energy to bringing specific theories to perfection and, in this way, obtain the maximum output from applying them. This will usually imply concentrating on specific methods as well. In order to excel we must choose and focus. Specialization is unavoidable. The result will be relatively small and partial theories with a high degree of coherence.

On the other hand, we also need generalists who can integrate fragmented insights into a broader perspective. These researchers attempt to develop more general theories. In order to realize the suggested advantages of methodological pluralism, we need to bring the small and partial theories together. However, just as in the complementarity of the partly incompatible models, the complementary methods do not amount to one coherent super method. Consequently, we must take a loss of coherence as part of the bargain.

These are, of course, two ideal types of researcher. Most researchers are somewhere in between the super specialist and the broad generalist. However, it is useful to distinguish the two ideal types because they have two different regulative ideals. The specialist's regulative ideal is that of coherence; associated methodological ideals may be that of logical consistency and strict adherence to specific methods. The generalist's regulative ideal is that of completeness; associated ideals may be that of inclusiveness and richness. These two ideals are in tension with one another: they cannot both be completely realized, yet they are both invaluable.

At this point, it will be clear that we need both types of researcher. Interdisciplinarity resulting in rich general theories is only possible with the help of devoted specialists inspired by strict methodological ideals, valid within specific disciplines. Reversely, specialization is only possible if there are generalists who provide new input from other disciplines, making knowledge and insights from other research traditions available and inspiring new hypotheses.

Five Types of Pluralism

In Part One, I have set out to understand the phenomenon of pervasive *theoretical pluralism*: the existence of a large variety of philosophical theories and concepts of law. I asked the question: how is it possible that the most brilliant theorists of our time not only disagreed about law, but even were at pains to fully understand one another? I have concluded that there are a number of different explanations for this. In this closing section, it may be helpful to summarize my argument so far. I will do this by distinguishing four other types of pluralism.

The most important type is what may be called *conceptual pluralism*. The concept of law is a plural concept that is open to a variety of legitimate but incompatible conceptions, both because it is essentially ambiguous and because it is essentially contested.[33]

The most important and novel explanation for theoretical pluralism presented in this book is that law is an essentially ambiguous concept, a concept which refers to a dynamic phenomenon that can only be described and modelled in at least two different ways that are each essentially incomplete and that are partly incompatible with one another. Because there are at least two incomplete and partly incompatible models to understand and describe law, a unifying theory is not possible. (Again, the sceptic among the readers about my radical claim may stick to a more moderate claim: with the current state of our knowledge, these models must be regarded as provisionally incompatible and, thus, a unifying theory is not yet possible.) A

---

33 Olsen and Toddington (*Architectures of Justice*, pp. 29ff.) criticize a Selznickian pragmatist approach as advocated by Sanne Taekema and, largely similar to the one I defend here. They believe that it would imply that we have to 'accept the inevitability of a vast plurality of conceptions of the phenomenon of law, and thus accept, in effect, the failure of the project of establishing a critical legal science'. It is not clear why they believe that a plurality of conceptions of law would be problematic, let alone why this would make a critical legal science impossible. The latter position could only be defended if criticism is impossible without substantive ethical foundations; but, as many critical philosophers in the pragmatist and hermeneutical traditions have demonstrated, this is an unwarranted assumption. For a discussion of hermeneutical approaches to justification see, for example, Warnke, *Justice and Interpretation*.

second explanation for the pervasiveness of theoretical pluralism is that law is a second order essentially contested concept. It is essentially contested whether or not it is essential for law to be oriented towards certain values, such as legality. Furthermore, among those who hold that law is oriented towards certain values, it is contested which values these are.

Two other types of pluralism are connected with conceptual pluralism. In this chapter, I argued that there is also a legitimate variation in definitions, which may be called a *definitional pluralism*. Because law is a plural concept, there are many definitions that may be adequate in specific contexts, even though they will always neglect certain aspects of law in general. The search for the distinctively legal is in vain; we must accept that law is a concept that can best be analysed in terms of a dynamic family resemblance. Which stipulation is most adequate will depend on the context, the purpose, and the specific types of law that we want to study.

The last type of pluralism that I have discussed is *methodological pluralism*. This is, like definitional pluralism, a consequence of conceptual pluralism. Because the phenomenon of law can be modelled in different ways, it can also be studied in different ways, using different methods. These methods may be hermeneutic, like the methods of traditional doctrinal research and of historical, linguistic and philosophical analysis. They may also be empirical, for example, methods used in legal sociology and in law and economics. Each of these methods may help us to understand the complex phenomenon of law better, but neither has a monopoly on being the only or even the most adequate method.

The explanation of pervasive theoretical pluralism may be found primarily in conceptual pluralism, but it is also associated with the other two types. Each of these four types of pluralism belongs to the level of theory. The idea of pluralism in Part One applies to theories, concepts, definitions and methods, respectively, but not to the phenomenon of law itself.

However, we may also find pluralism in law itself, what is usually called *legal pluralism*. For example, there is the variation in jurisdictions (British law versus Dutch law), in legal traditions (Common Law versus Civil Law), in fields of law (criminal law versus tort law), and in types of law (customary law versus legislation). There is also the phenomenon of global legal pluralism, a pluralism of legal orders such as domestic law, EU law and international law. These are different types of pluralism that have not been discussed in Part One, but which will be central to Part Two.

Of course, these forms of pluralism in law itself are not completely unrelated to theoretical pluralism. I have argued that the adequacy of specific concepts, definitions and methods is to be determined within specific contexts. Positivist theories of law, for example, may have been fairly adequate in the context of nineteenth-century Europe after the great codifications, but may be much less adequate in the context of international law. As we will see in Part Two, the variation in law itself may, therefore, be a further explanation for the pervasive pluralism in legal theory.

PART II
LEGAL INTERACTIONISM

Chapter 6
What is Legal Interactionism?

The Challenges for Legal Theory in the Twenty-First Century

In Part One, I developed a pluralist framework that allows us to understand why competing theories in jurisprudence may all embody a partial truth. It depends on the context and the issue studied which specific theory is most adequate. After this analytical groundwork, we are now in a position to construct a general theory of law and morality: a general theory – not a universal one. I cannot claim that it is universally valid; it can only be adequate in some contexts.[1]

The context I am interested in is that of modern Western democracies governed by the rule of law at the beginning of the twenty-first century. The theory developed in this part may be more or less adequate in other contexts too, but I will not discuss those here. The simple practical reason for this restriction is, of course, that modern Western democracies are the only contexts which I know reasonably well.[2] However, the more fundamental reason is that to do otherwise would very much broaden the variation of contexts to be addressed, and this might impair my attempt to develop a robust theory of law and morality. The broader the range of application, the more vague the theory will become. My approach is already, in various respects, quite broad-ranging, as it does not restrict itself to state legal orders. An attempt to include societies other than Western democracies would likely make it impossible to say anything meaningful.[3] Those who are familiar with other legal orders can analyse which parts of my theory are useful and which should be dismissed when they set out to construct a theory that is most adequate for those legal orders. Perhaps we may then discern some similarities among a broader variation of legal orders. However, I suspect that those similarities will be

---

1 This rejection of a claim to universal applicability of a theory of law is in line with both Selznick's and Fuller's contextualism. See Rundle, *Forms Liberate*, p. 6: '[Fuller] never suggested that his claims were to be accepted as universally applicable, in the style of general jurisprudence'. See also Cotterrell, *Politics of Jurisprudence*, 254.

2 My perspective is thus, in the words of William Twining, 'self-consciously quite parochial, reflecting my own biases and limited knowledge' (Twining, *General Jurisprudence*, p. xiii).

3 This contextual limitation also means that the theory developed in this book cannot be tested on the basis of hypothetical or real examples from non-democratic regimes that systematically violate basic moral precepts. If a reader argues that my theory will not answer problems like the validity of Nazi laws, he is correct; the context is simply a different one. In order to be able to deal with such problems, the basic ideas behind the theory might be of assistance, but the theory in itself cannot be applied to such problems.

less interesting than some of the characteristics that we might observe when we limit our focus.

In the sociological literature we can find dozens of terms denoting the processes of contemporary Western societies, such as industrialization, modernization and globalization. In some cases, these processes have already transformed into a new phase, as references to the post-industrial and postmodern society testify to. It is no use attempting to describe all of those processes. Instead, I will simply focus on four phenomena that are, in my view, most relevant for constructing a general theory of law. These are the ever-increasing amount of black-letter law produced by the state; the emergence of horizontal and interactional forms of law; the existence of global legal pluralism; and the highly dynamic character of the societies in question.[4]

First, there has been an enormous increase in state regulation, also known as the regulatory explosion. Modern states have created vast numbers of statutory rules and other types of regulations, usually in the form of black-letter law. Some of these rules are primarily directed at the state's bureaucracy or at societal organizations that are largely dependent on the state, such as those in the fields of health care, welfare and education. Many of these regulations focus on the smallest details. Other such regulations are directed at citizens and businesses. The result of this creation of these vast quantities of black-letter law is that it is impossible to know all of it, let alone observe it. Hence, this situation has made it difficult for citizens to be guided by the rules; consequently, there is an increasing risk that they simply evade or ignore them altogether. The paradoxical result of the regulatory explosion is that regulation becomes less effective as an instrument to guide the behaviour of citizens, businesses or state and semi-state bureaucracies.

Second, there is a gradual emergence of a different type of law, which is not based on top-down regulation, but on more horizontal processes of ordering.[5] State institutions play no role in the development of this law, or if they do play a role, it is merely that of one of the various partners in this process. This is interactional law, a type of legal order that usually emerges in the more or less horizontal interaction between various parties such as citizens, businesses, non-governmental organizations and state actors. The international legal order is one example of this. There is no central world government, so the notion of law as a top-down regulation by the state is simply not feasible. Indeed, as Brunnée and Toope show,

---

4 There is a wealth of literature on each of these four phenomena. I do not claim to be original in describing them; they are nowadays widely accepted, probably with the exception of horizontal and interactional forms of law. I just discuss them briefly in order to sketch the challenges of legal theory.

5 Of course, this is not a new type of law; on the contrary, customary law has always been an important part of law. However, in the context of public law (for example, in administrative law, international law and health law) the prominent role it plays is relatively new.

it is not even true that national states are the only actors in the scene.⁶ Businesses, non-governmental organizations and the media all play a role in the formation of a legal consciousness and the emergence of legal practices. Moreover, as a result of economic globalization, at the international level the interactions between businesses and between businesses and states are as important as interactions between states.⁷ Furthermore, the legal structure of these interactions is usually organized around contracts, covenants and similar horizontal instruments. However, the phenomenon of horizontal interactional law is certainly not restricted to international law and the world economy.⁸ It can be found at many levels in rapidly changing fields of society where state law is unable or too slow to respond to rapid developments, for example in self-regulation, ethics codes and covenants between consumer organizations and businesses.

Third, we can no longer deny global legal pluralism, in the sense of a plurality of legal orders that are partly intertwined and partly autonomous.⁹ If we look at a country such as the Netherlands, we may discern at least four major legal orders: domestic Dutch law, European Union law, the law of the Council of Europe, especially the European Convention on Human Rights, and international law.¹⁰ None of these legal orders can be completely reduced to the other, yet none is completely autonomous either. For example, the European Convention on Human Rights has formally a higher authority than Dutch domestic law; yet, with its margin of appreciation partly determined by the question of whether there is a European consensus, it also respects domestic law and incorporates it into its own case law. Moreover, at the level of implicit understandings and legal doctrine, there is a strong dialectical interplay between domestic legal orders and the law of the European Convention, as judges in the European Court have been thoroughly socialized in their own domestic legal order and, thus, cannot help but bring their own legal culture to the table when partaking in arguments on the cases before them. Certainly, legal pluralism is not restricted to normative orders that

---

6   Brunnée and Toope, *Legitimacy and Legality*, p. 5. See also Klabbers, 'Constitutionalism', pp. 91–4.

7   See Berman, 'Global Legal Pluralism', p. 1162: 'we see communities of transnational bankers developing their own law governing trade finance and the use of modern forms of *lex mercatoria* to govern business relations'.

8   As I will discuss below, interactional law need not always be fully horizontal. However, horizontal interactional law is certainly the most important type and, in my view, it is this type of law that constitutes a major challenge for contemporary theories of law.

9   See Twining, *General Jurisprudence*, for an extensive discussion of how studies of law (and especially jurisprudence) should take a great variety of legal orders and the relations between various levels of ordering seriously.

10 International law, moreover, consists, on the one hand, of a more general interactional law and, on the other hand, of a great number of relatively autonomous legal orders associated with more specific international treaties and organizations, such as the World Trade Organization (WTO), the World Health Organization (WHO) and various UN and regional organizations.

directly or indirectly derive from the authority of states. It includes many non-state legal orders as well, such as norms made in 'tribal or ethnic enclaves, religious organizations, corporate bylaws, social customs, private regulatory bodies, and a wide variety of groups, associations and non-state institutions'.[11]

Fourth, it is important to take note of the highly dynamic character, both of Western societies and of law. Society and technology change rapidly. This means that the law must respond to new problems and new issues, such as biotechnology. Beyond this, law must also be responsive to changing social views with regard to such issues as euthanasia or embryo selection. As a consequence, law has to adapt rapidly, but it usually has serious problems keeping up with the rapid pace of societal and technological changes. Moreover, the processes of social and legal change are often not very smooth and coherent. One segment of society may already have completely adapted to the requirements of globalization, whereas another segment may still be struggling with its consequences. In some legal fields adaptation to globalization may proceed smoothly (for example, when legal norms are developed on the basis of contracts devised by large multinational law firms), whereas other fields lag behind. Legislation and adjudication frequently fail to provide rapid responses. This presents an important challenge for every theory of law, as such a theory must account for the fragmented process of change. Any legal theory, if it is going to be useful, cannot simply focus on a coherent legal doctrine as it exists on 1 January 2014, but must also be capable of helping us understand ongoing trends and processes.

My analysis will start with the first two phenomena. When we combine them, we may conclude that there are two orthogonal directions in which law is developing. On the one hand, there is an ever-increasing number of top-down regulations produced by the state, resulting in an enormous amount of black-letter law; on the other hand, there is an emergence of horizontal interactional law. Currently, the major traditions in legal philosophy are not able to deal with this dual development adequately. Legal positivism may largely suffice for understanding top-down state law, but cannot include horizontal interactional law. Natural law theories do not help us understand most of the large body of instrumentalist state law. Nor do they help us understand most of horizontal law. Dworkinian interpretivism is helpful in the context of a well-developed legal order in which authoritative institutions such as judges can critically reconstruct the body of law, but not in the context of a fragmented international legal order or, more generally, in the context of horizontal law, where secondary institutions are still largely lacking.

Enacted Law and Interactional Law

What we need, therefore, is a theory that does justice both to positive law, produced by legal authorities, and to horizontal interactional law. We can build

---

11 Berman, 'Global Legal Pluralism', p. 1172.

here on Fuller's distinction between implicit law and made law, discussed in Chapter 3 above.¹² Fuller does not explicitly define both, but presents them in his discussion of two pure types of law, customary law and legislation, respectively. Implicit law may be described as 'a set of reciprocally adjusted expectations that functions as a basis for order between the parties'.¹³ Implicit law finds its implicit expression in the interaction itself, whereas made law is the explicit formulation by an enactment of a legislature or some other lawmaking institution. In made law, the formulation of the norm is supposed to precede the action not only in time, but also as the source of the law. In implicit law, the formulation – if at all – comes only after it has emerged in the interaction, and the interaction remains the primary source of the law, even after it has been formulated.

The two terms are, in my view, unfortunate. In a sense, every law is made law because law is a human construct – this holds true as much for customary law as for statutes. Moreover, the term 'implicit' suggests that once a norm is explicitly formulated – if only in order to explain to the newcomer what the norms are – it can no longer count as implicit law. It might also suggest that once a contract has been made in a longstanding business relationship, the law with regard to that relationship suddenly becomes part of made law.

For these reasons, I prefer two other terms that Fuller uses elsewhere: enacted law versus interactional law.¹⁴ Enacted law is law that comes into existence as the result of an explicit enactment by a legal authority – for example, a legislature, a court, but also an official in an organization, such as the head of a university who makes rules regulating the behaviour of students or staff. Interactional law is law that comes into existence through a gradual process of interaction in which a standard of conduct emerges that is considered to give rise to legal obligations. Thus, the two names refer to two different sources of law, enactment and interaction.

It may be helpful at this point to explore the characteristics of both ideal types of law in detail. In modern societies, enacted law takes the form of black-letter law, usually consisting of a set of rules. Enacted law is explicitly produced as law by institutions that claim the authority to make law and to pronounce authoritative statements regarding its contents. The most important ones are, of course, legislatures and courts – but these are certainly not the only ones. Many government organizations and officials have delegated regulatory power and can produce regulations that are considered binding upon those who are subject to their powers. Moreover, in every organization of a certain scale, whether it is a

---

12 Fuller, *Anatomy of Law*, pp. 43–84.
13 Fuller, *Principles of Social Order*, p. 286. Although Fuller does not present this formula as a description of implicit law, David Luban rightly remarks that it can be used as a definition of implicit law (Luban, 'Rediscovering Fuller's Legal Ethics', p. 206).
14 In *Principles of Social Order*, at p. 232, Fuller uses the terms enacted law and authoritatively declared law as synonyms for made law. Interactional law is used in *Morality of Law*, at p. 221 and p. 237.

governmental organization or a business, there are some officials or institutions that set internal rules for the employees and for those who are dependent on their services. Other such examples are churches, professional associations and even soccer clubs: these organizations may also have law-producing authoritative institutions.

Gerald Postema explains the concept of enacted law (or, in his terminology, made rules) as follows:

> Made rules are given canonical verbal formulations by a determinate author at a reasonably precise date. The practical force of made rules depends on the authority of their makers or the offices they occupy. Thus, made rules presuppose both authors and relations of authority and subordination.[15]

Enacted law emerges out of vertical relationships. That need not be the commanding authority of an absolute dictator, but the relationship is one between the lawmaker and the subject. Of course, in a democratic legal order, the subject as a voter can also influence the lawmaker indirectly; moreover, the person or persons constituting the lawmaking institution are also subject to the rule of law. However, the institution that produces the law, the legislature, stands in a vertical relationship of authority to citizens. Similarly, a general assembly of the members of a private association can produce enacted law and thus bind its members. Although in this case the underlying horizontal element is strong (all members having an equal vote), the actual enactment reflects a vertical relationship, as the group decision produces norms that are obligatory for each member. The general assembly and the individual member stand in a hierarchical relation of authority.

Both in democratic laws and in rules enacted by a general assembly, the vertical order is embedded in a more horizontal order. Nevertheless, the vertical aspect of authority is essential in enacted law. There are authoritative institutions that claim to have lawmaking and law-enforcing authority. This type of law can usually be described in the familiar frameworks of legal positivism, like a union of primary and secondary rules (H.L.A. Hart) or an institutionalized system claiming authority (Joseph Raz).[16] However, for a full understanding of enacted law, we need to go beyond legal positivism because the reason why enacted law has obligatory force cannot be fully understood from within a legal positivist framework.[17] As we will see, one of Fuller's central theses is that enacted law is embedded in a reciprocal pattern of interactions between citizens, legislators and other officials.

For a description of interactional law (or implicit rules), we may also turn to Gerald Postema:

---

15 Postema, 'Implicit Law', p. 256.
16 Hart, *Concept of Law*; Raz, *Authority of Law*.
17 See Postema, 'Implicit Law', p. 260.

[I]mplicit rules arise from conduct, not conception. Verbal formulations may more or less accurately capture the rules implicit in the conduct, but the formulations are always post hoc and strictly answerable to the conduct. No formulation is authoritative in virtue of its public articulation alone. Although implicit rules arise from the conduct of determinate agents, typically they have no precise date of birth and no determinate authors. They presuppose no relations of authority and subordination; thus, their practical force depends neither on authority nor on enactment, but on the fact that they find 'direct expression in the conduct of people toward one another'.[18]

The crucial point here is that, in social interaction, we must be able to rely on the predictability of at least most of the actions of other individuals (and of the state). Otherwise we cannot achieve our own purposes and guide our own behaviour. Therefore, social interaction requires 'relatively stable mutual expectations of behavior'.[19] These expectations 'emerge over time from a process of mutual accommodation and adjustment of expectations and actions of interacting agents'.[20]

It is this ongoing practice that is the basis for the obligatory force of interactional law. Interactional law is usually implicit in the interaction, but it can be made explicit by formulating the rules and putting them on paper. For example, the continuing relationship between business partners can be laid down in a contract, and this may acquire a certain legal status in its own right.[21] However, often the contract will not be followed to the letter because the underlying practice requires adaptation, and both partners will understand the need for these adaptations. For the partners in the contract, the implicit interactional law is more authoritative than the written contract. As long as this orientation to the underlying practice is considered to be the basis of the obligatory force we can speak of interactional law, even if the norms have also been formulated in contracts, treaties, codes, or even statutes.[22]

Interactional law is relatively stable, but it is certainly not unchangeable. It may change as a reaction to new circumstances. For example, Postema argues that it is possible to change interactional norms and still remain faithful to the interactional expectancies, when the actors are guided by the purpose of the practice of

---

18 Postema, 'Implicit Law', p. 257, quoting in the last sentence Fuller, 'Human Interaction and the Law', in *Principles of Social Order*, p. 232.
19 Postema, 'Implicit Law', p. 257.
20 Postema, 'Implicit Law', p. 258.
21 See Fuller's analysis of the interactional foundations of contract law in *Principles of Social Order*, pp. 244ff. Contract also has strong elements of made law; see Fuller, *Anatomy of Law*, pp. 70–71.
22 However, when and in so far as the written texts become an independent source of obligatory force, we are leaving the domain of interactional law and replacing or supplementing it with enacted law or contract.

interaction and the idea of reasonableness.[23] Let us assume that I always take care of the neighbours' cats during their holidays, and vice versa. If they put a note in my mail box asking me to do so next week over the upcoming holidays and I do not reply telling them no, and they know I am in town, I have implicitly accepted an obligation to take care of the cats. This obligation holds even if I unexpectedly have to leave to take care of my mother who has suddenly fallen seriously ill. In that case, I have, at a minimum, an obligation to ask someone else to feed the cats, even though this means that someone else – whom my neighbours may not even know – will have to enter their house. This is a reasonable reinterpretation of the implicit understanding between my neighbour and myself, guided by our primary purpose: to keep the cats alive and healthy.

Interactional law usually arises out of interactions with a horizontal character, but may also arise out of interactions with a more vertical dimension. The clearest examples of interactional law are, indeed, horizontal orderings, but that does not mean that there is no interactional aspect in vertical relationships.[24] Interactional law is based on a principle of reciprocity, and that reciprocal relation need not be fully horizontal. There can also be reciprocity between a boss and an employee. Similarly, interactional elements may be present in a reciprocal relation between state and citizens, but how far that relation is basically vertical or has more horizontal characteristics may vary.

Indeed, interactional expectations are also present in vertical power relationships, when a person in power gives orders to citizens and the citizens decide to accept and obey those orders, or do so only in part. Even in an autocratic state, when the state uses statutory norms to regulate the actions of its citizens, the interactional element is still present and essential. The state orders specific actions, but the citizens have to acquiesce to the norms in order to give them effect. In some cases, these patterns of interaction and reciprocal expectations may intensify and acquire, in the opinions of all actors involved, obligatory force; then we may even speak of interactional law in a predominantly vertical relationship. For example, state enforcement agencies frequently accept that the official rules are not followed to the letter, and citizens then expect the agencies to tolerate a certain margin of rule infringements. The citizens may feel that the state violates these interactional legal norms (or customary law) if those infringements are suddenly nevertheless prosecuted – a legal argument that sometimes has been accepted by courts. This example shows how even vertical relationships are often characterized by a combination of enacted and interactional law.

It may appear as if these are two completely different systems of law. However, they are not. They are intertwined. There are always interactional elements presupposed by enacted law and, especially in modern complex societies, enacted

---

23 See Postema, 'Implicit Law', p. 258.
24 See Fuller, *Principles of Social Order*, p. 190.

elements that influence interactional law.²⁵ Enacted law must be interpreted in order to be applied, and for that interpretation we must rely in part on moral considerations as well as on the interactional legal norms that are accepted in society or in relevant subsections of it.²⁶ Moreover, there are certain implicit principles of interpretation that are not often formulated in enacted law itself but that are fully part of the interpretive practice, as, for example, the principle that in case of conflict, a newer statute has more weight than an older statute. Such principles may be considered part of the interactional law that makes enacted law possible.

A more fundamental illustration of how enacted law presupposes interactional law is Fuller's internal morality of law.²⁷ If a legislator wants to enact law, he does not have full licence to do whatever he wants. In order to make law that can act as guidance to those subject to it, he must respect the eight principles of legality; otherwise he will simply fail to draft a law that can guide behaviour. For example, if the legislator does not publicize the laws, the citizens cannot act on them; if the laws are inconsistent or vague, they will simply not know what they are expected to do. Many legal positivists have regarded these principles as mere demands of effectiveness. If a legislator wants to be effective, he should respect them. However, this misses the fundamental point.²⁸ For Fuller, legislation is embedded in a framework of interactional expectations based on reciprocity. The legislator expects the citizens to follow the law, but the citizens also expect the legislator to be reasonable. In a democracy, the vertical relationship is not merely that of (in Hart's famous terms) 'a gunman situation writ large',²⁹ but is part of fundamental expectations with regard to the various roles in society. A citizen is expected to act as a responsible citizen and the legislator is expected to act as a responsible legislator. The legislator must enable citizens to guide their actions and pursue their own aims within the context of a stable legal framework. The ideal of the rule of law and the ideal of democracy as a common enterprise to govern society responsibly are central to these interactional expectancies. If the legislator violates the eight principles of legality – or, more fundamentally, the expectations following from this normative order – he loses legitimacy and weakens the bond of reciprocity between legislator and citizens. In extreme cases, citizens will no longer take account of the laws because following them can no longer be seen as

---

25   See Fuller, *Anatomy of Law*, pp. 57–84, where he presents various examples of how implicit elements are present in made law, and vice versa. See also Macdonald, 'Legislation and Governance', pp. 284–93.

26   Fuller, *Anatomy of Law*, pp. 57–60.

27   Fuller, *Anatomy of Law*, p. 60: 'Every exercise of the lawmaking function is accompanied by certain tacit assumptions, or implicit expectations, about the kind of product that will emerge from the legislator's efforts and the form he will give to that product.' Fuller uses 'legislator' here in the interpretation which is common in the European Civil Law tradition as the personified lawmaking authority. I follow him in this respect.

28   See Rundle, *Forms Liberate*, p. 92 and *passim*.

29   Hart, 'Positivism and Separation', p. 603.

a reasonable demand. Thus, the possibilities and constraints of enacted law are embedded in interactional law. It is this reciprocal relationship between legislator and citizens which is the basis for the internal morality of legislation. Those positivists who reduce the eight principles to demands of effectiveness can only do so because they mistakenly take the relationship between legislator and citizens as merely one of a unidirectional exercise of authority. Fuller, on the contrary, would argue that even if the superficial relationship is one of a unidirectional exercise of authority, it can only give rise to valid obligations if it is embedded in an underlying interaction based on reciprocity.

The reverse also holds true: interactional law builds on enacted law. Modern societies are so strongly permeated by enacted state law that there is no longer such a thing as a private realm completely free from the influence of enacted law. When patterns of interactions emerge and form interactional law, this is not a purely spontaneous process. The actors will have been strongly influenced, sometimes consciously but usually unconsciously, by the norms of the state legal order when they think about the terms of cooperation. There is usually a dialectical interplay between citizens' ideas about what is reasonable and fair and the principles laid down in statutes.[30] Statutes often codify customary law, but they also modify it; and, moreover, they make one uniform code. If a statutory norm has been in the books for 200 years (which is the case in many European countries with Napoleonic codes which were introduced in the early nineteenth century), then this has also, in various direct and indirect ways, influenced the popular legal consciousness and general practice. In as far as this has happened, interactional law builds upon enacted law. Moreover, each one reinforces the other.

An example of such a mutual reinforcement of interactional law and enacted law is the contract. From the perspective of state-enacted law, contracts are binding because a statute says so. Most European civil codes contain a provision to that effect. From the perspective of interactional law, however, contracts are binding because they explicitly formulate what was already implicitly understood as a set of mutual obligations on the basis of a cooperative relationship. The fact that the norms of interactional law and enacted law converge implies that contracts contain a strong obligatory force. We should not be reductionist here and try to reduce the force of the contract to only one of the sources; both are a source in their own right. There is no need to try to base all claims to validity and bindingness on merely one source. Both interactional law and enacted law can give rise to legal obligations, and if they both point in the same direction, the obligatory force is only reinforced.

We must add even more complexity to the story. The contract itself is also a source of law in its own right.[31] Once it has been signed, it constitutes a relatively

---

30 On this interplay see Macdonald, 'Legislation and Governance', p. 288.

31 In *Anatomy of Law* (at p. 117) Fuller distinguishes four mechanisms of law: 'legislative enactment, customary law, contractual law and adjudicative law as exemplified in the common law system'. Each of them contains a mixture of (in Fuller's terminology)

autonomous legal order, based on mutual consent. The terms of the contract are the primary sources of the obligations following from it; both the underlying interactional law and the enacted law on contracts are, from this perspective, only secondary sources. So there are three perspectives on the meaning of the contract. Each of them can claim to give an explanation for why the contract can create obligations; each of them provides part of the truth.[32]

A Non-Reductionist Approach

The theory developed in this chapter may be called legal interactionism.[33] In a pluralist approach, legal interactionism takes seriously interactional law, but tries to do justice to enacted law as well. My account has close affinities with the interactional account of international law recently presented by Jutta Brunnée and Stephen Toope; however, it differs from their view in developing a more pluralist approach, in line with the later work of Lon Fuller. I will discuss their theory first and then discuss how it should be adapted in order to make it more adequate in dealing with pluralism.

---

implicit and made law, but the mixtures differ. Even so, legislative enactment and customary law can be seen as embodying the ideal type of made law and implicit law, respectively. Here Fuller's broad use of the phrase 'sources of the law' may cause confusion. Each of the four mechanisms can be a source of law in the narrow sense of the phrase, meaning that it can be the basis for legal obligations. In Fuller's broader sense of the phrase, each of them is also a source for the obligatory force of the law. However, this obligatory force must, if I understand Fuller correctly, be grounded in the mixture of made and implicit elements. In this respect I differ from Fuller, as I argue that contract derives its obligatory force not only from enacted and interactional law, but can be also seen as an obligatory force-creating mechanism in its own right. The same might hold in Common Law countries for adjudication, which can both be seen as deriving obligatory force from enacted law and interactional law and as a source of obligatory force in its own right.

32 *Mutatis mutandis* we could say the same about international treaties. They are both the basis for a legal order in their own right and rely on the underlying interactional practice of legality as the source for their obligatory character. Brunnée and Toope, *Legitimacy and Legality*, p. 69 neglect the first aspect when they consider positive law as merely an element of interactional law.

33 Fuller's theory has been called interactionist by various authors, for example, Brunnée and Toope, *Legitimacy and Legality*, p. 24, and Witteveen, 'Rediscovering Fuller', pp. 31–2. Witteveen argues that interactionist views on law can also be found with Montesquieu, American pragmatism and the sociology of Georg Simmel. Brunnée and Toope use the term 'interactionalism' for their own position. As my account is more similar to Fuller's than to Brunnée and Toope's, on those points where they differ, I prefer the word interactionism. To emphasize that it is a theory about law and not about human interaction in general, I have added the word legal. Legal interactionism, as constructed in this book, is strongly embedded in American pragmatism and symbolic interactionism, but my central thesis that law is an essentially ambiguous concept diverges from the mainstream in those two traditions.

What is essential for law, according to Brunnée and Toope, is not form or authoritative institutions, but the fact that (at least some) citizens and other actors are obligated.[34] This is because legal norms can inspire fidelity and a feeling of obligation. Fidelity is not produced by authorities that regard law simply as a command to their subjects. Citizens may obey if these commands are backed up by threats, but they will not feel obligated; commands will not create a distinctive legal legitimacy. In order to produce fidelity, legal norms must be grounded in shared understandings and built, maintained (and sometimes destroyed) in a continuing practice of legality. According to Brunnée and Toope, there are three requirements for the emergence and continued existence of law.

The first of these requirements is a community of practice in which some shared understandings and moral commitments emerge. These understandings need not be substantive; they can be very minimal and largely procedural. 'It is possible to imagine law rooted in thin shared moral commitments, such as autonomy and communication.'[35] Indeed, these two commitments form the basic foundation for interactional legal practices, as the principles of legality presuppose and reinforce the idea of autonomous actors and the possibility of communication between them on the meaning of the norms.[36] For example, for basic rules of contract law, it may suffice to have a common notion of free consent or autonomy and of transaction.[37] For international law, the shared understandings are often very thin indeed, but they may become more substantive in the process of continued interaction and discussion. The starting point may be no more than the common acknowledgement that we need norms or procedures to coordinate when and how force is allowed, or the shared understanding that we should find means to avoid global warming beyond dangerous levels.

The second requirement is that, on the basis of these shared understandings, there is a practice of legality. A practice of legality is a practice of norm creation and norm application which adheres to the eight principles of legality as developed by Lon Fuller in *The Morality of Law*. Brunnée and Toope hold that if the creation of norms and their application do not match up with these principles, then those norms are not fully law. The norms created not on the basis of these principles of legality may sometimes be effectively followed as commands backed up by threats, but they lack full legal character, even if they have the formal characteristics often found in (but not defining of) law. Or it is possible that the norms created are simply not followed by any other actors than the norm creators themselves, as

---

34 Brunnée and Toope, *Legitimacy and Legality*, p. 55.
35 Brunnée and Toope, *Legitimacy and Legality*, p. 32.
36 Both autonomy and communication are gradual terms; we do not need full autonomy (whatever that may be) or completely undisturbed communication to make law possible. But it may be that decreased autonomy and partly blocked communication channels diminish the legal quality of law.
37 Brunnée and Toope, *Legitimacy and Legality*, p. 32.

they do not feel included or taken seriously as autonomous actors. In both of these cases, the norms do not evoke a sense of legal obligation among the norm subjects.

The third requirement is that of a continuing practice of legality. In international relations, law creation is not the simple result of an act of will of some authorities; it is a continuing project and challenge. Here, Fuller's eighth principle, the congruence between norm and official action, is especially important for the continual reconstruction of law. If legal norms are no longer taken seriously by the participants in a practice they become a dead letter and lose their legal character.

This is, in a nutshell, Brunnée and Toope's basic argument. It seems a plausible account of how interactional international law may emerge in certain circumstances. However, there are two related points of criticism that I want to explore. The first concerns their suggestion that every practice of legality must be characterized by the eight principles which Fuller developed for the process of legislation. The second concerns their suggestion that, at least in the field of international law, interactional law is the only source of law and that all other types of law should be ultimately derived from interactional law.

Fuller developed his eight principles of legality as an internal morality of legislation, of the 'enterprise of subjecting human conduct to the governance of rules'. In his book *The Morality of Law*, he seems to suggest that the eight principles constitute the internal morality of law in general.[38] However, in his later work he acknowledges that legislation is only one of the possible legal processes and that each process has its own internal morality. According to Kenneth Winston, the five main legal processes are contract, mediation, legislation, adjudication and managerial direction.[39] This list is not exclusive: there are other less important processes, such as elections and lottery, and new ones may emerge.[40] Although some of the eight principles of legality for legislation may be relevant to these other legal processes, they need not. For example, in *The Morality of Law*, Fuller argues that only five of the eight principles apply fully to managerial direction.[41] The internal moralities of adjudication, mediation, contract and managerial direction thus are all different because they emerge from the specific demands of the process.[42]

---

38 See Winston, 'Introduction', p. 44.

39 Fuller did not include international law in his analysis. It could be regarded as a legal process *sui generis* or as a mix of contract and legislation. Whatever qualification we choose, it certainly is not merely legislation, and thus the simple application of Fuller's eight principles to international law is questionable. For a similar criticism see Krisch, 'Review of Legitimacy and Legality'.

40 See Winston, 'Introduction', p. 41. In *Principles of Social Order*, at pp. 188–9, Fuller presents a list of nine processes (including the five discussed here), emphasizing that other principles have been left out.

41 Fuller, *Morality of Law*, p. 208.

42 For an overview of the types of legal processes and their distinct characteristics, see Winston, 'Introduction', p. 48.

Moreover, there is a contextual variation as well that needs to be addressed. Fuller's internal morality of legislation is typical of legislation in a more or less democratic context, in which citizens are treated as autonomous persons. The internal morality of interactional international law, as developed by Brunnée and Toope, is typical of international law at the beginning of the twenty-first century. In a critical reaction to their theory, Christian Reus-Smit suggests that, before the nineteenth century, there was a different set of international legal practices and that these were connected with different criteria of legality. He convincingly argues that we should not 'treat Fuller's criteria of legality as though they were *the* criteria of legality'.[43] There is no reason to assume that practices of legality always have the same characteristics; on the contrary, it is plausible to assume that there is variation with regard to context and to types of law.

At this point, Philip Selznick's analysis of legality may provide a helpful supplement and correction to Brunnée and Toope's theory. Selznick argues that law is a normative system oriented towards the ideal of legality.[44] Although the core notion of legality can be formulated as 'the progressive reduction of arbitrariness in positive law and its administration', the interpretation of the ideal may vary and develop to include more substantive elements.[45] Legality is a complex ideal, consisting of a set of constitutive values.[46] In the context of democratic legislation, these values lead to Fuller's eight principles of legality; but in other contexts, the values may be associated with a different internal morality and, thus, with different sets of principles of legality.[47]

Ideals are more open to interpretation than principles; in different contexts different aspects of the ideals may be emphasized.[48] Moreover, ideals are also more open to evolution. Therefore, if we focus on law as a practice (or set of practices) oriented towards the ideal of legality, it may be easier to discern change and variation. Consequently, understanding practices of legality, not in

---

43 Reus-Smit, 'Obligation through Practice', p. 347 (italics in original). He argues that criteria of legality are always historically and contextually contingent.

44 Selznick, 'Sociology and Natural Law'. On Selznick, see also the intellectual biography by Krygier, *Philip Selznick*.

45 Nonet and Selznick, *Law and Society in Transition*, p. 108. This formulation of the ideal of legality is a recurring phrase in Selznick's work; see Taekema, *Concept of Ideals*, p. 113.

46 Taekema, *Concept of Ideals*, p. 141.

47 Olsen and Toddington, *Architectures of Justice*, pp. 31–2 argue that these 'master ideals' can only be constructed with recourse to moral judgment. In my view, this is correct because, as Dworkin has convincingly argued, legal interpretation is always intertwined with moral argument. However, it does not follow that we need a foundationalist theory of ethics, as Olsen and Toddington suggest. When understanding a legal order in light of its leading ideals we need not assume 'the objectively rational defensibility' of our interpretation of these ideals.

48 For a more elaborate discussion of ideals, see Van der Burg and Taekema, *Importance of Ideals*, and Chapters 7 and 9 hereunder.

terms of Fuller's eight principles of legality but in terms of the more fundamental ideal of legality, leads to an account that is more pluralist and dynamic. In this reconstruction, Brunnée and Toope's theory of interactional international law and Fuller's theory of legislation are not rejected but put into context. They may be regarded as robust theories for particular forms of law in particular historical contexts. If we want to broaden our scope, we must accept that there are more ways in which the ideal of legality can be implemented than merely through the eight principles of legality as developed by Fuller.

The second criticism mentioned above is that Brunnée and Toope are mistaken to suggest that interactional law is the only source of law. In this respect they differ from Lon Fuller's book *Anatomy of the Law*, when he discusses two sources of the law (implicit or interactional law and made or enacted law).[49] I have already discussed the various sources of law above, so I will not repeat my analysis here. I concluded there that a legal theory must recognize both interactional law and enacted law, as well as other sources such as contract and treaty, based on the possibility of creating obligations by mutual consent.

Legal interactionism, in the pluralist account advocated here, holds that the obligatory force of enacted law and contract is embedded in an interactional pattern. In a sense, therefore, it regards interactional law as primary because without a general pattern of interaction in which enacted law is accepted as obligatory, enacted law may come close to being merely the exercise of brute force. However, legal interactionism, as I understand it, does not reduce the obligatory force of contract or enacted law to that of interactional law. Both may also constitute a legal order in their own right which can create obligatory force once it has emerged. Therefore, interactional law is not the sole foundation of enacted law or contract. However, the obligatory force of each of the legal orders is reinforced when there is congruence between the deeper interactional law and the black-letter law of enacted law and contract.

The term 'legal positivism' is, of course, associated with positive law in the sense that it takes positive law as the primary source of law, and in some versions even as identical with law. Philip Selznick and Ronald Dworkin have used an analogous phrase, 'legal naturalism', for their own positions. Both authors are not simple natural law thinkers, and they use this term to indicate their affinity with a valuable core in natural thinking without completely accepting substantive natural law as the basis of their thinking.[50] Similarly, the term 'legal interactionism' is used

---

49 For a similar criticism, see Krisch 'Review of Legitimacy and Legality', p. 208. Krisch argues convincingly that Fuller's horizontal elements operate in a vertical framework, and that this vertical dimension is ignored in Brunnée and Toope's translation of Fuller to international law.

50 Selznick, 'Sociology and Natural Law'; Dworkin, 'Natural Law Revisited'. As far as I know, Dworkin has never repeated this use of 'naturalism' in connection with his own position. Clearly, both authors have a very different and much richer conception of naturalism than the reductionist version suggested by Brian Leiter in *Naturalizing Jurisprudence*.

to indicate a special focus on interactional law without regarding interactional law as the only source of law.[51]

Legal interactionism does claim that enacted law that is not embedded in an interactive practice is not fully law. There must be some congruence between interactional law and enacted law; otherwise the obligatory force of enacted law is weakened. Enacted law is embedded in a broader interaction and in that sense we could say that interactional law is primary.[52] Enacted law without any basis in interactional patterns simply is no law at all, but mere fiction. If someone claims that he is the supreme legislator and everyone should listen to his laws, while no one does, there is simply no law and, instead, probably just a lunatic. There must be at least some minimal practice in which individuals act according to what is claimed to be law, underlying the claim to authority.

However, legal interactionism does not take a reductionist position. Except for the extreme case of the lunatic, we cannot say that enacted law is fully dependent on interactional law. Enacted law can and usually does create its own legal order. Once this legal order has come into existence, it creates a dynamic of its own and may create an obligatory force of its own. This is the core of truth in Hart's usually unnoticed switch from a practice model to a product model, discussed in Chapter 3. Once secondary rules have emerged and, with them, a legal doctrine and legal authorities have come into existence, a new legal order has been created. The mistake of positivists is, however, that they suggest that therewith interactional law ceases to exist or that it is completely superseded by the new order of positive law. Even so, the true insight of positivism is that a new legal order has emerged, and that this new legal order of enacted law cannot be completely reduced to interactional law. As long as there is at least a minimal congruence between interactional law and enacted law, they both have a separate existence as legal orders. There may be tensions between the two legal orders as there rarely is full congruence. There is also substantive overlap as in normal situations there is much congruence. However, both positivists and interactionists must accept that once the two legal orders exist, one cannot be fully reduced to the other.

Relative Pluralism

At this stage, we must deepen the analysis of pluralism in two ways. First, there is not one state legal order and one order of implicit law; there are thousands of them. Roderick Macdonald argues that in fact every organization within the state

---

51 Part Two of Fuller's *Anatomy of Law* is programmatic in this sense, as it is named 'The Sources of Law'. The plural implies that both of the two types of law are sources for the obligatory force of law.
52 See Fuller, *Principles of Social Order*, p. 250.

bureaucracy creates its own mini legal order.[53] Indeed, it is part of the larger state bureaucracy, which is embedded in a broader state legal order. However, that does not make each mini legal order a fully integrated part of that broader legal order, as in the ideal type of Weber's rational bureaucracy. For example, each department usually has its own legal culture with many implicit understandings of 'how we do things here' – understandings which may be at odds both with those in other departments and those underlying the official legislation. Thus, even if the department is part of the state bureaucracy, it also creates a partly autonomous legal order of its own. What holds true for departments may be all the more true of independent agencies within the public sphere, such as environmental or educational agencies. Each of them, once created, acquires a life of its own and creates its own legal order with implicit understandings and explicit guidelines that may contradict statutes even if they are supposed to have a higher legal status.

Second, a similar point must be made with regard to more horizontal forms of order, such as customary law or contract. There is not one order of customary law; there are thousands of orders. Each different network of citizens in a specific context develops a normative order of its own. This may largely be identical to that of other networks and groups, but may differ on specific points. The same holds true with regard to the internal law of businesses, professional associations and churches.

This suggests a very broad form of legal pluralism. However, it is not an unbounded anarchy of independent legal orders. None of the legal orders in question is fully autonomous. They are not insulated from society or from the state – they cannot help but interact with other legal orders. For example, if two citizens want to formulate their business relationship in the form of a contract, they will first encounter the state legal order and its civil code. They may use this code as an instrument to give effect to their informal agreement, but they may also find it to be an obstacle in their way, because what they agreed upon cannot be given legal effect within the restrictions of the state legal order. An example is the non-enforceability in many state legal orders of surrogacy contracts or of labour contracts that require working more hours than the legal maximum. Even then, they may still ignore the state legal order and agree between them that they will consider it irrelevant. One of them may later find it a problem if he wants to enforce the agreement, because a court will not accept it as valid. However, as long as no state courts are involved, the parties can still choose to consider their contract as binding upon them.

Thus, the relations between the various legal orders may be those of harmonious co-existence and overlap, but they may also be fraught with tension. Sally Falk Moore has introduced the phrase 'semi-autonomous fields' for legal orders that are partly shielded from the state's legal order.[54] However, her analysis merely focuses on the relation between the state legal order and the normative order of one social

---

53 Macdonald, 'Legislation and Governance', p. 283.
54 Moore, 'Law and Social Change'.

field, which is semi-autonomous with respect to the state legal order. For this reason I prefer the phrase 'relative autonomy', used by Sanne Taekema.[55] On the one hand, relative autonomy implies that there is only partial autonomy; on the other hand, it indicates that the relatively autonomous legal order stands in relation to other social practices and legal orders, and to non-legal practices and society at large. These other legal orders include the state legal order, but also customary law or the internal disciplinary law of professional associations. Instead of a binary relation between the state legal order and the normative order of the semi-autonomous field, we comprehend a dense network of relatively autonomous legal orders interacting with many other legal orders and practices. Of these other legal orders, the state legal order is only one, even if usually the most important one.[56]

We may even go further and also call the state legal order a relatively autonomous order. One obvious reason for this is the existence of an international legal order and, in Europe, the legal orders of the European Union and the Council of Europe. These legal orders increasingly influence the state's autonomy. A second reason is that the state's legal order is also interacting with those thousands of legal orders on its territory, both internally (the legal orders within the state's bureaucratic and legal organizations) and externally (the legal orders of customary law, contracts and private organizations).

This is not a radical pluralism, but what we might call soft or relative pluralism.[57] The legal orders are no insulated orders, but are open and are quite closely knit. Relative pluralism agrees with Fuller that there are tens of thousands of legal orders around, but emphasizes that they are not free-floating, as they are embedded in the larger network of society.[58] To what extent they are autonomous with respect to one another may vary, but they are never completely closed off. The internal legal order of a radical religious sect, for example, may be more autonomous in relation to state law than the internal legal order of a state housing agency; yet both are only partly autonomous.

Many readers might wish to raise an objection at this moment. Perhaps I am right in arguing that there is a great plurality of normative orders here, but is

---

55 Taekema, *Concept of Ideals*, p. 189, where she also uses the term 'limited autonomy'.

56 Relative legal pluralism is a description of the intertwinement of multiple legal orders from a global or social perspective. The effect on individuals and groups has been characterized by Boaventura de Sousa Santos as 'interlegality': the everyday life of individuals and social groups 'crosses or is interpenetrated by different and often contrasting legal orders and legal cultures' (*New Legal Common Sense*, p. 97).

57 Relative legal pluralism must be distinguished from what John Griffiths calls pluralism in a weak sense ('What is Legal Pluralism?', p. 5). The latter is the recognition (often by a colonial power) of parallel legal regimes for different groups in the population within the framework of an overarching and controlling state legal system. Relative legal pluralism is the existence of competing legal orders, none of which can legitimately claim to be the overarching order.

58 Fuller, *Morality of Law*, p. 125.

that *legal* pluralism? Does this approach not lead to such a wide variety of legal orders, often conflicting, that positive law loses its distinctive advantage that it is an unambiguous and simple guide for our actions? Should we not, therefore, simply take the position that only positive law, originating in state institutions, is law?

Such an intuitive response will surely be expressed by many citizens, and certainly by almost all lawyers (including me), when confronted with an analysis leading to pervasive legal pluralism. The strength of this intuition shows how deeply we are influenced by the dominant identification of law with state law.[59] State law is, in modern societies, the most visible part of law, and the part which is most easily accessible because it takes the form of black-letter law. However, as the analysis above shows, this is an unjustified bias. Once we become aware of this implicit bias in our thought, we may become more open to perceive at least some forms of legal pluralism. Nevertheless, even then the question may arise: is legal pluralism really as pervasive as I have argued?

My reply to this objection is twofold. First, I would point out that nowadays some minimal form of legal pluralism is hard to deny even for the staunchest of positivists. As I argued above, for member states of the European Union, there are at least four relevant major legal orders: domestic law, EU law, the law of the Council of Europe and international law. Although these legal orders are partly intertwined, they are also relatively autonomous. Once we have accepted that international law, the European Union and the Council of Europe constitute distinct legal orders, this minimal form of legal pluralism – of what may be called global legal pluralism in the narrow sense – must be accepted as well.

So the question is not so much whether legal pluralism exists, but whether it is as pervasive as I claim it to be. Should we consider the internal norms of an association or a church as distinct legal orders? Are contracts and treaties and, indeed, even the interactional norms emerging on the shop floor also legal orders in their own right, or can their legal force always be reduced to state law – in as far as they should be considered law at all? In other words, what makes a normative order into a legal order?

This question has already been discussed in the previous chapter, in which I argued that, in general, a broad type of definitional pluralism is justified. If, for practical purposes, we really need to decide whether a normative order is legal or not, varying stipulations of the distinctively legal might be justified in different contexts. Therefore, we might now ask whether, in the context of Western liberal democracies, legal interactionism does provide a specific theory of what characterizes a normative order as legal.

The key to a legal interactionist perspective on legal pluralism is the insight that law can exist in degrees and encompasses a wide range of phenomena. A normative order can be more or less law. The idea that a legal order need not be fully law to be at least partly law holds true as much for the legal order of a weak

---

59 See Brunnée and Toope, *Legitimacy and Legality*, p. 6.

or failing state as for the legal orders constituted by the global climate regime or a professional medical association. We may sometimes therefore talk of emergent or incipient law.[60] Interactionism implies a gradualist conception of law. Therefore, most interactionists eschew a clear demarcation criterion of law because it would not do justice to the gradual processes underlying the emergence or decline of a legal order. So what we need is a dynamic conception of law which is sensitive to the emergence and decline of a legal order and to the gradual existence of law. Developing an ideal type of law, of law in a fully evolved stage, may help us reach a fuller understanding of its variation.[61]

In an interactionist view, law is a normative order. It emerges from intermeshing normative expectations between citizens, embedded in a practice of legality. As Selznick has argued, law is a normative order oriented towards the ideal of legality.[62] We should add that law is not only oriented towards the ideal of legality, but also towards other distinctively legal ideals such as justice, and to ideals that are not distinctively legal, such as democracy.[63] In this practice of legality, the normative expectations may gradually thicken (or weaken) and the institutional character of the legal order may also become thicker (or weaker). Secondary rules and law-enforcing institutions may emerge; the implicit rules may be formulated on paper (if only to make them more easily accessible to all parties and to newcomers); and even specific legal subpractices may emerge, such as adjudication and legislation.

Now, if this is the ideal type of a mature legal order, we can also see how various other elements that are often suggested as distinctive characteristics of law might fit in. In a complex society, relying on gradual processes of change may not be very effective. Therefore, it may be necessary to have institutions or rules that govern how the contents of the law will be determined, how it will be changed, and how it will be applied. Moreover, for effective discussion about the legal norms, it is helpful if these rules are explicitly formulated.[64] Therefore, in

---

60   For both terms see Selznick, *Law, Society and Industrial Justice*.

61   I focus on an ideal type of law in its fully evolved stage rather than on a unified concept of law as the combination of various characteristics of law. The latter attempt would fail because of the conceptual pluralism which I advocated in Chapter 5. Brian Tamanaha (*Realistic Socio-Legal Theory*, pp. 122ff.) has convincingly criticized attempts to combine what he calls two categories of the concept of law, that of lived law and of enforced law (two categories that largely correspond with interactional law and enacted law), in one concept of law. An analysis based on the ideal of a fully evolved stage in which interactional law and enacted law mutually reinforce each other is not vulnerable to his criticism because it does not presuppose a conceptual union.

62   Selznick, 'Sociology and Natural Law'.

63   Taekema, *Concept of Ideals*, p. 188. For a more elaborate discussion of law's orientation towards ideals, see Chapters 7 and 9 hereunder. Like legality and justice, democracy is an ideal that is not restricted to state law; it may have implications, for example, for participation in industries, in voluntary associations and churches, and in horizontal settings.

64   See Peters, 'Law as Critical Discussion'.

a complex society, law will usually be black-letter law, whether in the form of state law or in the form of contracts. Furthermore, it will improve the efficacy of law enormously if there are effective sanctions and institutions that enforce those sanctions. However, it is worth remarking that even in a fully developed phase there need not be a connection with the state; effective enforcement can be guaranteed in many ways.

This leads us to the following ideal typical description of law in its fully evolved stage. Law is a normative order, embedded in a practice of legality. There are secondary rules of recognition, change and adjudication. The norms are explicitly formulated, usually as black-letter law, and there is congruence between enacted norms and interactional norms. There is an effective enforcement mechanism and sanctions may be applied.

However, if law can exist in degrees, there are various respects in which it can be less law than at the fully evolved stage. Effective sanctions and enforcement mechanisms can be missing, as is often the case in international law. Explicit formulation of the norms may be absent, as is often the case in interactional law. Even a practice of legality may be largely absent, as may be true in state bureaucracies, where internal regulations seem more like general commands, and in dictatorial regimes. Finally, a well-known pathology of legal orders is that there is little congruence between enacted law and interactional norms. In all these situations we may still say that there is law, but that it is a lesser law.

Of course, if all these characteristics are missing, there is no law at all. So the question remains: what is minimally necessary in order to characterize a normative order as legal? From the above analysis it may now be clear why we cannot give a general answer to this, let alone suggest a simple cut-off point below which there is no law. Not only would every cut-off point be arbitrary, but it is also true that it is all those characteristics together that may justify calling a normative order law. To take the example of bureaucratic commands in the form of directives within the state bureaucracy: they are explicitly formulated on paper; there are secondary rules of recognition, change and adjudication; there may even be sanctions for the civil servant who does not obey them; but there may be a very minimal practice of legality underlying them. In such a situation, it may be still justified to call them law if we look at the whole picture.

Of course, we could stipulate a cut-off point and, for certain purposes, simply say that some normative orders are law and some are not law. That is completely legitimate as long as we acknowledge that it is our stipulation which is the basis for the distinction, and as long as we give good reasons for the cut-off point so that it is not merely arbitrary. This is exactly what Brunnée and Toope do when they make the practice of legality the distinctive criterion in international law.[65] The practice of international law needs a clear baseline of what is law and what is not. From the internal point of view, participants (and that includes legal scholars such as the authors) may suggest a criterion for when to call something law. Such a criterion

---

65 Brunnée and Toope, *Legitimacy and Legality*.

cannot be completely arbitrary; there is no discretion here. In Ronald Dworkin's terms, it must meet the requirements of fit and justification.[66] Yet, Brunnée and Toope's suggestion is reasonably defensible, though contestable. Other authors, focusing on different legal phenomena, may prefer a different criterion.

Returning now to the question of legal pluralism, it is clear that legal interactionism indeed implies a broad form of legal pluralism. Normative orders which have a number of those characteristics but lack others may be called law, although each of these orders may lack different characteristics. Interactional legal orders lack explicit formulation, international legal orders may lack effective sanctions, and so on. The metaphor of a dynamic family resemblance, as discussed in the previous chapter, is once again insightful in this context. There are many ways in which law can half-exist, so there cannot be only one distinctive criterion to distinguish the legal from the non-legal.

The Dynamic Interplay between Relatively Autonomous Legal Orders

In this chapter I discerned four contemporary phenomena that an adequate theory of law must address. These are: the emergence of interactional law, especially with a more horizontal nature; the increase in state regulation resulting in enormous amounts of black-letter law; global legal pluralism; and the increasingly dynamic nature of law and society. In response to the first two phenomena, I developed a theory of legal interactionism that can address them. The primary reason why legal interactionism is the most adequate descriptive theory of contemporary law in Western democracies is that it can do justice to both the vast quantities of state-enacted black-letter law and the emergence of interactional law in various areas of law. Moreover, it can also do justice to the undeniable fact of global legal pluralism. Legal interactionism is the most adequate theory for the purpose of undertaking this challenge.

We can further elaborate this analysis by returning to the idea developed in Part One, that law is an essentially ambiguous concept. There are at least two ways we can model law (or similar phenomena such as morality), and they are partly incommensurable. Therefore, we must switch between these two models. There are various reasons why legal interactionism can be enriched by the insight that we need those two different models to fully understand law.

First, some of the legal orders can best be analysed in a practice model and others using a product model, though the best insight is obtained if we use both models. For state-enacted law, the product model offers a reasonable description, whereas for interactional international law the practice model is most adequate. Yet, as I have argued above, state-enacted law is embedded in a practice of legality and it requires interpretive and argumentative practices to be applied. Therefore, we may also need the practice model to understand the underlying patterns of

---

66   Dworkin, *Law's Empire*, p. 239.

interaction. Similarly, in international law there is an emerging legal doctrine; the emergence of this doctrine can best be studied by alternating between the practice model and the product model.

Second, the relatively autonomous legal orders (for example, those of EU law and domestic law) are intertwined and continuously interact with one another. The interaction between two legal orders can only be fully understood if we switch between the two models. In the product model, we can identify the overlap and differences between the different legal doctrines, but we cannot understand how they mutually influence one another. The dialectical interplay between the different legal orders is a process that can only be studied when focusing on the interactional practice, on the arguments being used in both legal orders and on the underlying normative convictions.

The double process of legal fragmentation and intertwinement of legal orders is not only restricted to the interplay between two legal orders. For example, to understand Dutch health law, we must be able to understand four major legal orders: Dutch domestic law; the law of the European Union (which is, in fact, in itself an amalgam based on various treaties); the law of the European Convention on Human Rights; and various international legal orders based on separate treaties. However, there are even more legal orders that are relevant, from the standard contracts used in insurance practice to the internal disciplinary law of the Dutch medical association, and to the implicit understandings in medical practice. Of course, academic jurists try to construct a coherent whole out of this collection of partly distinct and partly intertwining legal orders, and write treatises on 'Dutch health law' as if it constituted a coherent whole, with only a few gaps. But such a doctrinal construction does not do justice to the full plurality of normative orders and the tensions and conflicts between them. Here we must switch between attempts to construct law as a static coherent normative order and approaches that do superior justice to the dynamic interplay between various relatively autonomous, even if substantively overlapping, legal orders. To understand this dialectical interplay, we must switch between the two models of law. For example, we can study the legal order of the European Union and Dutch domestic law by comparing the black-letter law and the doctrine of both. However, using such a static analysis enables us merely to see how they differ and overlap, and perhaps how the doctrines converge in time, but not how they influence one another. For this analysis we need to switch to a practice model.

The intertwinement between those legal orders is not a stable one; it is an inherently dynamic phenomenon. The legal orders are relatively autonomous and thus continuously interact with one another. It is mainly because of the dynamic character of this interaction that we must switch between the two models. It is now time to tackle the most difficult question: how to understand the dynamics of legal orders.

Chapter 7
Understanding the Dynamics of Law

An Internal Point of View

My suggestion at the end of the previous chapter was that in order to fully understand the dynamics of law, we must switch between two models. We need the product model in order to identify how legal doctrine develops over time. If we want to know precisely what changes, then the simplifying model of law as a product is essential; we must be able to describe the legal norms that were valid in, for example, the year 2000, and then see how the legal doctrine has developed since then. However, in order to understand why this has changed and what the underlying trends are, we need to move to the practice model. Only then can we fully apprehend the underlying dynamics, the ambiguities and developments in legal understandings, the emergence of new patterns of interaction, and the gradual adaptation in interaction to changing circumstances and changing convictions.

Indeed, legal interactionism and its combination of the two models are especially illuminating when we focus on the phenomenon of change. In a legal interactionist view, 'law is the work of its everyday participants, a continuous effort to construct and sustain a common institutional framework to meet the exigencies of a shared existence, to resolve recurrent conflict, and in general to realize the aspiration of just and harmonious relations among citizens'.[1] In this idea of law as a continuing collective project of citizens, the possibility of change and even the need for change are inherent. Law is in a process of continuous change, just like society in general. Statutes are sometimes changed quite radically, sometimes only in minor ways; case law usually develops through smaller steps, and so does the implicit law regulating commercial practice or medical practice. Changes in legislation and case law may be the most explicit kinds of changes, but they are certainly not the only ones.

The question is: how can we understand and explain the dynamics of law? The easy answer is to take an external point of view and analyse the way in which the law changes as a result of social, economic and political developments. But even if this is an important part of the answer, it is still only part thereof. We should also look from the internal point of view for the potential for change inherent to law itself. If there were no such potential, it would be much more difficult for external forces to change the law, as law is at least a partly autonomous institution.[2]

---

1 Winston, 'Introduction to Revised Edition', p. 3.
2 Watson, *Evolution of Law*, argues that legal development is mainly determined by the resources and limitations inherent in the legal culture and tradition; societal needs

In order to develop a theory of legal dynamics, we need to look at both models. In the next section, I will study legal dynamics within a practice model. I will then analyse it within the framework of a product model. The fourth section is a case study, reflecting on the development of law and ethics in the field of biomedicine, illustrating many of the themes that have been discussed in this chapter and the previous one.

Change in the Practice Model

The two models are clearly different with regard to change. Law as a practice is a dynamic model, whereas law as a product focuses on the static side of law. It is, therefore, not difficult to identify the potential for change when we take a practice perspective. It is obvious that law can be changed in processes of explicit lawmaking, such as legislation and adjudication. Similarly, the law changes when doctors discuss euthanasia and practise it, and gradually develop criteria for whether and when it may be considered part of good medical practice. In those practices where law is merely an implicit dimension of interaction, there is a potential for change in the fact that each new interaction implies a recreation of the interactional legal norms. Even if this recreation usually entails the mere application and reinforcement of the norms involved, application of norms is never purely mechanical and always involves a creative act in which these norms may be slightly altered.

Most legal orders know specific practices (or secondary rules) of changing, interpreting, and applying the law. Usually, this is the responsibility of legal authorities, in particular of legislatures and courts. Part of the answer to the question of how the law changes may be found in those institutions. Law changes because these authorities implicitly or explicitly decide to do so.

However, this is only the tip of the iceberg. A legal interactionist analysis provides a much broader view of the dynamics of law. It does not only focus on the moment of decision by legal authorities, but also includes the process leading up to that decision and the process after the decision has been made. We should not only look at the final vote in parliament, but also include the discussions and negotiations leading up to that vote, both in the parliament buildings and in society at large. During the process leading up to the final decision, a new legal consciousness may already emerge. Statutes are often a codification of interactional norms that emerged in society or specific practices such as medical practice or commercial practice, and we should also take the emergence of interactional norms in those practices preceding the legislation in account. Furthermore, the work of lawmaking is not done when a statute has been passed; it still needs to

---

and influences only play a minor role. His statement may be too strong, especially for the modern regulatory state, but he is certainly right in emphasizing the importance of inherent sources for legal change.

be seen whether the statutory norms are accepted as binding by everyone, and whether they effectively regulate behaviour. In other words: whether the statute is transformed into interactional law. Because legal interactionism studies both black-letter law and interactional norms, it casts its web much wider when it studies legal change.

A similar point may be made with regard to adjudication. In law schools and law textbooks, usually the focus is on the contents of the final decisions of highest courts. The law changes because, and when, the majority of the highest court says so. However, if we accept that law is a discursive practice, we should also pay closer attention to the arguments that were not accepted in the highest courts, such as dissenting opinions (in those jurisdictions where they exist) or the opinions of independent advisors such as the Advocates-General at the European Court of Justice. They may not yet have the support of a majority, but in many cases they are the heralds of future change. Moreover, in light of the relative pluralism of legal orders, we should not only focus on the judicial opinions within one legal order, but should also study developments in other jurisdictions. The judicial dialogue between courts in different jurisdictions may be an important factor in legal innovation.[3] However, the greatest chance of legal innovation is in the lower courts, in their decisions and arguments. Lower courts often try out new solutions for new problems long before these problems finally reach the highest court. In a sense, the lower courts are the experimental laboratories of the judicial system. Sometimes these innovations may be *extra legem* or even *contra legem*. If we want to understand change in the judge-made law, we should get rid of the myopic focus on the case law of the highest courts.

A further expansion of our understanding of change is possible if we do not regard the state legal order as one coherent system, but pay attention to the internal tensions. There may not only be tensions between higher courts and lower courts, but also between the ordinary courts and functional courts, such as military courts or medical disciplinary courts.[4] More importantly, the state legal order's lawmaking capacity exists beyond the national parliament and the courts. Internal regulations of administrative agencies and regulations and policies made by local councils are also part of the state legal order. Often the innovations in regulation

---

3 For judicial dialogue, see various contributions to the special issue of the *Utrecht Law Review* on *Highest Courts and Transnational Interaction* 8 no. 2 (May 2012). Robert Ahdieh argues that judicial dialogue and dialectical review (a hybrid form of judicial dialogue and appellate review) can encourage innovations. Attention should also be paid to the use of *obiter dicta* as a signalling device by higher courts and international courts and tribunals (Ahdieh, 'Between Dialogue and Decree', pp. 2064–8 and pp. 2072–7).

4 For a curious example, see ECtHR, *Nejdet Şahin and Perihan Şahin v. Turkey*, 20 October 2011, No 13279/05. Some families of victims of a military plane crash were awarded pensions under the Anti-Terrorism Act by domestic administrative courts, whereas families of other victims of the same crash were denied those pensions by military courts. The Court argues that 'the possibility of conflicting court decisions is an inherent trait of any judicial system which is based on a network of trial and appeal courts'.

may be found there. In Dutch health law, innovations (for example, with regard to regulating euthanasia) were often made by medical disciplinary courts and ethics councils.

Drugs policies provide other examples where local governments often find more creative ways of dealing with drug use than the inert national states. Most experts nowadays agree that most national policies on repressive drugs (especially the 'war on drugs' in the United States) have failed, and that we should develop ways of regulating and controlling drug use rather than aiming at an ineffective legal prohibition. However, at the national level, it is often impossible to create statutes legalising drugs, let alone regulating and controlling their production, for example, through a state monopoly and a system of taxation. Even the Netherlands (which has effectively legalized the possession of small portions of soft drugs through prosecution guidelines) has so far refrained from taking the final step of legalization and state control of production and sale – partly because of its international obligations under various treaties.[5] However, throughout the world, various municipal or regional authorities have ignored national law and developed pragmatic solutions of tolerance and non-prosecution with regard to possession of lower amounts of soft drugs and experiments such as needle-exchange and medical organizations supplying drugs. Here again, legal interactionism provides a wider perspective on legal development as those local and functional lawmaking agencies are also included.

By accepting a wide pluralistic perspective on a variety of practices rather than constructing law as a coherent legal doctrine, legal interactionism can pay more attention to tensions within the state legal order. Those tensions between the relatively autonomous legal orders of state agencies and local agencies, of lower courts and functional courts, may often signal the emergence of new law, and of increasing support for new norms. However, to get a full view of emergent law, we must also look outside the state legal order. Most legal conflicts are not brought before the courts as they are settled outside the judicial system. Many legal norms develop as interactional norms long before they are formally codified in legislation. Eugen Ehrlich's famous warning is nowadays as valid as ever: 'the center of gravity of legal development lies not in legislation, nor in juristic science, nor in judicial decision, but in society itself'.[6]

Reflection and discussion on legal norms occur outside the legal institutions as well, in academic journals and newspapers, on the Internet and in pubs. Citizens, professions and the business world often develop new norms in response to new situations or changing moral opinions. They may use contracts to formulate them. For example, before states formally recognized marriages or partnerships between same-sex couples, lawyers had been drafting cohabitation contracts for many

---

5 On Dutch drugs policy, see Van Dijck, 'Drug Policy in the Netherlands'; Buruma, 'Dutch Tolerance'.

6 This quote is from the 'Foreword' to Ehrlich, *Fundamental Principles of the Sociology of Law*; see also p. 390 for a slightly different formulation.

years. The enforceability of these contracts or of some clauses through the state judicial system may sometimes have been dubious, but that did not imply that they were not considered as binding by those involved, including usually many third parties which were formally not bound to such private contracts. To legal theorists who recognize state-made law as the only framework, such contractual clauses may have seemed void; but to many citizens they were not.

Often the emergent norms are simply a form of customary law or custom. Even if citizens do not think of their non-conformist practices as having the binding force of law, these practices may still weaken the legal quality of state legal norms. For example, in many big cities, red traffic lights are habitually ignored by pedestrians. The official rules on traffic lights are still legally valid, and not completely ignored; yet infractions are usually not or only selectively prosecuted. This means that the practice does not completely invalidate traffic lights rules, but it does considerably weaken them. In some other cases, courts may even regard standing business practices as having the force of law, being able to justify emergent norms that are a violation of statutory norms.[7]

All these phenomena must be part of a complete analysis of legal change in a practice model. The decisions made by highest courts and state parliaments are only the tip of the iceberg. If we want to understand legal change, we need to cast a wider net. Legal interactionism, with its acceptance of relative pluralism and interactional law, offers therefore the best perspective to understand change in the practice model.

The Role of Ideals in Legal Dynamics

In the practice model, the potential for change is, thus, easy to identify. What exactly these changes involve, however, can be better understood by using the product model. In the practice model, we can discern changes in interaction patterns or observe that parliament has passed a new statute. To determine more in detail what these changes imply, we should discuss them in terms of legal texts, doctrines, or statements of positive law. However, legal doctrine is not merely the passive product of changes in legal practices. It has a logic of its own, with inherent possibilities and limitations. If there were no potential for change in law as a product, it would be much more difficult to change it. Therefore, we should also look at the legal doctrine, this supposedly more static dimension of law, and determine wherein lies its potential for further development. This may seem like a curious suggestion. Legal doctrine is often presented in legal textbooks in an ahistorical way, as a coherent system of rules and concepts. Even if it is admitted that there are small gaps and minor inconsistencies in the doctrine, it is taught that

---

7 For example, in a famous decision the Dutch Supreme Court relied on a trade custom that contravened statutory law (Hoge Raad 3 maart 1972, NJ 1972, 339 (*Maring/Assuradeuren*).

these irregularities can be solved in line with the general system of rules. In such an approach, major changes seem impossible. Law may work itself pure, but it cannot transform itself in more radical ways.

Obviously, this image of limited change does not do justice to reality – not even if we restrict our analysis to enacted law in the state's legal order. Positive law changes in many ways, and not only via legislation but also via judge-made law. The judiciary obviously changes the law – sometimes in very radical ways – even if in most legal orders there is an ideology that tries to minimize the creative impact of their interventions. In order to understand the dynamics of case law, we must find the sources that the judges can appeal to in order to change the existing legal doctrine.

Usually, the reason to change the law is that new concrete problems or more general issues arise for which the legal doctrine either offers no clear solution or suggests a solution that is inadequate. This may be the reason why a change in the law is required, but it does not offer an explanation of where the source for the change can be found within the doctrine. The potential for change is to be found, rather, at the other end of abstraction, at the level of purposes, principles and ideals.[8] When confronted with issues regarding genetic tests or information technology, basic notions such as privacy or autonomy provide guidance and inspiration. Furthermore, we also see new dimensions of those old notions. For example, that autonomy may also be relevant with respect to information connected with one's personality, such as a genetic predisposition or even consumer patterns, is something new – and constitutes new dimensions of the old concepts of autonomy and privacy. The ideals behind those concepts may provide inspiration for dealing with new cases.[9] Only in the light of new cases do we see the inadequacy of the current legal doctrine and find recourse to the potential for change inherent in the underlying ideals, with their surplus of meaning.

---

8   The idea that principles play a major role in legal development is not uncommon, the modern classic being Dworkin, *Taking Rights Seriously*; see also the analysis in Cotterrell, *Politics of Jurisprudence*, p. 23. The idea that ideals and purposes also play such a role is perhaps less standard but has been suggested by various authors, including Fuller, *Morality of Law*; Nonet and Selznick, *Law and Society in Transition*; Dworkin, *Law's Empire*; Peters, 'Law as Critical Discussion'; and Taekema, *Concept of Ideals*. See Nonet and Selznick, *Law and Society in Transition*, p. 81: 'When Fuller underscores the centrality of purpose in the legal enterprise or when Dworkin and Hughes look to principle and policy as foundations of legal reasoning, they express the modern aspiration for a legal order that is effective in dealing with change.' For a more elaborate analysis of ideals and their role in legal dynamics, see Van der Burg and Taekema, *Importance of Ideals*. Ideals may be understood as values that are usually not completely realizable. They are usually partly implicit in legal, moral and political practices and are often difficult to formulate exactly.

9   That abstract ideals need not always be the best possible guide, and especially not when they are cut loose from their basis in legal and empirical reality, is illustrated by Blok, 'Ideal of Data Privacy'.

In this way, ideals provide a source of inspiration for change. The need for change lies elsewhere, outside the doctrine, in new cases and issues; but the sources of new ideas which may help to deal with these new cases and issues are to be found in the ideals themselves. Ideals are, of course, not the only source of new ideas – imaginative thinking may also be inspired, for example, by moral theories or even by literature and art, and it may also borrow from other legal orders.[10] Nevertheless, because ideals – and their connected principles and purposes[11] – not only have a surplus of meaning but (in any case the legal ideals I discuss here) are also part of the law itself and thus share its authority, they are the first source to turn to when we encounter a need for internal change.

These ideals may sometimes be codified, directly or indirectly, but never completely. The ideals of legality and justice themselves are not codified in Dutch law, but some more specific implications in the form of the principle of legality (Article 1 Dutch Penal Code) and the principle of equality (Article 1 Dutch Constitution) have been laid down. Even if these slightly more specific principles are codified, it does not imply that their meaning is unambiguous and uncontroversial. On the contrary, these principles are essentially contested, and their interpretation is open to development. This is because their meaning can only be determined in light of both the context and the underlying ideals.

In the product model, ideals (and principles and purposes) thus provide a source for change in the legal doctrine.[12] When the provisional equilibrium of legal doctrine is disturbed by new problematic cases or more general issues, they may offer guidance and orientation for revision of the doctrine. However, because they do not offer clear and unambiguous answers, and always need to be interpreted, when we do appeal to ideals we are forced to leave the safety and certainty of established legal doctrine. We must enter a practice of normative argument about the best possible solutions of the concrete cases or the legal approach to more general issues in light of those ideals. To determine the implications of the general ideals and principles, to elaborate a revised legal doctrine and to construct solutions to new cases, we must participate in an argumentative practice of law.[13]

In discussions, ideals may provide a common frame of reference. They are a common starting point in a pluralist practice. They can be catalysts in promoting an

---

10 For the influence of ethical analysis on law (and vice versa), see Van der Burg 'Law and Ethics'; for inspiration via literature, see Nussbaum, *Poetic Justice*; for influences by other legal orders, see Watson, *Evolution of Law*.

11 For the relation between values and principles (as optimization requirements), see also Alexy, *Theory of Constitutional Rights*, Chapter 3. I prefer 'ideals' rather than 'values', to emphasize that ideals can never be formulated exactly and, therefore, always have a surplus of meaning that enables legal dynamics.

12 I merely identify the potential for change in ideals in general terms here. The questions regarding when and why participants in the legal practice will indeed appeal to ideals, to which ideals an appeal is made and whether this appeal to ideals is successful cannot be discussed in these general terms.

13 See Dworkin, *Law's Empire*, p. 14; Peters, 'Law as Critical Discussion'.

open debate. Such a debate may lead to legal change through judicial interpretation and legislative action, but also because it results in shifting interpretations by society or by specific sectors or professions. The surplus of meaning, and the fact that they will never be completely realized, even if they are at least partly realized in law, makes it possible to have different interpretations regarding what the underlying ideals imply for the societal problems with which we are confronted, and what would be the best way to realize them more fully.[14]

Legal ideals, thus, play a role in both models. In the product model, they are authoritative sources within the legal doctrine that provide inspiration and guidance for reconstructing the doctrine. In the practice model, they offer a frame of reference for discussion, reflection and action. They do not, however, only play a role in each of the separate models; they also play a role in the continuous interaction between the two models in the social reality of law.

Once we appeal to ideals in order to provide answers for hard cases – for which the present legal doctrine is inadequate – they serve to promote a switch from the product to the practice model. We are then forced to leave settled doctrine and reopen the debate about the construction of the doctrine. In fact, lawyers do this continuously when they apply statutes, construct contracts and wills, or argue a case in court. In all such cases, they participate in legal practices and reconstruct legal doctrine. However, the orientation towards ideals requires them do this more explicitly because ideals bring a source of ambiguity and controversy into the practice which cannot be ignored. Whereas lawyers usually construct the doctrine and the various products based thereon as unambiguous and uncontroversial, as settled positive law, the appeal to ideals unsettles this and makes an open discussion about the content of the legal doctrine unavoidable. The openness of ideals leaves room for multiple interpretations and these should be confronted in the discursive practices of law.[15]

However, when we participate in the various practices that creatively interpret, reconstruct and discuss the law, we cannot go on debating forever. It is essential that law also provides provisional closures. One of the core values of law is legal certainty. This value reminds us that we cannot debate forever, and reorients us to the notion of law as a product. Law is most effective when it is clearly formulated, when there is a provisionally settled doctrine, an authoritative judicial decision or a contract. Only if we attempt to formulate rules and principles can law help us orient our behaviour and offer solutions for concrete problematic cases. Therefore, we must try to reformulate the law, to reconstruct the doctrine, to make verdicts and contracts. There may be a continuous debate about the construction of the law, but this debate should also lead to provisional closures by legislatures enacting

---

14 We should beware of a simple instrumentalist view of the relation between these ideals and the means. For a good analysis of the dialectic relationship between means and ends, see Westerman, 'Means and Ends'; see Selznick, *Moral Commonwealth*, p. 328.

15 Of course, sometimes the debate will end by an authoritative conclusion, for example, by a judge ignoring this pluralism before the debate has really begun.

a statute, by judges pronouncing a judgment and by legal scholars formulating a legal doctrine.

Consequently, we switch continuously between the two models. The ideal of legal certainty forces us to reconstruct the legal doctrine and bring the debate to a provisional closure. On the other hand, other ideals open legal doctrine to internal criticism, and offer inspiration and guidance for revision. There is thus a dialectical relationship between the two models, which opens the way to legal change without destabilizing the law completely. In this dialectical process, legal ideals provide a bridge between the two models. They force us to open and then again to provisionally close the legal doctrine, thus keeping the change within acceptable limits.

We may conclude that ideals promote the dynamics of law in various ways. First, they offer a potential for ideas, for new principles and practical solutions when the existing doctrine is in need of revision. Second, they force us to leave the certainty of legal doctrine and enter an explicitly argumentative practice. Third, they provide a common frame of reference in the ensuing discussion. And finally, they stimulate us to reach at least provisional conclusions.

Although the above analysis has focused on judicial lawmaking, it can be applied to interactional law as well. Sometimes the current interactional norms simply are no longer adequate in light of new problems or changing moral and social opinions. Changing interactional norms is, of course, possible with mutual consent of all the parties involved in the practice, but in order to convince other parties that they should change the current practice, arguments are required. The best argument is usually to point to the underlying purposes, principles and ideals of the existing practice, show that the current norms are no longer in line with these fundamental ideas and then suggest a new norm which does a better job. Indeed, in discussions on changing the interactional norms, the appeal to purposes, principles and ideals will be even more useful than in discussions about revising case law, as there is no authoritative formulation that needs to be explicitly overturned. A similar analysis may be applied to implicit norms that are not changed as the result of explicit discussions, but simply by changing interactional patterns. These implicit changes can only be understood by other participants in the practice if they can be understood as following from the underlying ideals and meet the standards of reasonableness.[16]

The Emergence of Health Law[17]

It is now time to put the theory to the test. I have claimed that legal interactionism provides a better framework than legal positivism for understanding the dynamics

---

16 See Postema, 'Implicit Law', p. 258.
17 This section is partly based on, and includes fragments from, a more elaborate study in Van der Burg, 'Bioethics and Law'.

of law. The history of the emergence of health law since the 1960s provides a good example to demonstrate this claim.[18]

Until the sixties, in most Western countries health law did not yet exist as an independent discipline or field of law. Specific rules of health law were virtually non-existent. State law largely upheld and respected professional autonomy, and only marginally interfered with medical practice. It upheld a great deal of discretionary power for doctors. Of course, there were some rules in criminal law, enforcing moral norms such as the prohibition of abortion, euthanasia, (assisted) suicide and various sexual practices like adultery, prostitution and homosexuality. However, regulation was mostly self-regulation by the medical profession with some form of disciplinary law. Indeed, the medical profession was regulated by interactional norms taught, partly by example, during training on the spot by more experienced professionals. The internal norms of the profession were implicit in medical practice rather than being extensively elaborated by lawyers; they were strongly intertwined with what was known as medical ethics. Medical ethics was the ethics of good medical practice, of being a good doctor. There was no elaborate body of guidelines and rules, either in moral philosophy or in law.

Professional practice was strongly paternalistic and moralistic. Doctors were expected to act for the good of the patient and to know what this good was, both in the moral and in the non-moral sense of the word. Patients were often not given full information about the diagnoses of their illnesses, especially if the prognosis was dim. In the field of psychiatry, the patient's best interest, as judged by the psychiatrist, was the basic criterion for non-voluntary treatments and institutionalization. Insofar as the determination of the patient's good demanded moral evaluation, this was seldom explicitly acknowledged; nor need it be, because the moral norms were considered non-controversial, being based on a traditional (usually religious) morality that was largely accepted by all in society, or by all in the subgroup to which both doctor and patient belonged. In a sense, we might even say that moralism and paternalism were not clearly distinguished, simply because the moral evaluations involved in judgments about the patient's good were so uncontroversial that they largely remained implicit.

This internal regulation of medical practice worked efficiently because external legal and bureaucratic interference was marginal and doctors could simply make their own decisions, without having to discuss them extensively with patients or staff. As long as their decisions and actions were embedded in a morally decent traditional practice and were accepted by all as authoritative, good medical treatment was guaranteed. However, since the sixties, it became increasingly clear that this reliance on interactional law with a strong moralistic and paternalistic character encountered serious problems.

---

18   For an analysis of this intertwinement, see also various studies in Freeman, *Law and Bioethics*; Rothstein, 'Role of Law'.

First, the paternalism and moralism of medical practice came under attack. The general emancipation process in which citizens claimed their rights did not leave medicine untouched. Withholding information about the true nature of a disease was no longer deemed acceptable. Both as a result of the general trend towards emancipation which started in the sixties and as a result of specific factors in the field of biomedicine, patients claimed their rights and wanted to control their own lives. Moreover, traditional morality had changed rapidly, resulting in a more pluralist character of modern societies. Free citizens wanted to control their own medical and psychiatric treatment because it was up to them to decide which treatment was for their good, not only in a non-moral sense but also in a moral sense. They claimed the freedom to decide whether they wanted to have a child or not and whether an abortion was morally justified. They wanted to decide themselves whether further suffering was an acceptable part of their dying process or whether they wanted to avoid further suffering through euthanasia or assisted suicide.

Second, the reliance on implicit, interactional law had the disadvantage that it could only deal with relatively gradual adaptations. The traditional legal and moral norms did not provide solutions to the problems that arose as a result of rapid changes in society, technology and health care practice. Societal structures and processes were changing so rapidly that an appeal to the moral tradition and trust in a gradual adaptation of implicit morality to changing circumstances simply was no longer adequate. Professional morality would have lost contact with social reality if it had not become an explicit object of open, critical discussion, reflection and adaptation. Technology posed many new problems to which traditional morality did not offer answers – issues like embryo research, organ transplants and the treatment of severely handicapped newborns that in the past simply would not have survived. Health care practice changed from a practice in which the individual physician had a personal relationship with a patient to a situation in which teamwork and interdisciplinary cooperation were normal. Each of these changes made it necessary to make moral and legal norms explicit so that they could be discussed, critically analysed and adapted to new circumstances or new opinions. They also made the need for explicit law more clearly felt, to guide those developmental processes and to prevent excesses as a result of normative uncertainty. When traditional morality no longer provided adequate guidance, and a new morality was still developing, society could no longer put its trust completely in the medical judgment because the risk of erring was too great.

These latter remarks already point to a third problem. Traditional practice knew no checks and balances, no external control mechanisms.[19] Even if almost

---

19 Moreover, the medical experiments and other violations of human rights during the Nazi regime offered a warning that medicine could also be seriously abused. George Annas argues that the emergence of American bioethics was also a response to the atrocities of the Nazi concentration camps, and that bioethics was born with international human

all medical professionals act in a decent or even highly laudable way, there will always be the need to correct the small minority of practitioners who do not. In a small-scale profession with strong mechanisms of social control, it may be largely adequate to trust informal and internal methods of correction and control, for example, through disciplinary proceedings. But in a more anonymous large-scale medical practice this simply does not suffice. Moreover, it does not give the patients adequate protection against and compensation for medical malpractice. Everyone with power runs the risk of abusing it; the more power the medical profession was given by modern technology, the greater was the need for control and checks and balances. In combination with the growing emancipation of patients, this led to an increasing demand for state intervention in medical practice.

These three problems led to the emergence of the new disciplines of health law and bioethics. The reasons for abandoning the old approach were both new normative opinions on paternalism and moralism, and responses to developments in Western society and in medical practice itself. The old approach was simply no longer generally accepted; nor was it functional in various respects.

Paternalism and moralism became problematic in light of newly reinforced liberal ideals of human rights and autonomy.[20] These ideals were already part of democratic legal orders, but in the sixties they became more prominent and provided a basis for criticisms of medical practice (as well as of many other practices and institutions in society). However, not only were they the basis for criticism, they could also be sources of inspiration for constructing new doctrines of health law and bioethics. The ideal of autonomy, for example, provided the basis for the doctrine of informed consent and various patient rights.[21] In order to have a broad discussion in society among practitioners and among specialists in health law and bioethics, it was necessary to construct legal and moral norms explicitly in the form of a doctrine. Thus the transformation from a practice model to a doctrine model was promoted by the need to openly discuss existing norms and construct alternative norms.

The problem of the slow adaptation of implicit professional norms to rapidly changing circumstances also provoked the transformation to a doctrinal model of law and morality. Professional morality was made more explicit and became an object of ethical reflection, discussion and reformulation in the light of changing circumstances. Changes in society, technology and health care practice resulted in the emergence of health law and bioethics as disciplines that supported this continuous process of reflection, discussion and reformulation. Changes in health

---

rights law. See Annas, *American Bioethics*. A similar argument can easily be made with regard to the emergence of health law and bioethics in various European countries.

20 See Sperling, 'Law and Bioethics'.

21 See Mason and McCall Smith, *Law and Medical Ethics*, p. 6: 'The concept of autonomy now pervades the whole of medical practice mirroring its general importance in contemporary moral philosophy.'

care practice, moreover, required that medical ethics was broadened to bioethics or health care ethics, and that medical law was broadened to health law, so that both included all health care professions (like nurses) and the organization of the health care system as a whole. Changes in society required that ethical and legal discussions were not confined to health care professionals, but that health care consumers were involved as well, which meant society as a whole.

The third problem mentioned above was that medical practice did not provide adequate mechanisms of control and correction, let alone the protection of patients and third parties. The most obvious institution for external control is state law. This meant that new legislation and regulations were needed in a practice that, so far, had not been used to much external regulation.

In the transformation process, the new disciplines of bioethics and health law profited from a close cooperation.[22] They had many things in common: no firm theoretical ground to stand on; demanding tasks; and, as is usual in a starting period, a very small number of competent ethicists and lawyers. Moreover, both disciplines often – though not always – had to struggle against the resistance of settled interest groups, especially physicians. But, most importantly, they had a common mission: to elaborate liberal ideals in a theoretically satisfying way and to implement them in health care practice.

In such a situation, it was only natural that both disciplines collaborate closely and find intellectual inspiration in each other's work.[23] Why not try to construe a theory on informed consent in a common effort by lawyers and ethicists? Why should lawyers not try to build on ethical theories regarding the status of the human embryo when developing suggestions for legislation on abortion or on embryo research? Moreover, it was not only intellectually helpful, but also strategically important to join forces if one of your aims was to change health care practice and opposition was strong.

Cooperation between both disciplines was made possible by the fact that both emerging disciplines used the same framework for analysis. Both health law and bioethics focused on law and ethics as a product, as a normative doctrine. They tried to develop new theories, principles, rules or concrete advice for the new problems that arose (or the old ones seen in a new light): the plight of psychiatric patients, the possibilities and risks of new technologies. Bioethicists tried to construct new moral guidelines and suggest solutions for concrete problems and moral dilemmas; often they also argued for new legal rules. Health lawyers also

---

22 See Leenen, 'Vijfentwintig jaar gezondheidsrecht', p. 21; Clouser and Kopelman, 'Philosophical Critique of Bioethics'.

23 The close cooperation and mutual inspiration are also visible in books on health law and bioethics. Many bioethics books extensively discuss court cases, (draft) legislation and self-regulation. Many health law books include elaborate discussions on the morality of, for example, abortion or euthanasia. And, most importantly, I know of no other field of law or ethics (with the exception of legal professional ethics) where so many books explicitly combine legal and moral analyses, even in their titles.

focused on products in the form of legislation, other types of regulation and judicial decisions. They continually tried to construct law as a coherent system of rules and principles. Thus, both disciplines had a similar orientation towards law and morality as a product.[24]

Moreover, bioethics and health law both used the same conceptual categories. In both disciplines, principles, patient rights, concrete rules and procedures take pride of place. This allowed (at least superficially) a translation of legal analysis into moral analysis and vice versa, an essential precondition for successful cooperation. Ethicists could participate in legal discussions because they largely used the same framework (though the precise meanings and roles of the principles and rights were usually not identical in law and ethics, a fact which was too often neglected by lawyers and ethicists alike). Lawyers could make a useful contribution to ethical discussions because legal experience often provided valuable insights into the way in which a moral right like that of privacy could be elaborated.

Thus, health law and bioethics both took a product view and both used the same conceptual framework. But the most important factor that guaranteed successful cooperation is that they were both committed to the same substantive ideals. Patient autonomy and patient rights – in other words liberalism – were central to the modern bioethical and legal discourse.[25] Because bioethics and health law shared this commitment to liberal ideals, they not only spoke the same language but also took similar stances, at a more theoretical and at a more practical level. Moreover, a theory based on autonomy and patient rights offered simple solutions for most of the problems that were central in the early days of bioethics and health law. On abortion and on euthanasia, on the plight of psychiatric patients and on medical experiments, the paradigm of patient rights gave a clear and simple answer: the patient has to decide. Against the traditional background of moralism and paternalism this was real progress. Moreover, autonomy meant that individuals were entrusted with the responsibility for moral dilemmas, rather than the law or society as such. Thus, the more subtle and controversial moral issues were effectively removed from the public sphere. This made it much easier, in modern pluralist societies, to reach an overlapping consensus on the moral issues that remained in the public sphere; who would oppose patient autonomy as such?

However, we should not only look at the disciplines of health law and bioethics, trying to elaborate a common doctrine, inspired by liberal ideals. Lawyers and

---

24 This is best exemplified by the central role the 'four principles of biomedical ethics' advanced by Beauchamp and Childress play in the ethical literature (see Beauchamp and Childress, *Principles of Biomedical Ethics*). Even many critics of 'principlism', such as Bernard Gert, take a product view and focus on moral rules instead of principles (see Gert, *Morality.*).

25 See Beauchamp and Childress, *Principles of Biomedical Ethics*, p. 78; Ippel, 'Gezondheidsrecht en gezondheidsethiek'; Schneider, 'Bioethics in Language of Law'. For a very critical analysis of this liberal – or, in his term, 'hippie' – value-orientation, see Trotter, 'Genesis of Totalizing Ideology'.

ethicists did not work in an ivory tower, but took part in a broader social debate – as did the health care practitioners themselves. During these debates health care practice did not passively wait for the legislature to come up with new norms; these norms were usually tested in practice before they were even discussed in formal legal institutions such as courts and legislatures. In fact, at the times the statutes were finally passed, most health law legislation was largely codification of norms that already had become interactional law and that had been accepted by large segments of health care practice, of patients and of health lawyers and bioethicists. Although the formulation in explicit doctrines enabled this process of discussion and gradual implementation of new norms, there was a continuing interaction between society, health law and medical ethics, and the health care professions. A good example of this is the emergence of new legal norms with regard to euthanasia in the Netherlands, where the role of legislation largely consisted of codification of already widely accepted norms. As the sociologists Griffiths, Bood and Weyers describe it, these norms had emerged in a broad interaction between a great many parties:

> The legal norms that currently seem to be valid have not emerged from legislation nor in any simple way from judicial decisions, but from interaction between the medical profession (in particular the Medical Association), interest groups (in particular the Association for Voluntary Euthanasia), the government, Parliament, the Health Council, the State Commission on Euthanasia, the Remmelink Commission (appointed to carry out empirical research concerning euthanasia and related practices), several groups of empirical researchers and other academic participants in the public discussion, the judiciary, the prosecutorial authorities, the medical disciplinary tribunals, the Medical Inspectorate, several political parties, a variety of social and religious organizations, the media and the 'public'.[26]

A group which should have been explicitly mentioned in this list of participants is ethicists: they were often asked for advice by the professions and interest groups; testified in court cases as expert witnesses; were members of the various committees and councils mentioned; and contributed to social discussions. Again, there was a strong intertwinement and cooperation between the disciplines of bioethics and health law. Similar descriptions may be given for many countries with regard to the emergence of norms with regard to issues such as in vitro fertilization, clinical trials and animal experiments, or human biotechnology.[27] These norms emerged from within the professional practice, and were discussed in broader contexts with ethicists, lawyers, interest groups and the public at large before they were finally codified in legislation.

---

26 Griffiths, Bood and Weyers, *Euthanasia and Law*, p. 43.
27 For the latter, see Poort, *Consensus and Controversies*.

In this brief and much too simplified sketch many themes recur that were discussed when developing the theory of legal interactionism. In the early years, medical practice was primarily regulated by implicit, interactional law. This interactional law was intertwined with traditional ethics and only loosely connected with state law; it constituted a relatively autonomous legal order. A doctrine of health law, either in the form of enacted law or of doctrinal presentations in treatises and textbooks, was virtually non-existent. For many legal positivists, it might look as if there was hardly any law, because there was little state-enforced law and the implicit medical law was hardly distinguishable from medical ethics. However, the pluralist approach of legal interactionism provides a more sophisticated framework that can do justice to the obligatory force that interactional law had for medical professionals. As I argued before, if we focus on interactional law, it is difficult to separate law from morality, and this holds true for the interactional norms of the medical professions. Medical ethics and disciplinary law were strongly intertwined rather than separated; they could even hardly be distinguished. Therefore, we may conclude that legal interactionism does provide a more adequate description of the interactional medical law in the early years.

Legal interactionism also provides an adequate framework for understanding the dynamics of the emerging health law. In reforming the implicit normativity of medical practice in response to rapid changes in society and technology, the appeal to fundamental ideals proved crucial. Moreover, the continuing cooperation between the disciplines of health law and bioethics makes much more sense within an interactionist framework than within a positivist one. Not only did these disciplines cooperate in elaborating new normative doctrines; the development of health law was the result of a continuing discussion in society at large as well as of a continuing experimenting with new norms in health care practice. As a result the role of courts and legislatures was relatively marginal in the initial development of those new norms. The pluralist and open perspective that interactionism offers allows us to study those societal discussions and developments in health care practice, whereas a strong focus on black-letter law would largely leave those discussions and developments out of sight. Therefore, we may conclude that this case study demonstrates indeed that legal interactionism provides a good framework for studying the dynamics of law.

Chapter 8
Three Apparent Anomalies in Modern Law

International Law

The general conclusion of the preceding two chapters was that legal interactionism provides an adequate understanding of legal pluralism and of legal dynamics. As pluralism and dynamics are pervasive in modern law, legal interactionism is a more adequate theory to describe modern law than the traditional competitors of legal positivism and natural law. Thus, we need a shift to a different paradigm.

At a more concrete level, this ability to do justice to pluralism and dynamics is also reflected in the understanding of phenomena that at first sight may seem legal anomalies or aberrations. For example, the dynamic interplay in many European countries between domestic law, European Union law and Council of Europe law can only be understood in the context of a perspective that does justice to both pluralism and dynamics. The standard view of law in which law is the product of state sovereign legal orders is strongly at odds with this contemporary reality. While we have this standard view in mind when looking at those intermeshing legal orders, this emerging global legal pluralism must be considered an anomaly. It is only when we take a legal interactionist approach that it becomes clear that these intermeshing legal orders are newly emerging legal phenomena that may embody a different type of law, but are law nonetheless.

In this chapter I will discuss three of these apparent anomalies: international law; the law based on the European Convention on Human Rights; and interactive, horizontal legislation. Each of these phenomena, in various ways, does not fit into the standard view of law, and is often criticized for that very reason. Legal interactionism provides a more positive approach. Not only can it see these phenomena as newly emerging variations of law – rather than as aberrations – it can also explain why these phenomena are an adequate response to the specific conditions of dynamic pluralism in the modern world. We may, therefore, regard these phenomena as part of a newly emerging interactionist legal paradigm.

International law is, as I have mentioned before, an oddity for most legal theories. There is no supreme sovereign and there are very few institutions with what resembles legislative, adjudicative and law enforcing functions. Moreover, there are no simple tests of pedigree as, on the one hand, some treaties that are the product of formal institutions and procedures remain a dead letter, whereas, on the other hand, customary law is a major source of law. Moreover, international law cannot be perceived as one coherent legal order, but is rather a loose network of different, relatively autonomous, legal orders – some global, some regional. Consequently, accounts of positivism based on authoritative sources, state institutions, or secondary rules are not quite satisfactory in really explaining international law. Moreover, the digital character of legal positivism – legal norms cannot half exist – cannot do justice to the phenomenon that in international law norms gradually emerge and can be said to become more law in the process. Indeed, Brunnée and Toope conclude that the dominance of an inadequate theory of law has dire consequences:

> The resulting picture of international law is rarely good, often ugly, and always distorted. [...] When we assume that the defining features of domestic law – and by extension of all law – are formal enactment by a superior authority, application by courts, and centralized enforcement, we are bound to see international law as a poor cousin. Most importantly, we risk misjudging how law operates in international society, obscuring its potential power, and misdirecting even the best-intentioned efforts to improve it.[1]

Their view of interactional international law, discussed in Chapter 6 above, obviously corresponds more closely to the phenomenon of international law than the simple black and white criteria of most positivist theories.[2] Indeed, it allows for more diversity than natural law theories, as it only requires a minimal shared understanding, which is largely procedural.[3] It merely requires the agreement that some form of coordination and common action is necessary on the basis of respect for autonomy and open communication, and that a practice of legality is the best method to tackle this need. Brunnée and Toope have an inclusive view of who can and should participate in the practices of legality in order to create law. Law 'is made through a variety of actors, including elites, the media, NGOs and "ordinary" citizens'.[4] The horizontal structure of international law includes not only horizontal relations between states, but also between states and other actors, and between those actors. Thus Brunnée and Toope offer a helpful pluralist understanding of international law, accepting that there may be many relatively autonomous practices of legality that are both regionally and functionally distinctive. For example, the legal order regulating water resource management in the Nile Basin is a relatively autonomous legal order, with no direct links with the legal order of the Council of Europe; but, indirectly, there are connections between these two orders, as both are embedded in the global network of emerging international law. They also offer a dynamic and gradualist

---

1 Brunnée and Toope, *Legitimacy and Legality*, p. 6.
2 Of course, they are not the only international legal scholars who regard interaction as central to our understanding of law. See, for example, Koh, 'Transnational Legal Process'. I will concentrate here, however, on the version of Brunnée and Toope, as they have attempted to develop the most consistent Fullerian or interactionist version of international law.
3 Brunnée and Toope, *Legitimacy and Legality*, p. 30.
4 Brunnée and Toope, *Legitimacy and Legality*, p. 5.

understanding of international law, showing how shared understandings can gradually take on a more substantive form.

Brunnée and Toope's theory of international law has great advantages over positivist alternatives. Not only does it take seriously the main source of international law, interactional law, but it also offers an explanation for the evolution of law from a very thin legal order to a gradually thickening order, where more substantive commitments emerge during the process. It acknowledges the role of soft law – so often criticized by positivists as inadequate or even dangerous – as an important and effective part of international law.[5] Moreover, it can do justice to the persistently horizontal and pluralist structure of international law. For the purpose of understanding that part of international law which is merely interactional, it provides a good analysis.

However, there is one point of criticism, mentioned in Chapter 6 above, which is worth exploring in more detail. Brunnée and Toope ultimately regard interactional law as the only source of law, and view the obligatory force of enacted law and state consent as reducible to the obligatory force of the underlying interactional law. Enacted law represents only a surface phenomenon according to Brunnée and Toope; positive law is an important method of fixing legal understandings but cannot create a legal order in its own right. However, although at the current stage of development of international law interactional law is the main source of law, it should not be regarded as the only source. Enactment and consent can also be the basis of relatively autonomous legal orders, even if they are embedded in broader practices of interaction and must be largely congruent with those practices in order to be legitimate. Moreover, many developed forms of international law present a mix of interactional, enacted and consensual elements. In other words, Brunnée and Toope do not take pluralism seriously enough.[6]

Indeed, their starting point is the idea of legal obligation; in their view the distinctive character of law is that it creates obligations. However, I would argue that we may discern at least three distinct sources of obligation in international law, each of them in specific circumstances creating a distinctive legal legitimacy. Brunnée and Toope are correct in arguing that some form of interactional practice underlies all sources of law.[7] If there is no practice based on reciprocity that supports the norm of *pacta sunt servanda*, no obligations can arise from state consent. However, once there is a practice in which the consent of states is taken to bind them and give rise to legal obligations, then consent has become a source of

---

5   Brunnée and Toope, *Legitimacy and Legality*, p. 50.

6   For a similar argument that Brunnée and Toope are not pluralist enough, see Reus-Smit, 'Obligation through Practice', p. 339.

7   I agree with Brunnée and Toope that there must be some form of interactional practice; however, in my view, this practice need not always be a practice of legality. Therefore, we cannot say that interactional *law* underlies all sources of law.

obligation in its own right.[8] Similarly, law-creating and law-applying authorities and procedures must find a basis in interactional patterns; otherwise they only remain dead letter.[9] But that does not exclude the fact that, once created and accepted, these authorities and procedures create a legal order of their own, and that their enactments may also create law.

Let me illustrate this point with the example of the law of the European Union. The European Union has emerged over the past 60 years as a major producer of black-letter law for 28 member states; though, as an institution, it started in 1951 by the passage of a rather weak treaty (the Treaty of Paris constituting the European Coal and Steel Community) between six member states which had been involved in a bitter war with one another only six years earlier. Brunnée and Toope's theory provides an adequate description of the early stages of the integration process here. Gradually, the weak institutions became stronger, and more substantive commitments found broader support and were implemented, leading to the creation in 1958 of the European Economic Community. The integration gradually became stronger and European institutions grew more powerful as stronger shared understandings emerged and the practice of legality underlying European law became more substantial. The next phase of even more intense cooperation began in 1992 with the transformation into the European Union.

However, Brunnée and Toope's theory becomes less adequate at the later stages of integration. The institutions of the European Union have now created a relatively autonomous legal order, with a life of their own, creating a law of their own, and going beyond the original treaties and the underlying interactional law. The original horizontal structures of the European treaties have been partly been transformed into more hierarchical structures. In many ways, the European Union nowadays looks like a federal state, whereas in various other ways it does not. However we might want to characterize the European Union, it is clear that its institutions have led to an immense production of black-letter law. Enactment has become a separate source of law within the European Union.[10]

We could try to reduce this black-letter law to interactional law but, as I have argued, this does not do justice to how these phenomena function. Enactments by the European Union's institutions create direct obligations. Consent can create obligations in its own right as well. A theory which recognizes a plurality of legal sources is, therefore, to be preferred. Legal interactionism can recognize a plurality

---

8   Thus, when they criticize authors who see state consent as the sole basis of international law, they are correct. However, that does not exclude the possibility that consent or, in other words, contract and treaty, is a source of law in its own right. See Chapter 6.

9   Brunnée and Toope, *Legitimacy and Legality*, p. 70.

10   In fact, for many member states the obligation to incorporate the European Union's black-letter law into the domestic legal order is a major factor in the current regulatory explosion.

of legal sources because it takes enacted law as well as interactional law seriously, and does not try to reduce all types of law to one basic category.

The European Convention on Human Rights as a Living Instrument

The second apparent anomaly is that of the case law of the European Court of Human Rights and, in particular, the role it constructs for itself. The Court in Strasbourg has repeatedly stated that the Convention is to be regarded as a living instrument which must be interpreted in the light of present-day conditions.[11] Thus, the Court holds a bold, dynamic view of the meaning of the Convention. This may seem to be an illegitimate claim for a court in the eyes of many politicians and legal theorists. It does not fit into the positivist Civil Law conception of the *trias politica* in which the judge should merely interpret and apply the rules, such as the written constitution and statutory law, enacted by the lawmaking authorities. Nor does it fit into the Common Law conception of a judge's role, which is more evolutionary but restricted by doctrines of binding precedent. Of course, domestic and other international courts are also, in reality, often activist in substantively reforming the law, but in their rhetoric they usually minimize their innovative role. Thus, the Court has often been criticized for overstepping its role as envisioned by the state parties to the Treaty of Rome.[12]

The Court's handling of pluralism is equally innovative and controversial.[13] The doctrine on the margin of appreciation holds that in many cases the balance between a human right, as protected in the Convention, and other state interests has to be struck by the domestic authorities. As long as there is no broad European consensus on issues such as state neutrality or recognition of transsexuals, the Court will not substantively rule on those issues.[14] Again, this is a strange role for a court that has been given responsibility to protect human rights, especially from the perspective of liberal-democratic theory. The justification for the existence of constitutional courts is usually a countermajoritarian one, implying that those courts are commissioned for protecting the rights of minorities against intolerant majorities.[15] By so openly accepting that a majority is not yet ready for what

---

11   See ECtHR, *Tyrer v. United Kingdom*, 25 April 1978, No. 5856/72.

12   Usually these critiques come from politicians and the general public in response to controversial decisions by the Court. For example, the *Hirst* case on voting rights for prisoners (ECtHR, *Hirst v. United Kingdom*, 6 October 2005, No. 74025/01) provoked outrage among British politicians and in the media. The *Lautsi* case on crucifixes in Italian public schools (ECtHR, *Lautsi v. Italy*, 3 November 2009, No. 30814/06 (Second Section), later overturned by the Grand Chamber in *Lautsi and Others v. Italy* on 18 March 2011) did so both in Italy and various other countries. For a more principled criticism, see Lord Hoffman, 'Universality of Human Rights'.

13   Krisch, *Beyond Constitutionalism*, pp. 143–51.

14   Yourow, *Margin of Appreciation Doctrine*, pp. 193–6.

15   See Dworkin, *Taking Rights Seriously*.

should be considered the right of the minority, the Court may seem to be forsaking its primary task.

Legal interactionism provides quite a different analysis, and a more positive evaluation of the Court's role in reinforcing, interpreting and implementing the Convention. The Court's role was to build a common legal order, almost from scratch, for a very diverse group of sovereign states with a recent history of war and extreme violations of human rights. This legal order focuses on the often politically unpopular task of protecting the rights of minorities (rights of majorities seldom need protection in a democracy). This specific circumstance makes the standard view of law (and of the role of courts in constructing law) completely inadequate. It is easy to misunderstand the Convention and the Court in terms of a domestic constitution or Bill of Rights and of a Supreme or Constitutional Court, like those in the US and Canada. Those courts can build on a common legal identity, a common political system, and they have a role in the domestic *trias politica* alongside the executive and legislative powers. The Council of Europe, currently consisting of 47 member states, has none of these aspects. Indeed, there is a Parliamentary Assembly and a Committee of Ministers (which are almost invisible for ordinary citizens), but they barely have any power and rarely meet. Each of the member states has its own political institutions and legal traditions. Thus, it is clear that we need a completely different framework from that of a constitutional court with a countermajoritarian role.

The best way to understand the Council of Europe is to regard it as a common project, developed in response to the atrocities of World War II. The shared understandings were that something like that could never be allowed to happen again, and that a Convention on Human Rights would symbolize this intention and guarantee human rights in Europe. The shared understandings were very minimal and primarily negative (no more Auschwitz); indeed, it took a long time before they were strengthened.[16] The Court's role in this context was to reinforce the shared understandings on which its legitimacy was built and to expand upon those shared understandings and create legitimacy for developing stronger norms. There were only very general and open principles in the Convention, thus making the role model of judges in the Civil Law tradition – who simply apply the statutory law – inadequate; there was very little clear doctrine to apply. There was hardly any common legal tradition in this broad plurality of states, thus making it impossible to choose the model of Common Law, as there was no common tradition that could be formulated by judges.

---

16   See Krisch, *Beyond Constitutionalism*, pp. 144–5: 'the Convention reflected a minimal consensus, and many member states believed it did not require changes to their laws and institutions. As we have seen, the Strasbourg organs have been careful not to raise these costs too suddenly: while giving Convention rights increasing bite over time, they did so in an incremental fashion that never departed too much from the level of rights protection already consolidated in member states.'

In such a situation, the Convention is best interpreted as a shared project, a common ambition. On the one hand, this project required the formulation of a legal doctrine regarding the meaning of those human rights. On the other hand, it required the building of legitimacy for this doctrine in a broad variety of member states. In such a project, three requirements were essential: it must be evolutionary, it must be pluralist and it must be communicative and argumentative.[17] And these three requirements can, indeed, be discerned in the practice of the European Court.

First, it is evolutionary. The central idea that the Convention is a living instrument is a response to the need to gradually strengthen and expand upon shared understandings. As we saw in Chapter 6, dynamics in legal doctrine is strongly promoted if ideals play a major role in legal doctrine, and this is true of the Convention. The process of evolutive interpretation has been made possible by the fact that the Convention is phrased in very broad and vague terms. These terms, however, are not merely vague – as such they would not provide much guidance. Both the rights and the exception clauses refer to fundamental ideals of human rights and democracy, which are open to continuous reinterpretation in light of changing circumstances and changing ideas.[18]

Second, the Court has explicitly addressed the issue of legal, social and moral pluralism in its doctrine regarding the margin of appreciation.[19] The Council of Europe includes countries as diverse as the Netherlands, Turkey, Russia and Liechtenstein. In the first decades of its existence, some member states were even fascist dictatorships. As it is far less known by the general public than the smaller European Union and, apart from the European Convention, has relatively little practical importance, it would be highly inadequate to characterize this loose collection of states as a political community. In such a diverse group, pluralism is simply a matter of fact. This is, for example, clear when we look at one of the standard exception phrases in most of the human rights clauses: that restriction is necessary in a free and democratic society to protect public morals. The moral standards vary greatly among the European countries and even within a country.

The risk of such a diverse plurality of states is that it may result in a low level of human rights protection. Since some universal rights are only respected in a very elementary way in some states, one possibility is that the court will

---

17 See Brunnée and Toope, *Legitimacy and Legality*, pp. 119–20: 'Therefore, when the stock of internationally shared substantive understandings is relatively thin, law-making may be more productively focused upon elastic, open-textured substantive norms, or upon norms that are aimed primarily at building legality. Such norms leave scope for a domestic margin of appreciation – and thus for diversity – and allow for the gradual building up of shared understandings and an attendant practice of legality.'

18 See *Christine Goodwin v. United Kingdom* (ECtHR 11 July 2002, No. 28957/95) where the Court emphasizes its dynamic and evolutive approach in light of the object and purpose of the Convention.

19 See ECtHR, *Handyside v. United Kingdom*, 7 December 1976, No. 5493/72.

settle for the lowest level of protection for fear of losing its legitimacy by setting too high a standard. The doctrine of the margin of appreciation is an interesting compromise which specifies that, whereas certain acts may be considered against public morals in the most conservative parts of Austria, for example, they need not be so in the more liberal and secularized Netherlands. Therefore, the level of human rights protection can be different in both countries. There may even be relevant differences within a given country. Thus, in the case of *Otto-Preminger-Institut*, the Court held that the movie *Das Liebeskonzil* could be prohibited in Tyrol, whereas it need not have arrived at the same conclusion had the state of Austria wanted to prohibit it in Vienna.[20]

Of course, disagreement is possible, whether or not the Court struck the right balance in this specific case.[21] From one perspective, the Court may have been too lenient, and did not do sufficient justice to the moral pluralism that exists within the region of Tyrol itself. As the movie was to be shown in a progressive film centre, we may assume that there were at least some citizens who did not think this movie was against public morals. Moreover, we may wonder whether a prohibition was really necessary. However we may wish to evaluate applications of the margin of appreciation to concrete cases and perhaps possible mistakes in the application, the basic principle of the margin of appreciation seems to be not only correct, but also indispensable for the purpose of dealing with pluralism.[22] Indeed, it takes into account local contexts and allows for a differentiation between contexts. It is, however, not an unlimited licence for states as it places the burden of proof on the member states. Member states have to convincingly demonstrate that the restriction is really necessary in a democratic and free state, and is required for the protection of public morals.

Not only does the burden of proof lie with the member state, it is also open to dynamic interpretation.[23] Whereas a certain restriction may seem justified or within the margin of appreciation now, it need not be so in the future. The Court's approach to pluralism is, thus, reinforced by its evolutionary approach. In a continent with such major cultural, political and religious differences and rapid changes, this is an indispensable strategy to prevent an originalist and minimalist interpretation. We should not immunize historically contingent doctrines against change with an appeal to the original intentions of the framers (which in light of the diversity among the contracting parties would only be a fiction anyhow).

---

20 ECtHR, *Otto-Preminger-Institut v. Austria*, 20 September 1994, No. 13470/87.

21 This is illustrated by the fact that the judgment was based on a majority of six judges, with a minority of three strongly dissenting judges.

22 See Gerards, 'Pluralism, Deference and Margin of Appreciation'. Gerards argues that the use of a 'margin of appreciation'-like doctrine might be of great value for the EU courts, such as the European Court of Justice.

23 See Brunnée and Toope, *Legitimacy and Legality*, p. 181, for a similar analysis on the process of progressive clarification of treaty terms with regard to the United Nations Framework Convention on Climate Change.

How fruitful such an approach can be is easily demonstrated with regard to the changing attitudes towards homosexuality. There can be no doubt that in the early fifties, in almost all European countries, homosexuality was deemed to be against public morals and it was generally accepted that it should not be treated as on a par with heterosexuality.[24] Views have changed enormously since then – although, as of yet, not in all member states. An originalist interpretation would have made it impossible to interpret the Convention in light of changing social attitudes and, thus, might have led to the conclusion that a prohibition of homosexual acts between consenting adults could be deemed necessary. The evolutionary strategy allowed the Court, however, to take a different approach in the *Dudgeon* case in 1981.[25] Whatever the merits of the argument for prohibition in the past, it was no longer considered necessary.

These two mechanisms, the margin of appreciation and the evolutive interpretation, make it possible for the Court to take account of changes in society. However, the Court goes beyond the merely passive role of simply following societal changes.[26] It also attempts to promote further changes in the member states by identifying processes of change and issuing warnings to reluctant member states that these ongoing processes may lead, in the future, to further changes in the case law. In some of its judgments, the Court held that social development in Europe has not yet advanced so far that a consensus has emerged, which implies that in the future it might.

Examples may be found in a number of cases regarding the legal recognition of gender change for transsexuals after sexual reassignment surgery. In the case of *Cossey*, the Court stated that there had been developments in recent years, both in the law of some of the member states and at the European level in the European Parliament and the Parliamentary Assembly of the Council of Europe, but that there was still diversity of practice. Therefore, there was still little common ground and, consequently, a wide margin of appreciation. However, it also explicitly stated: 'Since the Convention always has to be interpreted and applied in the light of current circumstances, it is important that the need for appropriate legal measures in this area should be kept under review.'[27] After a number of years, the Court finally deemed that the moment had arrived – that social acceptance of transsexualism was so broad that the argument of the British government was

---

24 The European Court of Human Rights did not discuss the prohibition of homosexuality until the *Dudgeon* case in 1981 (*Dudgeon v. United Kingdom*, 22 October 1981, No. 7525/76), but in *X v. Federal Republic of Germany*, No. 104/55, Yearbook I (1955–57), p. 228 (229), the Commission accepted a prohibition.

25 ECtHR, *Dudgeon v. United Kingdom*, 22 October 1981, No. 7525/76.

26 See Yourow, *Margin of Appreciation Doctrine*, p. 194: 'the Court absorbs and emanates social change'.

27 ECtHR, *Cossey v. United Kingdom*, 27 September 1990, No. 10843/84. Similar statements may be found in various other cases with regard to transsexualism, such as ECtHR, *Rees v. United Kingdom*, 17 October 1986, No. 9532/81.

no longer acceptable. In the *Christine Goodwin* case, the Court concluded that, in the light of recent developments, the matter no longer fell within the margin of appreciation and held that the refusal to give full legal recognition to gender reassignment constituted a violation of the European Convention.[28]

In this way, the Court participates in a dialogue with the member states, both with the courts and parliaments and with the societies. Its discursive culture, with its judgments containing elaborate argumentation and *obiter dicta*, and often with well-argued concurring and dissenting opinions, contributes to this dialogue. The legitimacy of the court can only partly rest on its legal authority; it must ultimately be built on serious attempts to convince the audiences in the various member states. Such attempts cannot rest on communication as a hierarchical command; they must take the reactions in the member states seriously. Therefore, the Court must try to engage in an open dialogue, both with the national courts and with the political institutions and public opinion in the member states; or, rather, as Ahdieh has argued, in a process of judicial dialectical review.[29] The margin of appreciation and the evolutive interpretation enable such a dialectic process.

These two mechanisms are indications of what may be called an interactionist paradigm of judging. In this paradigm, there is a continuous interplay between legal and social developments. There is acceptance of pluralism, but this plurality is not an everlasting, let alone general phenomenon – it may be subject to change. And in its communicative strategy, the Court explicitly promotes a dialogue with the member states to encourage them to take an evolutionary approach as well, and to make changes that are justified in light of changing social conditions.

Horizontal Interactive Legislation

An interactionist legal practice is not only emerging at the international level. It can also be found at the domestic level, for example, in the phenomenon of more horizontal types of legislation. In the Netherlands, for example, a number of authors have described the emergence of a new paradigm of legislation with names as symbolic, communicative and interactive legislation.[30] I will simply take as their most general heading the name interactive legislation.[31] Willem Witteveen

---

28   ECtHR, *Christine Goodwin v. United Kingdom*, 11 July 2002, No. 28957/95.
29   Ahdieh, 'Between Dialogue and Decree'.
30   For a critical overview, see various articles in Zeegers, Witteveen and Van Klink, *Social and Symbolic Effects*; Poort, *Consensus and Controversies*.
31   Of course, similar theories are found elsewhere too. Obvious sources of inspiration are Nonet and Selznick's idea of responsive law, Fuller's work on the internal morality of legislation and Kenneth Burke's rhetorical studies. Related ideas may be found in John Braithwaite's work on responsive regulation, Cary Coglianese's work on negotiated rulemaking and Mark Van Hoecke's idea of law as communication.

and Bart van Klink have focused on the communication processes after the passing of a statute, and described how, in some cases, the statute did not provide strict rules, but rather constituted a rhetorical framework which enabled further discussion among the participants in a legal community. They call this type of legislation symbolic or communicative legislation.[32]

Frans Brom and I have taken a broader view, and discerned similar interactive processes in the phase leading up to the passage of legislation into law, especially in legislation on ethically sensitive issues such as the regulation of biotechnology, anti-discrimination legislation and marriage.[33] We have named this process interactive legislation, as it builds on broad processes of interaction among a great number of societal actors at all stages of the norm-making and implementing processes. I argued that, at least in societal fields with a strong ethical dimension, the development of legal norms is shifting from a vertical model in which the legislator authoritatively sets standards for society, to a more horizontal, interactive process in which various social actors participate; and among them, the legislator has an important, though not necessarily central, role.[34] Similarly, the implementation, enforcement and control of legal norms is shifting from a vertical model in which government bodies are the main enforcing actor, to a more horizontal, interactive process in which various societal actors participate, among which government bodies have an important though not necessarily central role. Consequently, the separate processes of norm development and norm implementation are merging into one continuous process of norm development and implementation.[35]

The statute is no longer the central source of law; often it merely codifies the interactional law, emerging in society or in, for example, medical practice. Moreover, statutes often formulate open standards rather than strict rules. On the one hand, these standards may express the common values (or the values of the dominant group) and provide a common normative framework. The statutory formulation then has an expressive function. On the other hand, these standards may provide a common point of reference by which the norm addressees can be guided without presenting too many detailed and overly restrictive rules. Moreover, they invite active interpretation and discussion on

---

32 Witteveen and Van Klink, 'Soft Law'.

33 Van der Burg and Brom, 'Legislation on Ethical Issues'. In various publications, Willem Witteveen has also taken this broader view; in 'Significant, Symbolic and Symphonic Laws', p. 35, he argues that the texts of symbolic laws 'do not rest upon the expression of an authorial intention so much as upon an explication of what has emerged from the interactions between agents making law in the structured practices of a particular community and field of law'.

34 I summarized the model of interactive legislation in Van der Burg, 'Irony of Symbolic Crusade'; some fragments from pages 289–90 have been included here.

35 There is an interesting parallel here with Brunnée and Toope's argument that we should integrate lawmaking and compliance questions in international law. See *Legitimacy and Legality*, p. 98.

those interpretations, both among citizens and between citizens and the various legal authorities. Statutes then also have a communicative function.[36] Because of this continuing process of interpretation and implementation, and the strong focus on more general values and principles, moral and legal norm development are often strongly intertwined.

The model of interactive legislation has emerged in the specific context of the Netherlands, where it resonates with the tradition of an inclusive, consensus-oriented, consociational style of democracy. However, it is certainly not restricted to the Netherlands, as in countries such as Switzerland and Denmark phenomena with partly similar characteristics may be found.[37] Here, I am not primarily interested in the normative issue of whether interactive legislation is a desirable legislative practice, but rather how we can understand this phenomenon in its best light. As with the other phenomena discussed in this chapter, it has often been criticized as an anomaly or an aberration.[38] Interactive legislation is said to be undemocratic because it no longer focuses on the democratically elected parliament as the primary source of law. The use of vague norms and aspirations is said to provide little guidance to citizens, and leaves too much discretion to ethics committees.

However, from the perspective of legal interactionism, interactive legislation, indeed, makes sense. In its ideal typical form, it guarantees the congruence between interactional and enacted law, as the enacted law merely codifies the moral and legal norms and values that have emerged in the practice. Furthermore, it guarantees the continuing involvement of society, or the relevant sectors of it, in the implementation, and ensures that a similar congruence will be maintained when shifting circumstances make changes in the law necessary.[39] The formulation of open standards indicates that this process of interaction between enacted law and interactional law will never be completed, and provides for a flexible framework for the future elaboration of the law. The involvement of citizens and societal organizations, both in the legislative process and in the implementation process, can be regarded as an additional way of implementing democracy rather than as a competition with the democratically elected parliament. These characteristics, which are aberrations in the traditional positivist framework, can be seen in the

---

36 For these two functions of law in interactive legislation, see Van der Burg, 'Expressive and Communicative Functions'.

37 For an interesting comparison, see Poort, *Consensus and Controversies*. Poort concludes that in each of these three countries legislation on animal biotechnology may be characterized as interactive, although in Denmark only the process leading to the statute may be characterized as interactive; and neither of the two other countries fully realizes the ideal of a continuing interactive process after legislation has been passed. Stefan Grotefeld, 'Wie wird Moral ins Recht gesetzt?', also argues that the Swiss regulation of biotechnology can be understood in terms of interactive legislation.

38 See various papers in Zeegers, Witteveen and Van Klink, especially Pauline Westerman, 'Some Objections', and Jellienke Stamhuis, 'Communicative Law'.

39 This point makes it clear that interactive legislation is not to be identified with interactional law; it is rather the interplay between enacted and interactional law.

interactionist perspective as advantages as they enable legislation to fulfil a role in dynamic and pluralist contexts.

Moreover, interactive legislation takes pluralism and dynamics more seriously than do traditional approaches to law. It does not focus, as traditional theories of legislation do, on one moment when a law is created out of the blue, but instead regards that moment as a significant one in a continuing process of normative evolution and elaboration. Moreover, interactive legislation accepts that consensus must be built, both before the enactment and following the enactment. Thus, it does not presuppose consensus or the end of the discussion once a statute is passed.[40]

However, it should be emphasized that this is merely the ideal typical model of interactive legislation. Indeed, Lonneke Poort has demonstrated that, in reality, the dynamic process often gets stuck.[41] Her analysis is very instructive because it makes it clear that the shift to a more interactionist paradigm is not merely a question of different institutions, but also requires a different culture, which is more open to dynamics and social and moral pluralism. One major reason why in Denmark, after an interactive process of legislation, the process of further norm development got stuck was the positivist legal culture in that country. As long as lawyers expect that statutes create clear rules, and implementation means a clear case law with strong rules of precedent or *stare decisis*, there will not be much further normative development. The gaps will be filled and there will be a stable doctrine after all, as soon as there is a sufficient body of case law.

Another explanation of why a full interactive legislative process proved difficult to maintain was that in Switzerland and the Netherlands consensus was presupposed rather than actually created. There was a fiction of consensus rather than a broad acceptance of legitimate pluralism.[42] Both factors show the firm hold that the standard view of law, as discussed in the Introduction to this book, has over the minds of lawyers and non-lawyers alike. If you expect law to be a coherent and stable doctrine, interactive legislation is an aberration which must

---

40 As Poort has convincingly argued in *Consensus and Controversies*, consensus at the end of the interactive process will not always be possible. (For a similar critique, see Stamhuis, 'Communicative Law'.) We should therefore adopt a broad idea of interactive legislation in which continuing dissensus is accepted as a possible and legitimate outcome. The debate on the highly controversial Dutch Equal Treatment Act (see my 'Irony of Symbolic Crusade') is an example of interactive legislative process where a strong opposition remained alive.

41 Poort, *Consensus and Controversies*.

42 Similarly, referring to the legislative process of the Dutch Work Councils Act, Stamhuis, 'Communicative Law', p. 296, argues that the legislator imposed norms on norm addressees under the 'pretence' of consensus. Reviewing empirical studies of negotiated rulemaking in the United States, Cary Coglianese concludes that consensus should not be the goal of public participation in the regulatory process because consensus building is decidedly ineffectual: 'Alternative methods of public participation that do not demand agreement are the more realistic strategies for democratic engagement' (Coglianese, 'Does Consensus Work?', p. 182).

be remedied as soon as possible by developing a doctrine through mechanisms of case law, by judges or by advisory committees.

Again, there is a clear parallel to the analysis of interactional international law by Brunnée and Toope. With only minor adaptations, we could apply the quote from their book (p. 6) in the opening section above to interactive legislation:

> When we assume that the defining feature of legislation is enactment by a superior authority such as a democratically elected legislature, we are bound to see interactive legislation as a poor cousin. Most importantly, we risk misjudging how legislation operates in more horizontal settings, obscuring the potential advantages of interactive legislation, and misdirecting even the best-intentioned efforts to improve it.

The Emerging Interactionist Paradigm

This chapter has demonstrated that legal interactionism is not merely a philosophical theory of law, but also something to be found in legal reality. The three phenomena discussed in this chapter are illustrations of an emerging interactionist paradigm in legal orders. The emergence of this new type of law is a response to a changing world in which relative pluralism and dynamics can no longer be ignored. They cannot be ignored in legal theory; nor can they be denied in legal practice.[43]

The standard view of law which I described in the Introduction is at pains to understand these new legal phenomena. They can only be regarded as anomalies or aberrations or, at best, as defective forms of law. As long as we are caught in the framework of this standard view, we simply cannot do them justice. However, in light of legal interactionism, these phenomena do make sense; they can suddenly be perceived as adequate responses to a changing world. What is more, interactive legislation can be seen as the prototype of law, guaranteeing a dynamic and evolving congruence between enacted and interactional law.

The analysis of interactive legislation in this chapter demonstrated that interactionist law is what may be called a high-risk approach: it can easily fail to live up to its ambitions.[44] It requires not only a specific type of law – it also requires a different type of legal culture and attitude. As long as the participants in a legal

---

43 For another attempt to do justice to interaction, but strongly inspired by Habermas and Teubner, see Van Hoecke, *Law as Communication*, p. 11: 'human interaction and communication have to be at the center of any theory of law, rather than individuals or legal systems as such'.

44 The idea that interactionist law (a type of law with many similarities to responsive law) is a high-risk approach is inspired by Nonet and Selznick, *Law and Society in Transition*, p. 7. At p. 26 they make a similar point about the conditions for success: 'Yet, responsive law, in reaching for a complex achievement, makes great and perhaps excessive demands for competence and resilience in the political community.'

practice have a positivist attitude, they will treat interactionist law as failed law. They may develop a stable legal doctrine based on case law by ethics committees, thus further frustrating legal evolution once a statute is passed. Or, in the case of international law, they may treat it as non-binding because it lacks traditional lawmaking and law-enforcing agencies. The European Court in Strasbourg is, in this scenario, seen as a power usurping agency, encroaching on the national sovereignty of states, or, on the contrary, as a failed constitutional court failing to live up to its liberal-democratic role as the guardian of minorities.

These risks demonstrate that the realization of an interactionist legal paradigm is a continuing project which needs to be broadly supported in order to be fully effective. An important condition for the full realization of its promises is that we finally rid ourselves of the dominant view of law, and replace it with a more sophisticated, interactionist view.

Chapter 9
The Necessary and Contingent Relationship between Law and Morality

A Variable Relationship

What does legal interactionism imply for the relationship between law and morality? In Part One I argued that the relationship is variable. In a practice model, a strict separation is indefensible, but there may be great variation in how intensively and in what ways law and morality are connected. In a product model, we might try to construct law and morality as completely separate; but even if this separation were possible, it would only be the result of our construction, and certainly not of an empirical or conceptual necessity. In most modern legal orders, however, and even in a product model, a strict separation is at odds with reality as there is an increasing reliance on open norms and references to underlying principles and aspirations.

We may now connect this analysis with the distinction we have made in Chapter 6 between enacted law and interactional law. Interactional law is best understood within a practice model, enacted law within a product model of law. In interactional law, a strict separation between law and morality is impossible. It will often even be difficult to distinguish both, especially at the level of specific legal norms and arguments. Although the interactional legal order as a whole may be construed as distinct from other legal orders, and as distinct from morality, at the level of the elements of interactional law (such as norms and arguments) the legal and the moral dimensions are usually indistinguishable.

If we focus on enacted law within a product model, the pattern is reversed.[1] At the level of individual elements of enacted law we are often able to construct them as distinct and even largely separate from morality, whereas at the level of the legal order as a whole this is more difficult. We can frequently discern distinct sources of specific legal rules (the enactments), and these sources and their contents can often be identified without appeals to morality. However, it depends on the specific legal order how far the collection of these sources is considered to be the whole law, and in what ways, in the process of interpretation of these

---

1 If we do not focus on the products of the enactment, on the contents of statutes and court decisions, but rather on the processes of law creation, interpretation and application, then a practice model is more adequate. Both in legislative processes and in other argumentative practices, moral, political and legal arguments are intertwined and often even indistinguishable.

sources and the construction of the legal doctrine as a coherent whole, there is openness to morality. When a constitution refers to fundamental rights or tort law to open criteria such as reasonableness and fairness, in the interpretation of those norms we will often use references to ideals and principles that have a mixed moral and legal character. Therefore, in the construction of law as coherent doctrine, we cannot simply restrict ourselves to the sources, and some connection with morality is unavoidable. On the other hand, if a statute enacts a rigidly formulated speed norm of 100 km per hour, there may seem to be no need for a reference to morality, and the legal norm may be regarded as separate from morality. But as soon as we move from the specific enacted norm to the norm as it is applied in the context of the criminal legal system, the picture shifts. Then we may see that the norm is embedded in a context in which reference to morality in extreme cases is often unavoidable. For example, in most (if not all) legal orders, a speed limit may be violated in cases of emergency, with an appeal to general legal doctrines such as those of *force majeure*. However, in order to determine whether there is *force majeure*, we need to evaluate and balance the various interests at stake, and this balancing makes law open to moral reflection.

A preliminary conclusion, therefore, might be that the more a legal order is based on interactional law, the more open it is to morality. Reversely, the more a legal order is based on enacted law and rigid rules, the stronger the relative autonomy of the law. But these statements are so vague and general that they hardly say anything. In order to determine the relative intertwinement and the relative autonomy of law, we must try to understand the more specific factors that influence both. In the following section, I will discuss the factors that promote strong connections and intertwinement between law and morality. I will then discuss the factors that promote a strong relative autonomy of law. In the final sections, I will connect this analysis to the debate between legal positivism and natural law and argue that legal interactionism is not only an alternative to both theories, but that it also incorporates the core of truth found in both.

In the Preface, I argued that most studies on law and morality have a normative agenda, whereas I am interested in a descriptive analysis. In this final chapter, it may perhaps seem to some readers as if I finally endeavour on a normative project. Nevertheless, I want to emphasize that my project remains one of sociologically informed legal theory.[2] I try to explain how law and morality are partly intertwined

---

2   Cotterrell, *Politics of Jurisprudence*, p. 3 distinguishes legal theory as a subcategory of legal philosophy. He distinguishes it from those parts of legal philosophy 'concerned primarily with the moral *justification* of particular aims or policies related to or expressed in legal theory. [...] Legal theory aims to understand systematically the nature of law as a social phenomenon' (italics in original). However, he continues by making a confusing distinction between normative and empirical legal theory, as based on the contributions of legal philosophy and legal sociology, respectively. This is an unhelpful and, in my view, incorrect opposition because legal philosophy can also be non-normative, especially those parts that aim merely at understanding. I prefer, therefore, to use the phrase 'sociologically

and partly autonomous. I conclude that this intertwinement in the context of a liberal democracy, and the orientation of law towards certain ideals like legality and justice, result in a variable moral quality of law. Law is not a normatively neutral phenomenon; it has a necessary but contingent moral quality. Therefore, my descriptive analysis has normative implications. However, this analysis is not based on a normative theory as such, let alone that I try to develop a normative theory of how we should morally evaluate and improve the legal order.

As I have argued in Chapter 4, the term morality may refer to social morality, critical morality or the ideal law used as a critical standard for law. Although from an external point of view it may be possible to distinguish these three versions, from an internal point of view it is often impossible.[3] For a participant in society, social morality may largely seem to be justifiable and thus identical to critical morality in as far as she accepts social morality as her own. This is one more reason (apart from the reasons discussed earlier) why it is difficult to construct a valid definition of morality, even as a working definition. Just as there is no universal uncontroversial definition of law, there is no single definition of morality. Although for certain purposes a more specific stipulation might be useful, in the context of the analysis in this chapter it is not, as such a stipulation would suggest a definite precision which does not do justice to the variation in reality and, in particular, to the connections between the three versions. Therefore, in the following three sections I use the term morality descriptively in this broad sense, referring both to social morality and to views of critical morality and ideal law held by participants in a legal order.

In the final section, however, I discuss the philosophical debate on whether law has inherent moral value. Consequently, I cannot avoid speaking of a 'higher moral quality' of law in an evaluative sense because that is precisely what the debate is about. Nevertheless, when I do so, I do not presuppose, let alone defend, a specific normative theory. I only refer to widely accepted normative ideals such as democracy, justice and the rule of law and presuppose that these ideals are morally valuable. It is against the background of these rather uncontroversial normative standards that I discuss the possible variations in the value of law in terms of 'higher moral quality'. Again, my analysis remains descriptive, although it is phrased in evaluative terms, and although it definitely has normative implications.

The Partial Intertwinement of Law and Morality

Let us first discuss the reasons why law and morality are intertwined. The basic reason is that, in the patterns of interaction that constitute interactional law, the

---

informed legal theory' to designate a philosophical non-normative analysis of the nature of law which tries to incorporate insights from legal sociology.

3   Taekema, *Concept of Ideals*, p. 202.

moral and the legal dimensions often cannot be distinguished from one another. Individuals stick to an agreement both because it is a legal obligation and because it is a moral obligation. In interactional law, the normative force of obligations is often not differentiated; there is simply a feeling of obligation. If citizens are asked why they follow certain norms, the answers may both refer to the law and to morality as well as to mere custom or expediency. In general, it would be artificial to reconstruct patterns of interaction as if law and morality were really distinct. They are two aspects of the same phenomenon.[4]

However, the fact that law and morality intertwine does not mean that they are identical. The emergent legal order is embedded in a normative pattern of interaction, but cannot be reduced to it. Instead, it has a life of its own, characteristics of its own and, thus, partly differentiates itself from other legal orders. Legal obligations get a more precise and specific formulation, and once this happens, they can be seen as distinct from morality – even if they are still embedded in the broader interactional normative order. Even in simple contractual agreements, the products to be delivered may be specified in detail and put on paper. As soon as this happens, we can at least distinguish the specific legal obligations from the broader normative and moral order. Once law has come into existence, it may create obligations that no longer correspond with moral obligations. A distinction, however, is not a separation.[5] As long as the basis of the legal order is in interactional law, law and morality are strongly intertwined. The emergence of a distinctive legal order within this broader practice may give rise to a relative autonomy and, consequently, the intertwinement may become looser, but it will never completely disappear.

The second reason why law and morality are intertwined in interactional law is the interpretive and argumentative nature of law as a practice. As Ronald Dworkin has convincingly argued, once we regard law as a discursive practice, the legal and moral dimensions of the arguments merge in the discussion.[6] There may be exclusively legal arguments, for example, arguments referring to case law or statutes, but the collection of these exclusively legal arguments never constitutes a complete argument. Even seemingly clear texts may require interpretation, and every legal text is then to be interpreted in light of underlying ideals and principles. Moreover, legal practice is more than judicial practice, which is central to Dworkin's theory. In legislative practices, political, moral and legal arguments fuse when decisions are made to change the law. In mediation, ideals of fairness and equity may come to the foreground. In interactional practices and contract, appeals may often be made to reasonable interpretation in light of common sense and

---

4 See Cane, *Responsibility in Law and Morality*, pp. 13–15. He argues that the relationship between law and morality is symbiotic; they are both parts of a rich tapestry of practices.

5 Compare Schauer, 'Nature of Nature of Law', p. 462, arguing that 'two things which cannot be demarcated may nonetheless be differentiated'.

6 Dworkin, *Taking Rights Seriously*, p. 149.

implicit understandings. Views of what ordinary citizens or professionals believe to be the positive law often are intertwined with (and even indistinguishable from) views of what they believe would be reasonable and fair.

So the interpretive and argumentative character of law is a central factor in the intertwinement of law and morality. However, this intertwinement is variable, as legal practices may differ with regard to how open they are towards morality. In highly formalist judicial practices, informed by a legal positivist culture, the intertwinement may be very loose, as the only type of argument that is allowed is an argument that cloaks itself as a literal interpretation of a text.[7] In legislative practices, the intertwinement may be stronger because legislatures usually have wide discretion to change the law – even if they still have to remain faithful to the underlying legal order in order to avoid contradictions and violations of constitutional principles and fundamental rights. In interactional law between citizens, the intertwinement may be strongest – they will often regard the law made in the capital as a mere décor against which they have to act out their moral-legal understandings of what the norms, implicit in their practice, require.[8] However, there is never full identity between law and morality or full separation. Even in the most formalist and positivist adjudication and bureaucratic implementation, there will still be the possibility for interpretation in which moral dimensions influence legal decisions. Interpretive discretion may be narrower the more black-letter law, in the form of rigid rules, is available – but it will never be completely absent.

This brings us to the third aspect which has to be taken into account to understand the variable connections between law and morality. This is not merely connected to law as an interactional practice or as an interpretive and argumentative practice, but also to law as a doctrine. The more important in legal doctrine ideals, principles, fundamental rights and open norms are, the more there is room for argument and interpretation.[9] These elements of law can only be understood in partly moral terms; in order to interpret these terms we must refer to morality.

This is what inclusive positivists have accepted, and in light of the increasing importance of general principles, fundamental rights and open norms in contemporary law, it is hard to defend a position which does not accept these as part of positive law. However, in order to remain faithful to the basic positivist idea that there is some form of separation between law and morality, inclusive positivists tend to contain these appeals to morality and construct morality as some objective order outside the law. Otherwise, morality would simply be a part of the law, which means that there is not a contingent but an essential relation between

---

7 See Alexy, *Theory of Constitutional Rights*, p. 58, arguing that the more weight is given to what he calls formal principles, the stronger the prima facie character of rules is. In a formalist system where rules have a very strong prima facie character, and thus cannot easily be trumped by principles, there is little intertwinement with morality, and less openness to dynamics.

8 See Witteveen, 'Alternatieve regulering'.

9 See Chapter 7.

law and morality.[10] Perhaps in extremely static and homogenous societies, we could treat moral doctrine as an objective social source on par with other social sources such as legislation and judicial decisions. We might refer to empirical studies about the moral beliefs of the citizens for appeals to social morality, or we might refer to ethical treatises and religious teachings for appeals to critical morality. We might also ask ethical experts or religious authorities to testify on the contents of morality. Nevertheless, even in homogenous societies, the validity of these appeals might fail because the issue would be how to interpret vague and internally contradictory precepts in those moral doctrines, which would reintroduce full moral argument in the interpretation of the law. However, the most important criticism against such a social source view of morality is that we do not live in that type of society. The notion that morality is an uncontroversial fact that can objectively be ascertained by judges is simply not acceptable any longer. If legal argument necessarily refers to morality, it must refer to moral arguments rather than to moral facts.[11]

This analysis thus leads to a Dworkinian position, which makes argumentation a core element of law in which moral and legal arguments are fused and can no longer be separated. Consequently, we can only regard the relationship between law and morality as one of intertwinement. Although the intensity of this intertwinement is contingent, the intertwinement itself is unavoidable and therefore necessary. The contingency refers to the variation in how important ideals, principles, fundamental rights and open norms are in positive law. However, even if their importance is minimal, there is no legal order without implicit use of those standards and without concepts such as *force majeure* or fairness. There is always a necessary connection to morality, even in the most positivist legal cultures. Thus the relationship between law and morality is both necessary and contingent.

The Relative Autonomy of the Law

The grounds for a relative autonomy of the law vis-à-vis morality are all connected with a process of differentiation of a specific legal order from other legal orders, and from society and morality. There is not one distinctive characteristic here that stands out, but a number of factors that mutually reinforce one another. The emphasis on formality and procedure, and the reliance on black-letter law and rigid rules are usually associated with legal institutions such as courts and legislatures and specialized legal professions with their own technical language. Underlying

---

10 For a largely similar critique of inclusive legal positivism see Taekema, *Concept of Ideals*, p. 212.

11 A similar argument has been made convincingly by Dworkin in his 'Reply to Critics' in *Taking Rights Seriously*, pp. 346–8 with regard to the soft positivism of Soper and Lyons. Dworkin remarks that their position is no longer positivist in the usual meaning of that term.

all these characteristics is the orientation of law towards distinctively legal ideals such as legality and justice. Even if a full separation can never exist (except in the minds of legal theorists) there can be a relatively strong autonomy if all those factors work in the same direction.

The first factor in the differentiation process is that legal practices are oriented towards the core ideals of legality and justice.[12] The ideal of legality is not part of ordinary morality (although some of the values constituting it are recognized in ordinary morality as well); it is a distinctively legal ideal. It is the basis for values and principles such as due process and the eight principles of legality. As a result of the orientation to legality, form and procedure become more important in the life of law, and vice versa. The central importance of form and procedure in the life of law reinforces the orientation towards legality. Justice is the second core ideal of law, but it is also a wider political and moral ideal.[13] Although in the context of law, the emphasis is usually on more formal interpretations of these values, such as procedural fairness and non-discrimination, they can never be completely dissociated from the more substantive interpretations such as moral equality – the idea that every person is entitled to equal concern and respect. In so far as the law restricts itself to the more formal values of justice, it retains its autonomy; in so far as the law is also oriented towards more substantive values which law shares with politics and morality, it partly loses its distinctive character.[14]

Certainly, legality and justice are not the only ideals that are relevant in law. We may discern three categories of ideals. The first category is that of distinctively legal ideals – ideals that are internal to the law. Legality and justice are distinctively legal ideals; they encompass a number of legal values such as due process, legal certainty and equality before the law. The second category consists of those ideals that have been incorporated in law in such a way that a specific legal order cannot be understood without it. They have become internalized, part of the identity of law, although they are certainly not a core ideal in every legal order. At the same time, their incorporation in the legal order has also coloured them in specific ways. Two examples of these types of ideals are democracy and good governance. Even if the incorporation of democracy into legal orders goes back more than 2,000 years, it is clear that in most Western societies a more robust implementation only emerged during the last two and a half centuries. The legal implementation of good governance is of an even more recent date and is associated with the rise of administrative law. However, both ideals have become so strongly entrenched in the contemporary legal orders of Western states that we simply cannot understand

---

12 Selznick, 'Sociology and Natural Law'; Fuller, *Morality of Law*; Dworkin, *Justice in Robes*, pp. 171ff; Taekema, *Concept of Ideals*, p. 188.
13 For a more elaborate analysis of justice as a legal ideal, see Taekema, *Concept of Ideals*, pp. 191–4.
14 See Taekema, *Concept of Ideals*, p. 144: 'The ideal of legality is indeed supportive of the autonomy of the law, and the more it incorporates general social values the more open the law becomes.'

these legal orders without referring to the orientation towards those two ideals. In political theory, democracy and the rule of law are widely regarded as two interconnected ideals, two sides of the same coin – although, historically, they were clearly distinct ideals.[15] Indeed, they have become so strongly intertwined that, in our current interpretations, each refers to the other. When Fuller argues that the basic requirement of legality is open communication and a reciprocal relationship between legislature and citizens, he infuses legality with democracy. When we regard access to justice for citizens who feel that their rights have been violated as one of the elements of democracy, we similarly infuse legality in the ideal of democracy.

The third category of ideals is that of external, political ideals such as economic growth, solidarity and sustainable development. A culturally rich environment, good education, a good and affordable system of health care, and economic development are other examples of political ideals which influence the development of law. The law may serve these ideals, but it has not internalized them – they remain external to law. Law is merely an instrument in the service of those political ideals.

This ideal typical distinction between three categories of ideals provides a fruitful perspective on the relative autonomy of law. If a legal order is strongly oriented towards the internal ideal of legality, we may expect a strong level of autonomy. When a legal order is strongly oriented towards internalized ideals, there is more openness towards morality and politics; but we may still expect a relatively strong level of autonomy, as the internalization ensures that the legal order remains in charge. However, if external ideals dominate a legal practice, we may expect a weak level of autonomy, as law may easily become an instrument in the hands of the political leaders or of societal interests, or of both (the legislature in Berlusconi's Italy is an example of the latter).[16] The more strongly law is oriented towards its internal and internalized ideals, the more it is differentiated from both morality and politics.

A second factor in the differentiation process is the existence of distinctively legal procedures and institutions and, in connection with those institutions, the existence of legal professions.[17] Once these institutions have emerged they develop a life of their own, including specific procedures and formalities. Even though legislatures are, through their representative natures, still quite open to the indirect influence of social morality, they are also partly shielded from direct influence in many ways. Legislation often lags behind because of a certain built-in inertness in the applicable procedures. The tension in many countries between positive law and

---

15 See Habermas, 'Law and Morality'.

16 These three categories correspond with the three forms of law that Nonet and Selznick discern, in the order in which I have presented them: autonomous, responsive and repressive law. See Nonet and Selznick, *Law and Society in Transition*.

17 For the important role of the legal elite, with its own distinctive legal culture, in the relatively autonomous development of law, see Watson, *Evolution of Law*.

popular views on medical-ethical issues such as abortion and euthanasia are just an illustration of this phenomenon. Sometimes the law is more liberal, and sometimes it is the social morality that is more liberal; but it is clear that on many ethical controversies, statutory law does not simply reflect social morality. In Civil Law jurisdictions, the relative autonomy of courts may be much stronger, especially if a legal positivist culture is dominant, and statutory law is characterized by a reliance on strict rules rather than open norms. In those cases the dominant legal ideology, reflected in the doctrine, is simply to avoid explicit references to morality, unless there are specific statutory phrases that require courts to do so. In the old Common Law tradition, where a judge is expected to 'reflect and distil moral experience'[18] as embodied in the collective practices of society, the continuity between law and morality is much more powerful, at least in that part of adjudication which is to be regarded as common law rather than as statutory interpretation. In fact, the adjudication then builds on interactional law, which means that the strong intertwinement of law and morality in interactional law is also incorporated in the legal order. What is important to note from these examples is that there is not only variation in the intensity of the intertwinement and the extent of the relative autonomy, but also that the connections between law and morality may be qualitatively different. There are various methods through which legal orders regulate their interactions with morality, ranging from direct input through voting, to indirect incorporation through legal argument, and to formalistic attempts to close law off from morality. It is not a matter of a simple continuum between almost complete autonomy and almost complete intertwinement.

The third differentiating factor is the existence of enacted law or, more generally, the reliance on black-letter law. Especially when black-letter law is formulated in terms of rigid rules, it is often largely separated from morality. However, it is never completely separated, as we saw in the previous sections. This is, first, because individuated rules do not exist as isolated atoms. Instead, they are part of a legal order in which principles and ideals, but also vague clauses such as *force majeure* or equity, always play a role and, thus, the windows to morality remain open. Second, there is not a complete separation between black-letter law and morality because even the legal order based on black-letter law is always connected with the underlying interactional law. Nevertheless, it is in examining enacted law that we may find it easiest to present law as if it were closed off from morality – though we should always bear in mind that this is only a construction.

The fourth factor in the differentiating process arises out of the culmination of the previous three factors, but also reinforces them. It is that law tends to develop a technical language of its own. The longer a legal order exists and is recreated in legal institutions, with the help of the legal profession, the stronger this language tends to diverge from ordinary language. There are often good reasons for this, as ordinary language is imprecise and ambiguous. Attempts to draft statutes, wills or contracts in ordinary language (or translate them into a minority language without

---

18 Cotterrell, 'Common Law Approaches', p. 12.

a written legal tradition), therefore, will usually not completely succeed, as there is a reason why these technical terms have emerged in the way they have.[19] Even to lawyers, some legal phrases may seem outdated; yet they are often (although certainly not always) indispensable. This has led to a specific legal structuring of normative issues which may not always correspond with the way normative issues are discussed in moral debates.

These four factors are important in understanding to what degree, and in which ways, law is relatively autonomous vis-à-vis morality. However, this leaves us with the question as to how we should interpret this vague concept 'autonomy'. Is it like the autonomy of regions within a larger state, or is it like the autonomy of a citizen in relation to other citizens? Is law merely a specific subcategory of morality, and are legal arguments merely a subcategory of moral arguments?

The idea that law is merely a subcategory of morality[20] fails to take the distinctive character of law sufficiently seriously. In a product model of law this idea must be rejected outright, as many instrumental legal rules – such as traffic rules or tax rules – are normative (they prescribe or prohibit behaviour) but are not moral. Even in a practice model of law, when we focus on law as an argumentative and discursive practice, it is inadequate. The idea that law is merely a subcategory of morality ignores the fact that law has two basic sources: interactional law and enacted law. Law is both argument and power, or, in Fuller's terms, reason and fiat.[21] Once law has come into existence, it has a life of its own. It is like the offspring of two parents. Indeed, although every child owes its genes to its parents, its character cannot be reduced to these genes as, after conception, and even more so after birth, the child's interaction with its environment provides a formative experience. This life experience influences the child's personality, which is distinct, even, from that of an identical twin sibling.

Similarly, a legal order has two main sources, enacted law and interactional law, though it cannot be reduced to these sources. The precise mix of interactional law and enacted law is unique to a legal order and is continuously evolving as a result of the continuous interaction with the social environment. In this process, the legal order also develops some characteristics which make it distinctively legal

---

19 Cf. Fuller, *Morality of Law*, p. 45.

20 An idea which has been defended by various authors, for example, by Ronald Dworkin in his recent work *Justice for Hedgehogs*, p. 405; Beyleveld and Brownsword, *Law as Moral Judgment*, p. 119.

21 Fuller, 'Reason and Fiat'; see Alexy, 'Dual Nature of Law'. This dimension of power is present both in the creation of law, for example, by legal authorities, and in its application to reality. See also Cotterrell's analysis of *voluntas* and *ratio* as interdependent elements in legal doctrine (*Law's Community*, p. 319). For a similar critique regarding the practical implications of law, see Smith, *Law's Quandary*, p. 70: 'modern accounts that identify law with legal discourse, by virtue of that very identification, systematically distort and overlook law's distinctive discursive character'.

and which differentiate it from other normative orders.[22] Although there is often a strong intertwinement between a given legal order and morality, the legal order also maintains a relative autonomy.

Legal Interactionism as a Synthesis between Natural Law and Legal Positivism

We may summarize the preceding analysis: law is always partly intertwined with morality and partly relatively autonomous, and the mix of intertwinement and relative autonomy varies. The stronger the reliance on interactional law, the stronger the emphasis on law as an argumentative and discursive practice; and the stronger the orientation towards principles, ideals and open norms, the stronger the intertwinement between law and morality will be. The more the law is oriented towards distinctively legal ideals, recognizes legal procedures, institutions and professions, relies on black-letter law and rigidly formulated rules and uses a technical language, the more it will be relatively autonomous.

The relationship between law and morality is one of the core controversies in the debate between natural law and legal positivism. The debate usually centres on three themes. The first is whether law and morality can be separated; in the first section of this chapter, I have already argued that they cannot, because they are always partly intertwined. The second is whether the relationship between law and morality is merely contingent or necessary. The third (which I will discuss in the following section) is whether law, as an institution, has moral value or is morally neutral. In the remainder of this chapter I will show that on both latter themes legal interactionism is a third theory which tries to do justice to the valuable insights of both legal positivism and natural law theory.

The second theme is whether the connection between law and morality is necessary or contingent. Legal interactionism argues that it is both. On the one hand, it is necessary, although not so much in a conceptual sense as in an empirical sense.[23] Legal interactionism holds that in reality no legal order can be fully separated from morality and, consequently, that the connection between

---

22 In Chapter 5, I argued that the search for universal distinctively legal characteristics is misguided. In line with this analysis, my discussion of distinctively legal ideals, procedures and other characteristics should be understood as referring to (usually fairly general) characteristics that are distinctive for some legal orders, but not necessarily for all.

23 The distinction between these two senses seems to underlie Hart's emphatic rejection of a necessary connection between law and morality. Hart accepts that the minimum content of natural law and the need for sanctions are a 'natural necessity'; similarly, he accepts the principles of natural justice and legality as having at least some normative implications (*Concept of Law*, p. 199 and p. 207). Thus, he does not deny empirical necessary connections; he merely seems to deny the much stronger claim that these connections are conceptual necessities. However, hardly any contemporary natural lawyers defend this stronger claim.

law and morality is necessary.²⁴ On the other hand, it holds that the relationship is empirically variable and, therefore, contingent because the degree and form of intertwinement are variable.²⁵ There is not one universal sense in which law is always connected with morality, but there may be a variety of ways in which it is more or less closely connected.

This interactionist idea is central to the work of Selznick and Fuller (especially in his book *Anatomy of the Law*). Both authors try to do justice to the valuable insights of natural law and legal positivism. Indeed, legal interactionism, building on the work of those two authors, may be regarded as a synthesis between both philosophical traditions.²⁶ It includes and explains the positivist idea that law can sometimes fruitfully be constructed as separate from morality, and it explains under which conditions such a positivist construction may be largely adequate. At the same time, it does justice to the valuable insight of natural law: that law and morality are connected – even though it argues that these connections are variable and dynamic rather than conceptual.

The central idea behind legal interactionism is that the relationship between law and morality is not to be analysed at a conceptual, but at an empirical level.²⁷ Once we accept this basic premise, it easily follows that the relationship is necessarily variable and dynamic. If we regard the relationship between law and morality in this way, then we are in a position to do justice to more substantive claims of natural law. Fuller's most controversial suggestion was that his 'internal morality of law' was morality rather than mere expediency.²⁸ Selznick's most problematic thesis is that he connects his 'legal naturalism' to a specific view of human nature, which he

---

24   However, phrasing this relationship in terms of a 'necessary connection' or a 'natural necessity' seems to me to be not fully adequate, as it might suggest some empirical generalization about how two distinct phenomena must always hang together. Perhaps, we should rather regard it as an epistemological necessity: we cannot distinguish them completely, because they intertwine.

25   Alexy, *Argument from Injustice*, p. 26 makes a distinction between classifying and qualifying connections between law and morality. Legal interactionism holds that the connection is a qualifying one: a legal order can be a legal order and yet be partly legally defective if it does not fully meet certain standards, such as the principles of legality. The aspirational and gradual character of law is the main reason why the connection is qualifying rather than dichotomous and classifying.

26   However, legal interactionism, as I construct it in this book, differs from both theories on one essential point: it does not accept the universalistic claims of both authors with regard to human nature (Selznick) and law (Fuller). Legal interactionism is, instead, more consistently pluralist, pragmatist and contextualist.

27   See Rundle, *Forms Liberate*, p. 4: 'at no point in his writings does Fuller claim any necessary conceptual connection between the two'. For a similar interpretation of Fuller as making general empirical claims, see Brudney, 'Two Links'.

28   On this claim, see Rundle, *Forms Liberate*.

considers to be, at least in some respects, universal.[29] Similar claims to universality can be found in classic and modern versions of substantive natural law. It is this universalistic pretention that makes these theses so problematic. Moreover, they are inconsistent with the basic contextualist and pragmatist leanings of both Fuller and Selznick. Legal interactionism holds that neither of these claims can be regarded as universal, but that does not exclude the possibility that they are contingent, yet general. In this way, legal interactionism opens up a productive perspective for the purpose of reconstructing the substantive ideas of natural law.

In Chapter 5, I argued that none of the usual distinctive characteristics of legal positivist definitions of law could be regarded as universally valid. Such definitions involve, for example, the association with authority or with force and sanctions, and the existence of secondary rules. Yet, in those orders where these characteristics are present we must pay attention to them because they are characteristics that are relevant to that specific legal order. In fact, most of the suggested defining characteristics of law, though not universal, are fairly general. By replacing the search for universal characteristics of law with a search for both relatively general and particular characteristics, and by analysing whether and in which respects these characteristics are present, we can transform the conceptual theses about necessary characteristics of law into empirical research questions.

A similar strategy can be used with regard to natural law's search for universal connections between law and morality. There is a necessary intertwinement between law and morality, but there is variation in the degree and form of this intertwinement. Therefore, beyond this very abstract statement with regard to the connection, there can be no universal statements about the form this connection may take. However, this does not exclude fairly general statements about the connections that may hold for a group of largely similar legal orders. Many of the ideas that have been suggested by natural law theorists are, indeed, of a fairly general application. They are important aspects of law in so far as they are present in specific legal orders. Therefore, we should replace the search for universal connections between law and morality with a search for both relatively general and relatively particular connections between law and morality. In this way we can transform the naturalist theses into empirical research questions. The interesting question is not a conceptual one but an empirical one. The question should be how strongly they are intertwined in a specific legal order, and in what ways.

The Moral Value of Law

A third theme in the debate between natural law and legal positivism is whether law has an inherent moral value, or whether its existence is strictly morally neutral. As legal interactionism eschews essentialism and conceptual connections between

---

29 For a similar criticism on Selznick's view of human nature, see Taekema, *Concept of Ideals*, p. 152.

law and morality, we might be tempted to side with the positivist camp and hold that there is no inherent moral quality to law. Indeed, as a baseline, there is an important core of truth in the positivist position. As law has no inherent essential nature and is a variable phenomenon, and as dictators often use law as an instrument for evil purposes, it is obvious that the existence of law is, indeed, compatible with a highly immoral character. That is the truism in legal positivism.[30]

However, that is not all that can be said. There is a core of truth in natural law thinking that should be taken into account as well. Even if there is no necessary or inherent moral quality of law, there are fairly general contingent characteristics that may promote the moral quality of law. These are to be found in the inherent ideals embedded in the practice of law, which can only be understood against the background of how law is supposed to function in society. These ideals are not always realized; they can be merely latent in law. However, in order to function adequately, law must at least realize them in part.[31]

We should start, then, with how law can function in a society and what this implies about its moral quality. Why should we have an institution such as law at all? Why should citizens be expected to abide by its norms in the first place? The answer to these questions can be found, in part, and perhaps surprisingly, in H.L.A. Hart's argument for the minimum content of natural law.[32] Hart's argument is that if law would not advance the minimum purpose of survival, human beings would have no reason to voluntarily obey any rules, and the law could not function. Therefore, a legal order should, at minimum, contain rules protecting persons, property and promises.[33] This is the minimum moral content of every legal order in a democratic society: if it does not guarantee these things, it will not be able to command obedience in the long run.[34]

Yet, Hart is mistaken when he claims that legal orders that do not embody this minimum cannot exist. In the past century, we have witnessed many regimes of terror that were able to obtain the voluntary obedience of at least a part of the population. In these regimes, the law was an effective instrument for terror, and even Hart's minimum moral content of natural law was not respected. Hart argues that his argument is not conceptual but, instead, contingent on human nature as we know it. His claim is what we might call universally contingent – it

---

30   However, this truism is not distinctive for legal positivism, because it is shared by most of its opponents: 'Concerns about the status of unjust laws do not separate positivists from the other theorists who say they reject legal positivism.' Greenawalt, 'Too Thin and Too Rich', p. 11.

31   This pragmatist analysis of the role of ideals in law is strongly inspired by Taekema, *Concept of Ideals*.

32   Hart, *Concept of Law*, p. 193.

33   Hart, *Concept of Law*, p. 199.

34   A similar, but richer and stronger argument is made by MacCormick, *Institutions of Law*, Chapter 15. In his 'post-positivist' theory, this minimum includes entrenched and justiciable human rights (p. 277).

holds true for all human societies, with human nature as the constant variable.[35] In light of the counterevidence, his claim must be rejected as too extreme and too essentialist. Hart's argument about the minimal content of natural law also presupposes a specific type of society, as it is not appropriate for all societies. Therefore, the most we can aspire to is a general contingent theory of human society and human nature, a theory that applies to a fairly broad category of contexts. This is not a problem for interactionists, who accept that legal interactionism is only a fairly general, but not universal, theory. Hart's argument simply does not provide a universal minimal content of law, but only a fairly general minimal content.

Even so, the argument for a minimal content of natural law is not only more restricted, but also more potent than Hart had suggested. After all, why would the guarantee of survival alone be enough to provide citizens with reasons to voluntarily obey the law? Perhaps in a Hobbesian state of nature this might be enough, but in the context of democratic Western societies, citizens may and, in fact, do expect more than the guarantee of plain survival. Most importantly, to command obedience, the state must respect its citizens as autonomous persons. In fact, it is on this precise point that Lon Fuller is emphatically critical of Hart's theory.[36] He argues that, in order to command voluntary obedience, law must be based on a relationship of reciprocity between legal authorities and citizens.[37] Indeed, Fuller has a broader understanding of what is required for law to function adequately in an open and free society. His eight principles of legality are rooted in a much wider reciprocal relationship between the legislator and his subjects.

Fuller's account of legality can, thus, be interpreted as built on a similar notion to that of Hart's minimal content of natural law. It is the notion that law can only function well if it embodies certain moral ideals that it realizes, at least in part.[38] Whereas Hart restricts this to the minimal ideal of survival in a Hobbesian state of nature, Fuller has a richer conception, which might be regarded as Lockean in nature. Fuller's conception presupposes not a brutal state of nature, but a relatively well-ordered, open and minimally democratic society. In such a context, law can only function well if it is based on a reciprocal relationship between legal institutions and citizens. This reciprocal relationship should not only be based on the minimum, but should also bear the promise of more. It should, therefore, both meet the minimum requirements of legality and aspire to the fuller realization of the ideal of legality. Only if law has this dual nature may we expect it to function well in a modern democratic society.

---

35 Hart, *Concept of Law*, p. 199 uses the phrase 'natural necessity'.

36 Fuller, *Morality of Law*, pp. 184–6. See Rundle, *Forms Liberate, passim*.

37 I focus in the next two pages on state law, but, as I will discuss at the end of this section, a similar analysis might hold for non-state legal orders.

38 For this view on ideals see Taekema, *Concept of Ideals*, p. 178: 'They are inherent to social practices, meaning not that they are necessarily part of such practices but they are indispensable for the good functioning of a practice.'

As I have discussed the principles of legality extensively above, I will not go into further detail about them here. It is necessary to note, however, that even if the principles of legality are only realized to a very limited degree, at least some reduction of arbitrariness and some transparency will follow from principles such as generality and publicity.[39] The principle that law should be publicized (and usually even formulated into black-letter law) provides not only for transparency, but also creates an opportunity for critical discussion.[40] The principle of generality excludes some arbitrariness – although certainly not all – and it points to the formal principle of equality before the law. Therefore, even in a minimal form, the orientation towards legality would already imply a minimal moral quality of the law.[41] However, we should take a broader perspective than this; otherwise we will miss the central idea behind Fuller's theory. We should interpret these principles not as separate minimal requirements, but as a mutually dependent, and sometimes conflicting, set and, further, interpret them in light of their underlying ideal. This set of principles is necessary in order to maintain an open, reciprocal relationship between legislator and subjects. If we take this broader view, we can observe a much stronger moral quality of law as a result of its association with the ideal of legality.

We can now also understand how Hart's argument about human survival can be expanded upon. Here, as well, law should both guarantee the minimum and aspire to a fuller realization of the ideal of human flourishing.[42] Moreover, in connection with the human minimum of bare survival, we might add the legal minimum of constituting order, associated with the broader ideal of a legal order, an order built on the rule of law. The minimum of bare survival already provides for a minimal moral quality of law, but the aspiration to the fuller ideal provides for the promise of a higher quality.[43] A similar analysis can be made for the internal and internalized ideals of law. They are, at least partly, realized in legal orders in Western democratic societies, and they bear the promise of a fuller realization. Even at a minimal degree of realization, they already provide for some moral quality of the law; but in their potential for further implementation, they offer the promise of an even higher quality.

Perhaps, this sounds circular: law is good because it incorporates good values such as legality, justice and democracy. However, it is not a simple circular

---

39   For similar views see, for example, Raz, 'The Rule of Law and its Virtue', in *Authority of Law*; MacCormick, 'Natural Law and Separation' (less minimal than Raz).

40   Peters, 'Law as Critical Discussion'.

41   This is a prima facie statement; of course, in other respects a legal order may be so grossly unjust that the overall evaluation of law is a negative one.

42   See Selznick, *Moral Commonwealth*, p. 38 and pp. 443–5.

43   For our purposes, we can simply leave aside the question of whether the principles of legality should be called a 'morality' or not; it is not very important what we call them. Most important is that they are morally relevant in the sense that they promote the moral quality of the law.

argument, but a pragmatist one.[44] Law is a relatively autonomous practice, embedded in a wider network of other practices by which it is influenced, just as it influences those practices in turn. In Western democracies, we may discern various ideals that are essential for understanding the practice of law; each of them contributes to a higher moral quality of the law. They are contingent in the sense that the connection to those specific ideals is not a conceptual necessity or a universal tendency. Yet, they are generally contingent in the sense that, in so far as the law exists in the context of those democracies, the orientation towards certain ideals is an important characteristic of law and, thus, contributes to its moral quality. Moreover, some of these ideals need to be at least partly realized in order to make it possible for a legal order to function at all.

Both the minimum realization and the promise of a fuller implementation contribute to a higher quality of law.[45] Survival and order only point to the absolute minimum which should be present in every legal order in order to command a minimum level of voluntary cooperation; yet they also embody the promise of a legal order that promotes human flourishing. The internal ideals of law, in particular legality and justice, are associated with many procedural and formal values such as legal certainty and due process, and with more substantive values such as equal concern and respect. The internalized ideals of law – such as democracy, human rights and good governance – have become so much a part of some legal orders that those orders cannot be understood without also taking those ideals into account. Each of these ideals is partly latent, partly realized, and the degree of realization may vary.[46] Yet, the fact that they are intrinsically connected with the law, both as critical standards and in their partial realization, may contribute to an improved quality. There is a potential for further realization, which cannot be ignored, and this inevitably creates a potential for a further momentum towards an even greater realization of those ideals.[47] It is at this potential that Ronald Dworkin hints when he talks about the law working itself pure.[48] There is a minimum of realization and a promise of progressive interpretation.[49] It is this dual nature of law which provides for a necessary yet contingent moral quality of law in Western democracies.

---

44 In the end, circularity in pragmatism cannot be solved but merely alleviated: see Taekema, *Concept of Ideals*, p. 177; Coleman, *Practice of Principle*, p. 55.

45 Krygier, *Philip Selznick*, p. 29 emphasizes that Selznick's overarching preoccupation was with (quoting Selznick) 'the conditions and processes that frustrate ideals, or instead, give them life and hope'. Krygier adds 'The sequence of its elements is also significant: first, what *frustrates* ideals, then what gives them life and hope' (italics in original).

46 See Selznick, *Moral Commonwealth*, p. 444: 'There is *inclination* but not *necessity*' (italics in original).

47 Selznick, 'Sociology and Natural Law', p. 90 argues that normative systems have a 'natural potential for "envaluation"'.

48 Dworkin, *Law's Empire*, p. 407.

49 Selznick, *Moral Commonwealth*, p. 443: 'Law is not necessarily just, but it does promise justice.'

So far my discussion has focused implicitly on state law, but similar (even if not fully identical) arguments can be made with regard to other legal orders.[50] For every legal order it is important to understand the way it functions in the specific context in which it has emerged, and what functional requirements follow from that. These requirements need not be the same as those associated with state law and, therefore, the internal morality of such legal orders may differ as well. Very limited legal orders, such as the internal law of an association, need not guarantee the purpose of survival, as they can leave that to other legal orders; but, at the very least, these legal orders should not violate this purpose either. The requirements of legality may take various forms and may consist of different sets of principles. After all, Fuller's eight principles of legality are associated with the practice of legislation, whereas other mechanisms of social order have, according to Fuller, a different internal morality. However, the ideal of legality in the minimal sense of progressive reduction of arbitrariness and of providing some form of legal certainty is common to all forms. As they are all part of a broader network of legal orders, practices and society at large, they mutually influence one another.

This brings me to one last remark. Law does not exist in a societal void. This holds true for state law as well as for other legal orders, such as the internal law of churches and industrial organizations. I have argued from the beginning that legal interactionism is developed in this book as a contextual theory against the background of Western democratic societies that embrace the rule of law. That means that ideals such as democracy and equal respect and concern are part of the background culture and are at least partly inherent in the state legal order. As soon as another legal order emerges – whether it be at the international level of international law, the transnational level of companies or at the subnational level – it is influenced by these background understandings and it incorporates them, at least in part. In the internal dynamic of a legal order, these ideals and background understandings will also influence the interpretation and continuous reconstruction of the law of that non-state legal order.

In so far as these legal orders do not explicitly accept general ideals such as democracy, transparency or equality, this may lead to tensions and pressure to reform. A good example of this may be found in industrial relations, where Selznick saw the emergence of values of legality in the industrial context.[51] A similar example can be found in some traditional churches, which are under continual pressure from the broader society to accept general ideals such as democracy and liberalism or more specific ideals such as equal rights for women and equal recognition of same-sex relationships. For example, the problems of the Roman Catholic Church in a democratic context have become most clear to the general

---

50 Selznick, *Law, Society and Industrial Justice*.

51 The influence, however, is a two-way process. Many political discussions on the state are now phrased in economic terms such as consumers and clients, efficiency and cost-benefit analysis. This also results in a tension between values of legality, justice and economic values in the context of state law.

public in the wake of the various child abuse scandals and the inept handling of them by the church authorities. But there is a more fundamental problem under the surface here. These incidents point to a deeper tension between, on the one hand, a church with an authoritarian structure and an illiberal moral theology and, on the other hand, a society which is oriented towards liberal ideals of democracy, transparency, equality and autonomy.

To repeat: legal interactionism is thoroughly contextualist. That may exclude claims of universalism, but it need not exclude a search for the contingently general. Law cannot be separated from morality and, in this sense, there is a necessary intertwinement of law and morality; yet the degree of intertwinement and the form it takes are variable and, thus, contingent. Law is oriented towards certain ideals which are inherent in legal practice and which promote the moral quality of law. We might say that there is a certain potential, but the degree of realization is, again, contingent. Legal interactionism, with its roots in pragmatism, thus offers a perspective on doing justice to the core of truth in both legal positivism and natural law.

References

Ahdieh, Robert B., 'Between Dialogue and Decree. International Review of National Courts', *New York University Law Review*, 79 (2004), pp. 2029–63.
Alexy, Robert, *The Argument from Injustice. A Reply to Legal Positivism*, Oxford: Oxford University Press 2002.
Alexy, Robert, *A Theory of Constitutional Rights*, Oxford: Oxford University Press 2002.
Alexy, Robert, 'The Dual Nature of Law', *Ratio Juris*, 23 (2010), pp. 167–82.
Annas, George J., *American Bioethics. Crossing Human Rights and Health Law Boundaries*, Oxford: Oxford University Press 2005.
Beauchamp, Tom L. and Childress, James F., *Principles of Biomedical Ethics*, New York: Oxford University Press 1994 (fourth edition).
Berman, Paul S., 'Global Legal Pluralism', *South California Law Review*, 80 (2007), pp. 1155–1238.
Beyleveld, Deryck and Brownsword, Roger, *Law as a Moral Judgment*, Sheffield: Sheffield Academic Press 1994.
Blok, Peter, 'The Ideal of Data Privacy and the Development of Law', in: Wibren van der Burg and Sanne Taekema (eds), *The Importance of Ideals. Debating Their Relevance in Law, Morality, and Politics*, Brussels: Peter Lang 2004, pp. 219–30.
Braithwaite, John, *Regulatory Capitalism. How it Works, Ideas for Making it Work Better*, Cheltenham: Edward Elgar 2008.
Brom, Frans W.A., Vorstenbosch, Jan and Schroten, Egbert, 'Public Policy and Transgenic Animals. Case-by-Case Assessment as a Moral Learning Process', in: Peter Wheale, René von Schomberg and Peter Glasner (eds), *The Social Management of Biotechnology*, Aldershot: Ashgate 1998, pp. 249–63.
Brudney, Daniel, 'Two Links of Law and Morality', *Ethics* 103 (1993), pp. 280–301.
Brunnée, Jutta and Toope, Stephen John, *Legitimacy and Legality in International Law. An Interactional Account*, Cambridge: Cambridge University Press 2010.
Burke, Kenneth, *A Grammar of Motives*, Berkeley: University of California Press 1969 [1945].
Buruma, Ybo, 'Dutch Tolerance: On Drugs, Prostitution and Euthanasia', in: Sanne Taekema, Annie de Roo and Carinne Elion-Valter (eds), *Understanding Dutch Law*, The Hague: Eleven International Publishing 2011, pp. 205–43.
Cane, Peter, *Responsibility in Law and Morality*, Oxford: Hart Publishing 2002.
Cane, Peter, 'Morality, Law and Conflicting Reasons for Action', *Cambridge Law Journal*, 71 (2012), pp. 59–85.

Cane, Peter (ed.), *The Hart–Fuller Debate in the Twenty-First Century*, Oxford: Hart Publishing 2010.

Clouser, K. Danner and Kopelman, Loretta M., 'Philosophical Critique of Bioethics: Introduction to the Issue', *Journal of Medicine and Philosophy*, 15 (1990), pp. 121–2.

Coglianese, Cary, 'Does Consensus Work? A Pragmatic Approach to Public Participation in the Regulatory Process', in: Alfonso Morales (ed.), *Renascent Pragmatism. Studies in Law and Social Science*, Aldershot: Ashgate 2003, pp. 180–95.

Coleman, Jules, *The Practice of Principle. In Defence of a Pragmatist Approach to Legal Theory*, Oxford: Oxford University Press 2001.

Cotterrell, Roger, *Law's Community. Legal Theory in Sociological Perspective*, Oxford: Clarendon 1995.

Cotterrell, Roger, 'Why Must Legal Ideas be Interpreted Sociologically?', *Journal of Law and Society*, 25 (1998), pp. 171–92.

Cotterrell, Roger, 'Common Law Approaches to the Relationship between Law and Morality', *Ethical Theory and Moral Practice*, 3 (2000), pp. 9–26.

Cotterrell, Roger, *The Politics of Jurisprudence. A Critical Introduction to Legal Philosophy*, London and Edinburgh: LexisNexis 2003.

Davies, Margaret, 'The Politics of Defining Law', in: Peter Cane (ed.), *The Hart–Fuller Debate in the Twenty-First Century*, Oxford: Hart Publishing 2010, pp. 157–67.

Den Hartogh, Govert, 'Soziale und kritische Moral oder Wie sich "Protestantismus" in der Moralphilosophie und der Moralerziehung vermeiden lässt', in: Karl Golser and Robert Heeger (eds), *Moralerziehung im neuen Europa*, Brixen: Verlag A. Weger 1996, pp. 53–73.

Devlin, Patrick, *The Enforcement of Morals*, Oxford/London/New York: Oxford University Press 1965.

Dewey, John, 'My Philosophy of Law', in: *My Philosophy of Law. Credos of Sixteen American Scholars*, Boston, Mass.: Boston Law Book 1941, pp. 73–85.

Dickson, Julie, *Evaluation and Legal Theory*, Oxford and Portland, OR: Hart Publishing 2001.

Dworkin, Ronald, *Taking Rights Seriously*, Cambridge, Mass.: Harvard University Press 1978 [1977].

Dworkin, Ronald, 'Natural Law Revisited', *University of Florida Law Review*, 34 (1982), pp. 165–88.

Dworkin, Ronald, *Law's Empire*, London: Fontana 1986.

Dworkin, Ronald, *Justice in Robes*, Cambridge, Mass.: Belknap Press 2006.

Dworkin, Ronald, *Justice for Hedgehogs*. Cambridge, Mass.: Belknap Press 2011.

Ehrlich, Eugen, *Fundamental Principles of the Sociology of Law* (transl. W.L. Moll), New Brunswick: Transaction Publishers 2002 (orig. English transl. 1936 [1913]).

Finnis, John, *Natural Law and Natural Rights*, Oxford: Clarendon 1980.

Frankena, William K., *Ethics*, Englewood Cliffs: Prentice-Hall 1973.

Freeman, Michael (ed.), *Law and Bioethics*, Oxford: Oxford University Press 2008.
Fuller, Lon L., 'Reason and Fiat in Case Law', *Harvard Law Review*, 59 (1946), pp. 376–95.
Fuller, Lon L., *The Morality of Law*, New Haven: Yale University Press 1969 [1964].
Fuller, Lon L., *Anatomy of the Law*, New York: Praeger 1968; Westport, Conn.: Greenwood Press 1976.
Fuller, Lon L., *The Principles of Social Order. Selected Essays of Lon L. Fuller* (edited by Kenneth I. Winston), Oxford: Hart Publishing 2001 [1981].
Gallie, Walter B., 'Essentially Contested Concepts', *Proceedings of the Aristotelian Society*, 56 (1956), pp. 167–98.
Gerards, Janneke, 'Pluralism, Deference and the Margin of Appreciation Doctrine', *European Law Journal*, 17 (2011), pp. 80–120.
Gert, Bernard, *Morality. A New Justification of the Moral Rules*, New York: Oxford University Press 1988.
Glendon, Mary Ann, *A Nation Under Lawyers*. Cambridge, Mass.: Harvard University Press 1994.
Greenawalt, Kent, 'Too Thin and Too Rich: Distinguishing Features of Legal Positivism', in: Robert P. George (ed.), *The Autonomy of Law. Essays on Legal Positivism*, Oxford: Clarendon 1996, pp. 1–29.
Griffiths, John, 'What is Legal Pluralism?', *Journal of Legal Pluralism*, 24 (1986), pp. 1–55.
Griffiths, John, Bood, Alex and Weyers, Heleen, *Euthanasia and Law in the Netherlands*, Amsterdam: Amsterdam University Press 1998.
Grotefeld, Stefan, 'Wie wird Moral ins Recht gesetzt?', *Archiv für Rechts- und Sozialphilosophie*, 89 (2003), pp. 299–317.
Habermas, Jürgen, 'Law and Morality', in: Sterling M. McMurrin (ed.), *The Tanner Lectures on Human Values VIII*, Salt Lake City: University of Utah Press 1988, pp. 217–79.
Hart, H.L.A., 'Positivism and the Separation of Law and Morals', *Harvard Law Review*, 71 (1958), pp. 593–629.
Hart, H.L.A., *The Concept of Law*, Oxford: Clarendon 1994 [1961].
Hart, H.L.A., *Law, Liberty and Morality*, Oxford: Oxford University Press 1963.
Hart, H.L.A., 'Book review of The Morality of Law', *Harvard Law Review*, 78 (1965), pp. 1281–95.
Heidenheimer, Arnold, 'Disjunctions Between Corruption and Democracy? A Qualitative Exploration', *Crime, Law and Social Change* 42 (2004), pp. 99–109.
Hirsi Ali, Ayaan, 'Open brief aan burgemeester Job Cohen', *Trouw*, 6 maart 2004.
Lord Hoffman, 'The Universality of Human Rights', Judicial Studies Board Annual Lecture 19 March 2009 (http://www.judiciary.gov.uk/media/speeches/2009/speech-lord-hoffman-19032009).

Ippel, Pieter, 'Gezondheidsrecht en gezondheidsethiek', in: Wibren van der Burg and Pieter Ippel (eds), *De Siamese tweeling. Recht en moraal in de biomedische praktijk*, Assen: Van Gorcum 1994, pp. 33–48.
Jackson, Sherman A., *Islamic Law and the State. The Constitutional Jurisprudence of Shihāb al-Dīn al-Qarāfī*, Leiden: Brill 1996.
Kelsen, Hans, *General Theory of Norms*, Oxford: Clarendon 1991.
Klabbers, Jan, 'Constitutionalism and the Making of International Law. Fuller's Procedural Natural Law', *No Foundations. Journal of Extreme Legal Positivism*, 5 (2008), pp. 84–112.
Koh, Harold Hongju, 'Transnational Legal Process', *Nebraska Law Review*, 75 (1996), pp. 181–207.
Krisch, Nico, *Beyond Constitutionalism. The Pluralist Structure of Postnational Law*, Oxford: Oxford University Press 2010.
Krisch, Nico, 'Book review of Legitimacy and Legality in International Law', *American Journal of International Law*, 106 (2012), pp. 203–9.
Krygier, Martin, 'Selznick's Subjects', in: Robert A. Kagan, Martin Krygier and Kenneth Winston (eds), *Legality and Community. On the Intellectual Legacy of Philip Selznick*, Lanham: Rowman & Littlefield 2002, pp. 3–16.
Krygier, Martin, 'The Hart–Fuller Debate, Transitional Societies and the Rule of Law', in: Peter Cane (ed.), *The Hart–Fuller Debate in the Twenty-First Century*, Oxford: Hart Publishing 2010, pp. 107–34.
Krygier, Martin, *Philip Selznick. Ideals in the World*, Stanford: Stanford University Press 2012.
Lacey, Nicola, *A Life of H.L.A. Hart. The Nightmare and the Noble Dream*, Oxford: Oxford University Press 2004.
Lacey, Nicola, 'Out of the Witches' Cauldron? Reinterpreting the Context and Reassessing the Significance of the Hart–Fuller Debate', in: Peter Cane (ed.), *The Hart–Fuller Debate in the Twenty-First Century*, Oxford: Hart Publishing, 2010, pp. 1–42.
Leenen, Henk. J.J., 'Vijfentwintig jaar gezondheidsrecht', in: J.H. Hubben and H.D.C. Roscam Abbing (eds), *Gezondheidsrecht in Perspectief. 25 jaar Vereniging voor Gezondheidsrecht*, Utrecht: De Tijdstroom 1993, pp. 16–27.
Leiter, Brian, *Naturalizing Jurisprudence. Essays on American Legal Realism and Naturalism in Legal Philosophy*, Oxford: Oxford University Press 2007.
Leiter, Brian, 'The Demarcation Problem in Jurisprudence: A New Case for Skepticism', *Oxford Journal of Legal Studies*, 31 (2011), pp. 1–15.
Lesaffer, Randall, 'The Grotian Tradition Revisited. Change and Continuity in the History of International Law', *British Yearbook of International Law*, 73 (2002), pp. 103–39.
Lewis, David, 'Languages and Language', *Philosophical Papers*, New York: Oxford University Press 1983.
Lyons, David, *Moral Aspects of Legal Theory. Essays on Law, Justice, and Political Responsibility*, Cambridge: Cambridge University Press 1993.

Luban, David, 'Rediscovering Fuller's Legal Ethics', in: Willem J. Witteveen and Wibren van der Burg (eds), *Rediscovering Fuller. Essays on Implicit Law and Institutional Design*, Amsterdam: Amsterdam University Press 1999, pp. 193–225.

Macaulay, Stewart, 'Non-Contractual Relations in Business. A Preliminary Study', *American Sociological Review*, 28 (1963), pp. 55–67.

MacCormick, Neil, 'Natural Law and the Separation of Law and Morals', in: Robert P. George (ed.), *Natural Law Theory. Contemporary Essays*, Oxford: Clarendon 1992, pp. 105–33.

MacCormick, Neil, *Institutions of Law. An Essay in Legal Theory*, Oxford: Oxford University Press 2007.

Macdonald, Roderick A., 'Legislation and Governance', in: Willem J. Witteveen and Wibren van der Burg (eds), *Rediscovering Fuller. Essays on Implicit Law and Institutional Design*, Amsterdam: Amsterdam University Press 1999, pp. 279–311.

MacIntyre, Alasdair, *After Virtue*, Notre Dame: University of Notre Dame Press 1981.

Mackie, John, 'The Third Theory of Law', in: Marshall Cohen (ed.), *Ronald Dworkin and Contemporary Jurisprudence*, London: Duckworth 1984, pp. 161–70.

Mallat, Chibli, *Introduction to Middle Eastern Law*, Oxford: Oxford University Press 2007.

Mason, John Kenyon and McCall Smith, Alexander, *Law and Medical Ethics*, London: Butterworths 1994 (fourth edition).

Moore, Sally Falk, 'Law and Social Change: The Semi-Autonomous Social Field as an Appropriate Subject of Study', *Law and Society Review*, 7 (1973), pp. 719–46.

Nonet, Philippe and Selznick, Philip, *Law and Society in Transition. Toward Responsive Law*, New York: Harper & Row 1978.

Nussbaum, Martha, *Poetic Justice. The Literary Imagination and the Public Life*, Boston: Beacon Press 1995.

Olsen, Henrik Palmer and Toddington, Stuart, *Law in its Own Right*, Oxford: Hart Publishing 1999.

Olsen, Henrik Palmer and Toddington, Stuart, *Architectures of Justice. Legal Theory and the Idea of Institutional Design*, Aldershot: Ashgate 2007.

Osiander, Andreas, 'Sovereignty, International Relations, and the Westphalian Myth', *International Organization* 55 (2001), pp. 251–87.

Patterson, Dennis, *Law and Truth*, New York: Oxford University Press 1996.

Peters, Antonie A.G., 'Law as Critical Discussion', in: Gunther Teubner (ed.), *Dilemmas of Law in the Welfare State*, Berlin: De Gruyter 1986, pp. 250–79.

Poort, Lonneke M., *Consensus and Controversies in Animal Biotechnology. An Interactive Legislative Approach to Animal Biotechnology in Denmark, Switzerland, and the Netherlands*, The Hague: Eleven International Publishing 2013.

Posner, Richard A., *The Problematics of Moral and Legal Theory*, Cambridge, Mass.: Belknap Press 1999.

Postema, Gerald J., 'Implicit Law', in: Willem J. Witteveen and Wibren van der Burg (eds), *Rediscovering Fuller. Essays on Implicit Law and Institutional Design*, Amsterdam: Amsterdam University Press 1999, pp. 255–75.

Radbruch, Gustav, *Rechtsphilosophie* (edited by Erik Wolf and Hans-Peter Schneider), Stuttgart: K.F. Koehler 1973 [1932].

Rawls, John, *A Theory of Justice*, Cambridge, Mass.: Harvard University Press 1971.

Raz, Joseph, *The Concept of a Legal System. An Introduction to the Theory of Legal System*, Oxford: Clarendon 1970.

Raz, Joseph, *The Authority of Law. Essays on Law and Morality*, Oxford: Clarendon 1979.

Raz, Joseph, *Ethics in the Public Domain. Essays in the Morality of Law and Politics*, Oxford: Clarendon 1994.

Reus-Smit, Christian, 'Obligation through Practice', *International Theory*, 3 (2011), pp. 339–47.

Rhode, Deborah L., 'Legal Scholarship', *Harvard Law Review*, 115 (2002), pp. 1327–61.

Rokumoto, Kahei, 'Philip Selznick's Conception of Law and Legal Sociology', in: Robert A. Kagan, Martin Krygier and Kenneth Winston (eds), *Legality and Community. On the Intellectual Legacy of Philip Selznick*, Lanham: Rowman & Littlefield 2002, pp. 167–83.

Rothstein, Mark A., 'The Role of Law in the Development of American Bioethics', *Journal International de Bioéthique*, 20 (2009), pp. 73–84.

Rubin, Edward L., 'Law and Legislation in the Administrative State', *Columbia Law Review*, 89 (1989), pp. 369–426.

Rundle, Kristen, *Forms Liberate. Reclaiming the Jurisprudence of Lon L. Fuller*, Oxford: Hart Publishing 2012.

Ryle, Gilbert, *The Concept of Mind*, Chicago: University of Chicago Press 2000 [1949].

Santos, Boaventura de Sousa, *Toward a New Legal Common Sense. Law, Globalization, and Emancipation*, London and Edinburgh: Butterworths LexisNexis 2002.

Schauer, Frederick, 'On the Nature of the Nature of Law', *Archiv für Rechts- und Sozialphilosophie*, 98 (2012), pp. 457–67.

Schneider, Carl E., 'Bioethics in the Language of the Law', *Hastings Center Report*, 24 no. 4 (July–August 1994), pp. 16–22.

Scott, James C., *Seeing Like a State. How Certain Schemes to Improve the Human Condition Have Failed*, New Haven: Yale University Press 1998.

Selznick, Philip, 'Sociology and Natural Law', *Natural Law Forum*, 6 (1961), pp. 84–108.

Selznick, Philip, *Law, Society and Industrial Justice*, New York: Russell Sage Foundation 1969.

Selznick, Philip, 'Book review of *Anatomy of the Law*', *Harvard Law Review*, 83 (1969–70), pp. 1474–80.
Selznick, Philip, *The Moral Commonwealth. Social Theory and the Promise of Community*, Berkeley: University of California Press 1992.
Shapiro, Scott, *Legality*, Cambridge, Mass: Belknap Press 2011.
Shklar, Judith N., *Legalism. Law, Morals, and Political Trials*, Cambridge, Mass.: Harvard University Press 1964.
Singer, Peter, *Practical Ethics*, Cambridge: Cambridge University Press 1979.
Smith, Stephen D., *Law's Quandary*. Cambridge, Mass.: Harvard University Press 2004.
Sperling, Daniel, 'Law and Bioethics: A Rights-Based Relationship and Its Troubling Implications', in: Michael Freeman (ed.), *Law and Bioethics*, Oxford: Oxford University Press 2008, pp. 52–78.
Stamhuis, Jellienke, 'Communicative Law. A Quest for Consensus', in: Nicolle Zeegers, Willem Witteveen and Bart van Klink (eds), *Social and Symbolic Effects of Legislation under the Rule of Law*, Lewiston, NY: Edwin Mellen Press 2004, pp. 277–97.
Taekema, Sanne, *The Concept of Ideals in Legal Theory*, The Hague: Kluwer Law International 2003.
Taekema, Sanne, 'Introducing Dutch Law', in: Sanne Taekema, Annie de Roo and Carinne Elion-Valter (eds), *Understanding Dutch Law*, The Hague: Eleven International Publishing 2011, pp. 17–33.
Taekema, Sanne, 'Relative Autonomy. A Characterisation of the Discipline of Law', in: Bart van Klink and Sanne Taekema (eds), *Law and Method. Interdisciplinary Research into Law*, Tübingen: Mohr Siebeck 2011, pp. 33–52.
Taekema, Sanne and Van Klink, Bart, 'On the Border. Limits and Possibilities of Interdisciplinary Research', in: Bart van Klink and Sanne Taekema (eds), *Law and Method. Interdisciplinary Research into Law*, Tübingen: Mohr Siebeck 2011, pp. 7–32.
Tamanaha, Brian Z., *Realistic Socio-Legal Theory. Pragmatism and a Social Theory of Law*, Oxford: Clarendon 1997.
Tamanaha, Brian Z., *A General Jurisprudence of Law and Society*, New York and London: Oxford University Press 2001.
Trotter, Griffin, 'Genesis of a Totalizing Ideology: Bioethics' Inner Hippie', in: H. Tristram Engelhardt, Jr, (ed.) *Bioethics Critically Reconsidered. Having Second Thoughts*, Dordrecht: Springer 2012, pp. 49–70.
Twining, William, 'A Post-Westphalian Conception of Law. Review of *A General Jurisprudence of Law and Society* by Brian Tamanaha', *Law & Society Review*, 37 (2003), pp. 199–258.
Twining, William, *General Jurisprudence. Understanding Law from a Global Perspective*, Cambridge: Cambridge University Press 2009.
Van der Burg, Wibren, 'Bioethics and Law. A Developmental Perspective', *Bioethics*, 11 (1997), pp. 91–114.

Van der Burg, Wibren, 'Ideals and Ideal Theory. The Problem of Methodological Conservatism', in: Wibren van der Burg and Theo van Willigenburg (eds), *Reflective Equilibrium. Essays in Honour of Robert Heeger*, Dordrecht/Boston/London: Kluwer Academic Publishers 1998, p. 89–99.
Van der Burg, Wibren, 'Two Models of Law and Morality', *Associations*, 3 (1999), pp. 61–82.
Van der Burg, Wibren, 'The Expressive and the Communicative Functions of Law, *Law and Philosophy*, 20 (2001), pp. 31–59.
Van der Burg, Wibren, 'An Interactionist View on the Relation between Law and Morality', in: Wibren van der Burg and Sanne Taekema (eds), *The Importance of Ideals. Debating Their Relevance in Law, Morality, and Politics*, Brussels: Peter Lang 2004, pp. 197–218.
Van der Burg, Wibren, 'The Role of Ideals in Legal Dynamics', in: Arend Soeteman (ed.), *Pluralism and Law. Proceedings of the 20th IVR World Congress, Archiv für Rechts- und Sozialphilosophie*, Beiheft 91, Stuttgart: Franz Steiner 2004, pp. 28–33.
Van der Burg, Wibren, 'The Irony of a Symbolic Crusade. The Debate on Opening up Civil Marriage to Same-Sex Couples', in: Nicolle Zeegers, Willem Witteveen and Bart van Klink (eds), *Social and Symbolic Effects of Legislation Under the Rule of Law*, Lewiston, NY: Edwin Mellen Press 2005, pp. 245–75.
Van der Burg, Wibren, 'Essentially Ambiguous Concepts and the Fuller-Hart-Dworkin Debate', *Archiv für Rechts- und Sozialphilosophie*, 95 (2009), pp. 305–26.
Van der Burg, Wibren, 'Law and Ethics. The Twin Disciplines', in: Bart van Klink and Sanne Taekema (eds), *Law and Method*, Tübingen: Mohr Siebeck 2011, pp. 175–94.
Van der Burg, Wibren, 'The Work of Lon Fuller: A Promising Direction for Jurisprudence in the 21st Century', *University of Toronto Law Journal* (forthcoming).
Van der Burg, Wibren and Brom, Frans W.A., 'Legislation on Ethical Issues. Towards an Interactive Paradigm', *Ethical Theory and Moral Practice*, 3 (2000), pp. 57–75.
Van der Burg, Wibren and Taekema, Sanne (eds), *The Importance of Ideals. Debating Their Relevance in Law, Morality, and Politics*, Brussels: Peter Lang 2004.
Van der Burg, Wibren and Van Willigenburg, Theo (eds), *Reflective Equilibrium. Essays in Honour of Robert Heeger*, Dordrecht/Boston/London: Kluwer Academic Publishers 1998.
Van Dijck, Maarten, 'Drug Policy in the Netherlands', in: Sanne Taekema (ed.), *Understanding Dutch Law*, The Hague: Boom Juridische uitgevers 2004, pp. 167–87.
Van Hoecke, Mark, *What is Legal Theory?*, Leuven: Acco 1985.
Van Hoecke, Mark, *Law as Communication*, Oxford: Hart Publishing 2002.

Van Klink, Bart and Taekema, Sanne (eds), *Law and Method*, Tübingen: Mohr Siebeck 2011.
Waluchow, Wilfrid J., *Inclusive Legal Positivism*. Oxford: Clarendon 1994.
Warnke, Georgia, *Justice and Interpretation*, Cambridge: Polity Press 1992.
Watson, Alan, *The Evolution of Law*, Baltimore: The Johns Hopkins University Press 1989.
Westerman, Pauline, 'Means and Ends', in: Willem J. Witteveen and Wibren van der Burg (eds), *Rediscovering Fuller. Essays on Implicit Law and Institutional Design*, Amsterdam: Amsterdam University Press 1999, pp. 145–68.
Westerman, Pauline, 'Some Objections to an Aspirational System of Law', in: Nicolle Zeegers, Willem Witteveen and Bart van Klink (eds), *Social and Symbolic Effects of Legislation under the Rule of Law*, Lewiston, NY: Edwin Mellen Press 2005, pp. 299–315.
Williams, Bernard, *Ethics and the Limits of Philosophy*, London: Fontana 1985.
Wilk, Kurt, *The Legal Philosophies of Lask, Radbruch, and Dabin*, Cambridge, Mass.: Harvard University Press 1950.
Winston, Kenneth I., 'Is/Ought Redux. The Pragmatist Context of Lon Fuller's Conception of Law', *Oxford Journal of Legal Studies*, 8 (1988), pp. 329–49.
Winston, Kenneth I., 'Introduction to Special Issue on Lon Fuller', *Law and Philosophy* 13 (1994), pp. 253–8.
Winston, Kenneth I., 'Introduction', in: Lon L. Fuller, *The Principles of Social Order. Selected Essays of Lon L. Fuller* (edited by Kenneth I. Winston), Oxford: Hart Publishing 2001 [1981], pp. 25–58.
Winston, Kenneth I., 'Introduction to the Revised Edition', in: Lon L. Fuller, *The Principles of Social Order. Selected Essays of Lon L. Fuller* (edited by Kenneth I. Winston), Oxford: Hart Publishing 2001 [1981], pp. 3–23.
Witteveen, Willem J., 'Rediscovering Fuller: An Introduction', in: Willem J. Witteveen and Wibren van der Burg (eds), *Rediscovering Fuller. Essays on Implicit Law and Institutional Design*, Amsterdam: Amsterdam University Press 1999, pp. 21–48.
Witteveen, Willem J., 'Significant, Symbolic and Symphonic Laws', in: Hanneke van Schooten (ed.), *Semiotics and Legislation. Jurisprudential, Institutional and Sociological Perspectives*, Liverpool: Deborah Charles 1999, pp. 27–70.
Witteveen, Willem J., 'Alternatieve regulering. De vele gezichten van de wetgever', in: *Alternatieve regelgeving* (Handelingen NJV), Deventer: Kluwer 2007, pp. 1–66.
Witteveen, Willem J. and Van Klink, Bart, 'Why is Soft Law Really Law?' *RegelMaat* 14 (1999), pp. 126–40.
Wittgenstein, Ludwig, *Philosophical Investigations* (transl. G.E.M. Anscombe), Malden, Mass.: Blackwell 2001.
Wright, P. George, 'Does Positivism Matter?', in: Robert P. George (ed.), *The Autonomy of Law. Essays on Legal Positivism*, Oxford: Clarendon 1996, pp. 57–78.

Yourow, Howard Charles, *The Margin of Appreciation Doctrine in the Dynamics of European Human Rights Jurisprudence*, The Hague: Kluwer Law International 1996.

Zeegers, Nicolle, Witteveen, Willem J. and Van Klink, Bart (eds), *Social and Symbolic Effects of Legislation under the Rule of Law*, Lewiston, NY: Edwin Mellen Press 2005.

Index

adjudication viii, 69–70, 105n31, 121, 124, 139–40, 144, 159
Ahdieh, Robert B. 121n3, 144
argument
  fusion of legal and moral 20, 35–6, 60, 68–71, 154–6
  legal 43, 70–71, 121, 154–6, 160
  moral 5, 68–70, 74
Alexy, Robert 65n2, 125n11, 155n7, 160n21
Annas, George J. 129–130n19
Aquinas, Thomas 65
Aristotle 34
attitude 25, 32–3, 58, 148–9
Austin, John 41, 59, 65
authority 20, 98–104, 110, 135–6, 148
autonomous legal orders 6–7, 112
autonomy of law, relative 12–15, 97, 110–113, 116–7, 135–8, 152–61
autonomy, individual 106–8, 124, 130, 132, 165

Beauchamp, Tom L. 32, 132
Berman, Paul Schiff 6, 12n23, 85n22, 89, 97n7, 98n11
Bentham, Jeremy 24
Beyleveld, Deryck 19n3, 160n20
binding or obligatory force of law 13, 87–8, 100–105, 109–11, 123, 137
bioethics vii, 15, 127–34
black-letter law 96, 113–7, 138, 155, 159, 166
Blok, Peter 124n9
Bood, Alex 133
Braithwaite, John 144n31
Brom, Frans W.A. 14n27, 67n11, 145
Brownsword, Roger 19n3, 160n20
Brudney, Daniel 162n27

Brunnée, Jutta 13–15, 26, 29n36, 86–7, 89, 96–7, 105–9, 113n59, 115–6, 136–8, 141–2, 145n35, 148
Van der Burg, Wibren 14n27, 34n46, 41n2, 108n48, 124–5, 127n17, 145–6
Burke, Kenneth 144n31
Buruma, Ybo 122n5

Cane, Peter 58n20, 86n26, 154n4
certainty, legal 35, 74, 125–7, 157, 167–8; *see also* uncertainty
Childress, James F. 32, 132
Civil Law 8–9, 23, 139–40, 159
codification 1, 8, 10, 24, 88n29, 120, 125, 133, 145–6
coherence and incoherence 7, 11–12, 41–2, 51, 57, 60–63, 78, 89–90
coherent doctrine, law as 3–8, 23, 53, 117, 121–2, 152
coherent theories 31–2, 39, 41–2, 49–51, 54, 60–63
Clouser, K. Danner 131n22
Coglianese, Cary 144n31, 147n42
Coleman, Jules 13n26, 36n49, 63n31, 167n44
Common Law 8, 92, 104–5n31, 139–40, 159
communication 14n28, 106, 143–8
complete and incomplete
  descriptions and models 21–6, 28–9, 39–42, 49–51, 60–63, 90–91
  legal doctrine 4, 6, 24
  theories of law 11–2, 28–9, 57, 59–63, 78
concept, *see* law; morality
concepts
  and conceptions 41–9, 77, 91
  descriptive 46–8, 73

essentially ambiguous viii, 10–11, 26, 39–52, 53–4, 59–63, 66, 79, 84, 91, 116
essentially contested 40, 45–8, 73, 91–2, 125
evaluative and normative 46–7, 73
second-order essentially contested 47, 79, 84, 92
consensus 6, 97, 132, 139–43, 146–7
consent 105–6, 109, 130–131, 137–8
contextualism viii–ix, 8–12, 15–16, 86, 92, 95, 108–9, 162–3, 168–9
contract 13, 87–8, 101, 104–5, 109, 111–3, 122–3
Cotterrell, Roger 6n12, 8n16, 11n22, 79n4, 89n32, 95n1, 124n8, 159–160
customary law 26–9, 43–5, 80–81, 99, 104–5, 111–2

Davies, Margaret 43n6
Den Hartogh, Govert 67n11
democracy 46–8, 146–9, 157–8, 166–9
descriptive analysis ix, 152–3
Devlin, Patrick 6
Dewey, John 24n23, 75n24
Dickson, Julie 78
Van Dijck, Maarten 122n5
doctrine, legal 23–4, 35, 60–62, 72–4, 116–7, 123–7; *see also* coherent doctrine, law as; complete and incomplete legal doctrine; law; model
Dworkin, Ronald 8, 25n26, 29, 41, 47, 54, 59–63, 109, 115–6, 124n8, 139n15, 157n12, 167; *see also* Fuller, Hart and Dworkin, debates between
constructing legal doctrine 5, 60–62, 72
fusion of law and morality 65, 70, 108n47, 154, 156, 160n20,
interpretivism vii–viii, 1–2, 13n26, 19–20, 88, 98
law as an argumentative and interpretive practice 19, 26, 60–63, 125n13, 154
legal positivism 1, 36n48, 59–61, 156n11

social rules 26–7, 73n23
dynamic concept of law, *see* law
dynamic phenomena 39–42, 46, 50, 83–4, 117
dynamics of law 7–8, 98, 101, 116–7, 119–34, 139–48, 168
dynamics in society 7, 98, 119, 122–3, 127–34, 142–4

Ehrlich, Eugen 122
Einstein, Albert 48
electron 21, 39–42, 46, 48–9
emergent law 114, 122–3
enacted law 13, 15, 98–105, 109–110, 114–6, 137–8, 146, 151
ethical theory 32–4, 66–9, 72
Europe, Council of 12, 14, 97, 112–3, 135–6, 139–44
European Convention on Human Rights 97, 135, 139–44
European Court of Human Rights 8, 44, 97, 121, 139–44, 149
European Union 112–3, 117, 138

family resemblance 39, 83–4, 86, 92, 116
Finnis, John 19n3, 79
formalism 53–4, 71, 88, 155
Frankena, William K. 32n40
Freeman, Michael 128n18
Fuller, Lon L. 3n5, 47, 54–63, 65, 95n1, 124n8, 160, 167
implicit and made law 56–7, 62, 99–105, 109
interactionism 12–5, 105, 162–3
internal morality of law 54–6, 103, 107–9, 144, 162
law as a purposive enterprise 19–20, 26, 41, 54–6
legality 55, 79, 81–2, 106–9, 157–8, 165–6, 168
legal pluralism 56, 87, 110n51, 112
natural law 12n25, 55–7
theory of law ix, 54–63, 99–109
Fuller, Hart and Dworkin, debates between viii, 2, 52, 53–63, 85

Gallie, Walter B. 45–8
Gerards, Janneke 142n22

Index 183

Gert, Bernard 32n42, 132n24
Glendon, Mary Ann 23n16
global legal pluralism, *see* pluralism
Greenawalt, Kent 65n1, 164n30
Griffiths, John 6n13, 112n57, 133
Grotefeld, Stefan 146n37

Habermas, Jürgen 14n28, 148n43, 158n15
Hart, H.L.A. 20, 57–60, 72–3, 82, 103, 110; *see also* open texture; Fuller, Hart and Dworkin, debates between
    concept of law 47, 50, 59, 81
    discretion 41
    morality 5–6, 34, 67–8
    minimum content of natural law 79, 161, 164–6
    positivism 1, 20, 65
    primary and secondary rules 19, 36, 41, 51, 58, 69, 81, 100
    separation of law and morality 65, 67–8, 161n23
    social rules 26–7, 58, 73n23
    theory of law 8, 56–63
health law vii, 117, 122, 127–34
Heidenheimer, Arnold 48
Hirsi Ali, Ayaan 44n10
Van Hoecke, Mark 6n13, 8n16, 14n28, 45n11, 84n20, 89n32, 144n31, 148n43
Hoffman, Lord 139n12
Holmes, Oliver Wendell 4n6, 23
horizontal law 96–8, 102, 111, 136–8, 144–8

ideal or critical law, *see* legal philosophy, normative
ideal or critical morality, *see* morality
ideal theory 31, 34
ideals
    and legal change 123–7, 130–132, 141
    and law 31, 152–9, 164–9
    and morality 34
    as open standards 36, 73, 108, 124–5, 152–6
    definition 124n8
    distinctively legal 114, 157–9, 161, 167

liberal 130–32, 169
internal, internalized and external 157–8, 166–7
law as oriented towards 15–6, 20, 31, 47, 79, 108, 114
regulative 42, 61, 90
interactional law 13–5, 96–110, 114–6, 127–9, 134, 137–8, 145–8, 151–5, 159–61
interactionism, legal
    and change 119–127, 134
    and pluralism 13, 116, 134, 135
    as a synthesis between natural law and legal positivism 12, 15–16, 151–2, 161–9
    description 12–16, 105, 109–10, 116
interactionism, symbolic 13n26, 105n33
interactionist paradigm 14–15, 135–49
interactive legislation 144–8
international law 8–9, 28–9, 80–81, 86–7, 89, 105–9, 115–7, 135–8
interpretation 27–8, 69–71, 108, 125–6, 139–46, 154–6
Ippel, Pieter 132n25

Jackson, Sherman A. 51n26
judges, *see* adjudication
jurisprudence, *see* legal philosophy
justice 157, 166–7

Kelsen, Hans viii, 8, 19, 24
Kennedy, Jacqueline 83
Klabbers, Jan 9n18, 97n6
Van Klink, Bart 89n32, 144–6
Koh, Harold Hongju 136n2
Kopelman, Loretta M. 131n22
Krisch, Nico 107n39, 109n49, 139–140
Krygier, Martin 9n19, 13n26, 81, 108n44, 167n45

Lacey, Nicola 59n24, 63n31
language 50, 159–60
law
    as a doctrine 3–6, 23–4, 51, 58–62
    as an interpretive and argumentative practice 5, 60–62, 125–7, 154–5
    as a system of propositions 5, 58–59, 66

as associated with the state 20, 36, 80, 82, 84–6, 96, 113–5
concept 10–14, 21, 39–52, 53–4, 58–63, 77–89, 91, 114–6
dynamic concept 13–14, 53, 83–4, 114–6
gradual concept 15, 56, 114
definition 15, 19, 21, 51, 59, 78–89, 113–6, 153
models of 19–37, 50–51, 66, 69–75
moral quality of 16, 153, 163–9
sources of 15, 35–6, 60–61, 99–105, 109–10, 137–8, 155–6, 160
standard view 4–8, 14, 135, 140, 147–8
law and morality
distinction 36, 60, 65, 67, 69–72, 84, 134, 151, 154
intertwinement vii–viii, 15–16, 71, 74, 133–4, 152–6, 159, 161–3
relation vii–ix, 1–6, 15–16, 19–20, 47, 65–75, 151–169
separation vii–viii, 19–20, 65–75, 151–7, 159, 161–2
Leenen, Henk J.J. 131n22
legal, the distinctively 13, 78–87, 92, 158–61
legal philosophy (legal theory or jurisprudence)
bias and partiality 8–12, 77–8, 85–6, 90, 113
deadlock and intractable controversies 1–3
debates 1–6, 19–21, 47, 53–62, 65–6
normative 66–8, 71–2, 153
sociologically informed ix, 152
task and challenges 78–83, 95–8
legality
ideal of 31, 81–2, 108–9, 114, 157–8, 165–8
practice of 86, 105–9, 114–6, 136–8
principles of 103, 106–9, 165–6
legislation 54–6, 103–4, 107–8, 144–8; *see also* codification; interactive legislation; process; statute
Leiter, Brian 3n4, 79n3, 110n50
Lesaffer, Randall 7n15
Lewis, David 50

Luban, David 99n13
Luhmann, Niklas 14n28
Lyons, David 20n5, 54n1, 59n21, 65, 68, 156n11

Macaulay, Stewart 57n11
McCall Smith, Alexander 130n21
MacCormick, Neil 2n2, 68n15, 164n34, 166n39
Macdonald, Roderick A. 103–4, 110–111
MacIntyre, Alasdair 25n28, 34, 45
Mackie, John 62n30
Mallat, Chibli 9n21
margin of appreciation 97, 139–44
Mason, John Kenyon 130n21
Máxima, Queen 83
model, *see also* law; morality
ideal 31, 34–5
potentiality 30–31, 34
practice 20–37, 40–41, 52–3, 55–63, 69–71, 120–123
product or doctrine 23–4, 32, 40–43, 51, 52–3
Montesquieu 105n33
Moore, Sally Falk 6n13, 57n11, 111
moralism 128–32
morality 5–8, 32–5, 39–52, 58n20, 66, 72–3, 153–9; *see also* ethical theory
concept 39–52, 66, 77, 153
ideal or critical 5–6, 34–35, 66–7, 153
models of 32–5, 39–52, 66
reference to morality in determining the contents of law 4–6, 35–6, 43–4, 66–74, 141–4, 152
social 6, 34–5, 66–72, 153, 156–9
natural law 9–12, 14, 19–20, 57, 66n7, 98, 109, 161–5; *see also* interactionism, legal
classical 1–3, 5–8, 20, 55
minimum content of 11, 68, 79, 161, 164–6
procedural 12n25, 55
substantive 55, 79, 163
naturalism, legal 12n25, 109–110, 162
Nonet, Philippe 108n45, 124n8, 144n31, 148n44, 158n16

normative theory ix, 45, 153; *see also* ethical theory; legal theory, normative
Nussbaum, Martha 125n10

obligatory force of norms, *see* binding or obligatory force of law
Olsen, Henrik Palmer 2n2, 24n22, 75n25, 108n47
open norms and standards 36, 74, 145–6, 155–6
open texture 27, 59, 72–3
order
    legal 6–14, 79–84, 86–9, 109–17, 135–8, 154–68
    state legal 80, 87–8, 110–112, 121–3
    normative 111–7
Osiander, Andreas 7n15

Patterson, Dennis 26n30
Peters, Anthony A.G. 23, 25n27, 62n29, 114n64, 124n8, 125n13, 166n40
philosophy of law, *see* legal philosophy
pluralism, *see also* law, sources of
    conceptual 19–21, 39–52, 91–2, 114–6
    definitional 78–89, 92, 115
    legal 6–7, 12–15, 35–6, 92, 110–117, 135–8
        global legal 12–4, 97–8, 112–3
        relative legal 13, 110–117, 121–3
    methodological 89–92
    moral 7, 141–4, 147
    theoretical vii–ix, 1–4, 8–10, 19–21, 91–2
pluralist framework 9–12, 77–92
Poort, Lonneke M. 14n27, 133n27, 144n30, 146–7
positive law 23, 30–31
positivism, legal 1–7, 19–21, 35–6, 43–4, 47, 65–75; *see also* interactionism, legal
    inclusive or soft 36, 155–6
    exclusive 88
    source-based vii, 44, 88n29
Posner, Richard A. 8n17
Postema, Gerald J. 100–102, 127n16
practice, *see also* law; legality; model
    definition 25
    legal 60–61, 69–71, 74, 89, 120–123, 154–8, 169
    medical 128–34
pragmatism 13n26, 105n33, 163, 167
principles 36, 60–61, 73, 124–5; *see also* legality; rules
process
    legal 14, 69–70, 107, 120, 158
    legislative 54–5, 145–7
    model 40–41
product, *see* model, product or doctrine
purpose 27–9

Radbruch, Gustav 20–21, 31, 36, 42n5, 54n2, 79
Rawls, John 32, 34, 45, 72
Raz, Joseph 4n7, 8, 19, 81n9, 88n29, 100, 166n39
Realism, Legal 4, 23
reciprocity 55n5, 99–100, 102–4, 165–6
relativism 89–90
religion 26–8, 39–44, 168–9
Reus-Smit, Christian 108, 137n6
Rhode, Deborah L. 23n16
rights 129–132, 139–44, 155–6
Rokumoto, Kahei 82n14
Rothstein, Mark A. 128n18
Rubin, Edward L. 81
rule of law, *see* legality
rules
    and principles 23, 36, 60–61
    legal 28–30, 55–6, 99–101, 155n7, 159
    primary and secondary 58–9, 69–70, 81, 110, 114–5
    social 26–30, 73n23
Rundle, Kristen 55–56, 63n31, 95n1, 103n28, 162, 165n36
Ryle, Gilbert 22

sanctions 87, 115–6
Santos, Boaventura de Sousa 112n56
Schauer, Frederick 79n3, 83n16, 154n5
Schneider, Carl E. 132n25
Schroten, Egbert 67n11
Scott, James C. 22
Selznick, Philip ix, 67n11, 69n17, 95n1, 126n14, 163

fact-value distinction 75n24
ideals 31, 166–7
ideals and law 19–20, 47n18, 114, 124n8, 157n12
legality 79, 82n14, 108–9, 168
naturalism 12–13, 109, 162–3
pragmatism 13n26, 91n33, 163
responsive law 144n31, 148n44, 158n16
variation 9n19, 162
weak definitions and strong concepts 9n20, 51, 84n19
separation thesis, *see* law and morality, separation of
Shapiro, Scott 78n2
shared understandings 106, 138, 140–41
Shklar, Judith N. 25n25, 84
Simmel, Georg 105n33
Singer, Peter 32n43
Smith, Stephen D. 4n6, 23n20, 160n21
Sperling, Daniel 130n20
state, *see also* order; law
bureaucracy 111, 115
regulatory 81, 96, 98
Stamhuis, Jellienke 146–7
statute 104, 120–121, 144–9; *see also* codification; legislation

Taekema, Sanne 43n7, 65n2, 89n32, 108, 153n3, 156–7, 163n29
ideals 31n39, 79n6, 108, 114n63, 124n8, 157, 164–5
pragmatism 91n33, 164n31, 167n44
relative autonomy of law 112
Tamanaha, Brian Z. 8n16, 75n24, 80–1, 83–5, 114n61
Teubner, Gunther 14n28, 148n43
Toddington, Stuart 2n2, 24n22, 75n25, 91n33, 108n47

Toope, Stephen John 13–15, 26, 29n36, 86–7, 89, 96–7, 105–9, 113n59, 115–6, 136–8, 141–2, 145n35, 148
top-down regulation 81, 96, 98
Trotter, Griffin 132n25
Twining, William 6n14, 83n16, 85n23, 95n2, 97n9

uncertainty 7, 31, 35, 72–4; *see also* certainty, legal
unified theory 50, 91

values 46–7, 75n24, 125n11; *see also* ideals
variation, an eye for 8–10, 71, 75, 79, 83, 108
vertical relationship 100, 102–3, 109n49, 145
Vorstenbosch, Jan 67n11

Waluchow, Wilfrid J. 36n49
Warnke, Georgia 91n33
Watson, Alan 125n10, 158n17
Weber, Max 111
Westerman, Pauline 126n14, 146n38
Weyers, Heleen 133
Williams, Bernard 32n41
Winston, Kenneth I. 13n26, 55n4, 107, 119n1
Witteveen, Willem J. 14n27, 105n33, 144–6, 155n8
Wittgenstein, Ludwig 39, 83
Wright, P. George 1n1

Yourow, Howard Charles 143n26

Zeegers, Nicolle 144n30, 146n38